Schriften zum europäischen Management

Herausgegeben von/edited by
Roland Berger
München, Deutschland

Weitere Informationen zu dieser Reihe finden Sie unter
http://www.springer.com/series/12472

Die Reihe wendet sich an Studenten sowie Praktiker und leistet wissenschaftliche Beiträge zur ökonomischen Forschung im europäischen Kontext.

This series is aimed at students and practitioners. It represents our academic contributions to economic research in a European context.

Henning Diederich

Environmental Policy and Renewable Energy Equipment Exports

An Empirical Analysis

With a Foreword by Prof. Dr. Wilhelm Althammer

Springer Gabler

Henning Diederich
Essen, Deutschland

HHL Leipzig Graduate School of Management, Dissertation, 2016

Schriften zum europäischen Management
ISBN 978-3-658-13557-7 ISBN 978-3-658-13558-4 (eBook)
DOI 10.1007/978-3-658-13558-4

Library of Congress Control Number: 2016939253

Springer Gabler

This Springer Gabler imprint is published by Springer Nature
The registered company is Springer Fachmedien Wiesbaden GmbH

Foreword by Prof. Dr. Wilhelm Althammer

In many countries, increasing the share of renewable energies in the energy mix is a central element of both energy and climate policy. To achieve this goal, environmental economics offers a rich set of policy instruments, encompassing as diverse instruments as voluntary agreements, command and control policies and market based instruments. Not surprisingly, each country follows its own way in applying and mixing these instruments. Sometimes this implies conflicts between different interest groups concerning the costs of regulation. Especially industry representatives often fear that a new or a stricter regulation might harm them by inducing additional costs and a decline in competitiveness. This fear has strong impacts on policy, the high number of industry-specific exceptions and special provisions within the European Union's system of tradable carbon permits may serve as an example.

The view of environmental regulation as being detrimental to countries' competitiveness was already challenged by Michael Porter more than 20 years ago. According to the so-called "*Porter Hypothesis*", stricter environmental regulation could even improve countries' competitiveness by inducing technology and process innovation. This effect is assumed to be particulary pronounced for what Porter and his co-authors call *"well-crafted"* regulation, i.e. output-oriented, clear, and market-based instruments. Since the hypothesis was formulated rather opaque in the original publications, a broad body of literature has emerged about the question what Porter meant and how his hypothesis can be tested empirically.

This constitutes the framework for Henning Diederich's thesis. He analyzes a special version of the Porter hypothesis, according to which the improvement of competitiveness should especially arise in the environmental products and services industry. Here, he focuses on the suppliers of solar and wind power equipment and their export competitiveness and offers two major innovations. First, he uses a new database to measure innovation effects by patent activity. Second, he uses regulation data for a broad set of instruments and countries. This allows him to analyze two specific aspects: First, the question about the characteristics of a *"well-crafted"* regulation which fosters innovation and increases competitiveness; and, second, the contribution of different kinds of regulation to increase competitiveness according to the lead market theory.

I wish that his interesting findings find a broad audience, both among academics and business.

Leipzig, February 2016

Prof. Dr. Wilhelm Althammer

Sparkassen-Finanzgruppe Chair of Macroeconomics

HHL Leipzig Graduate School of Management

Preface

Inspired by my work as strategy consultant in the energy practice of Roland Berger and my personal interest in renewable energies and climate change, I have made the decision to dedicate my PhD studies to the field of environmental economics.

The focus of today's discussion on global warming and anthropogenic climate change is very much on the high cost of emission reduction, while the potential economic upsides, i.e. new jobs and export revenues from green sector products, often receive little attention. With my doctoral thesis I contribute to the empirical research on the so-called narrowly strong Porter Hypothesis and demonstrate that climate change mitigation and business interest are not competing ends but can be achieved simultaneously through well-chosen regulatory means.

I hope that this piece of research attracts the interest of academics and practitioners alike and contributes to the definition of state-of-the-art regulatory instruments which, at the same time, protect the climate and promote innovation and economic activity in the green sector.

Many people have supported me during the writing of my thesis and deserve a big thank you.

I would like to express my special gratitude to my doctorate supervisor Prof. Dr. Wilhelm Althammer for always being available for feedback and insightful discussions from the very beginning of the idea phase to the finalization of the manuscript and the preparation of the disputation. I would also like to say thank you to the entire team of the Sparkassen-Finanzgruppe Chair of Macroeconomics, the program management and support staff of HHL Leipzig Graduate School of Management, and Prof. Dr. Manfred Kirchgeorg and Prof. Dr. Henning Zülch as second assessor and chair of the examination board respectively.

I would also like to thank my employer, the Roland Berger GmbH, for admittance to the Roland Berger PhD Program. Thanks to their very generous financial support, I could fully dedicate myself to academic research over the full length of my educational leave. Moreover, I have very much enjoyed the regular exchange with my colleagues in the four-monthly doctoral circles. In this context, my special thanks go to Dr. Christian Krys for coordinating Roland Berger's doctoral program and for organizing our regular meetings. I would also like to thank my colleagues and fellow doctoral students Wenting Zhao, Stephan Baur, Johannes Distler, Bert Förster, Martin Hülsen, Pascal Lehnen, Markus Möhrle, Raphael Neuburg, Gerrit Remané, David Rody, and Christoph Wagner for their valuable comments and remarks.

Another big thank you goes to my family for encouraging me to pursue my doctoral studies and to keep up the spirit during the more challenging phases of the research project. In particular, I want to thank my beloved wife Christine for critically reviewing the manuscript and challenging my lines of reasoning, and our daughter Charlotte for persistently reminding me of the approaching submission date. I would also like to express my special gratitude to my parents, Hannelore and Hans-Günter, for always encouraging me to be curious, to pursue my goals, and most importantly to keep trying when things didn't go well on first attempt.

Essen, February 2016

Dr. Henning Diederich

Table of content

Table of figures

Table of tables

Table of abbreviations[1]

&	and
°C	degree centigrade
Δ	delta
%	percent
a	year (Latin: annum)
AHS	effectively applied tariffs
ASEAN	Association of Southeast Asian Nations
avg.	average
bn	billion
CAGR	compound annual growth rate
CAPEX	capital expenditures
CCMT	climate change mitigation technologies
CES	constant elasticity of substitution
CO	carbon monoxide
CO_2	carbon dioxide
cont'd	continued
CSP	concentrating solar (thermal) power
ctry.	country
DC	District of Columbia
dep. var.	dependent variable
dist.	distance
DIW	German Institute for Economic Research (German: Deutsches Institut für Wirtschaftsforschung)
EC	European Commission
ECB	European Central Bank
ed.	edition or editor
eds.	editors
e.g.	for example (Latin: exempli gratia)
EIA	U.S. Energy Information Administration
env.	environmental
EPIA	European Photovoltaic Industry Association
EPO	European Patent Office (or Organization)
eq.	equation

1 This table is restricted to in-text abbreviations and acronyms. For the description of variable abbreviations used in equations and output tables or in references on the same, refer to the table of variables or to the appendices indicated in those sections where these variables occur.

esp.	especially
est.	estimation
et al.	and others (Latin: et alii)
etc.	and so forth (Latin: et cētera)
ETS	see EU ETS
EU	European Union
EU-27	European Union of 27 countries
EU ETS	European Union Greenhouse Gas Emission Trading Systems
exp.	expenditures
FDI	foreign direct investment
FE	fixed effect
fed.	federal
G20	Group of Twenty
GDP	gross domestic product
geo.	geographic
GHG	greenhouse gases
GLS	generalized least squares
GMM	generalized method of moments
gov.	government or governmental
GREDEG	Research Group in Law, Economics and Management (French: Groupe de Recherche en Droit, Economie et Gestion)
GREQAM	Research Group in Quantitative Economics Aix-Marseille (French: Groupement de Recherche en Economie Quantitative d'Aix-Marseille)
GW	gigawatt
GWEC	Global Wind Energy Council
H_0	null hypothesis
H-O	Heckscher-Ohlin
HS	Harmonized System (of tariff nomenclature)
i.e.	for example (Latin: id est)
ICTSD	International Center for Trade and Sustainable Development
IEA	International Energy Agency
IIP	Institute of Intellectual Property
incl.	including
inno.	innovation
intro.	introduction
IPC	International Patent Classification
IRENA	International Renewable Energy Agency
IRR	incident rate ratio
IRS	increasing returns to scale

IV	instrumental variable
IZA	Institute for the Study of Labor (German: Forschungsinstitut zur Zukunft der Arbeit)
JPO	Japan Patent Office
kVA	kilovolt-ampere
kW	kilowatt
kWh	kilowatt hour
LCOE	levelized cost of electricity
LED	light emitting diode
MA	Massachusetts
max.	maximum
Mercosur	Southern Common Market (Spanish: Mercado Común del Sur)
mgmt.	management
min.	minimum
MIT	Massachusetts Institute of Technology
Mont.	Montenegro
MPRA	Munich Personal RePEc Archive
MRT	multilateral resistance term
MW	megawatt
n/a	not available
NAFTA	North American Free Trade Agreement
NBER	National Bureau of Economic Research
NBREG	negative binomial regression
n.e.s.	not else specified
NLS	non-linear least squares
no.	number
NO_X	nitrogen oxide
obs.	observations
OECD	Organization for Economic Co-operation and Development
OLS	ordinary least squares
p.	page
PACE	pollution abatement and control expenditures
PCT	Patent Cooperation Treaty
pop.	population
pp.	pages
PPML	Poisson pseudo-maximum-likelihood
PPP	purchasing power parity
PV	photovoltaics
R&D	research and development
RD&D	research, development, and demonstration
RE	renewable energy

reg.	regulation
regr.	regression or regressions
REN21	Renewable Energy Policy Network for the 21st Century
RePEc	Research Papers in Economics
resp.	respectively
RFF	Resources for the Future
rob.	rubustness
RTA	regional trade agreement
SO_2	sulfur dioxide
S&P (500)	Standard & Poor's (500)
std. dev.	standard deviation
STI	Science and Technology Indicators
UK	United Kingdom
UN	United Nations
UNCTAD	United Nations Conference on Trade and Development
UNEP	United Nations Environmental Programme
UNFCCC	United Nations Framework Convention on Climate Change
US/U.S.	United States
USD	United States Dollar
USPTO	United States Patent and Trademark Office
USSR	Union of Soviet Socialist Republics
var.	variable or varying
VAT	value-added tax
vol.	volume
vs.	versus
W	watt
w/	with
WEF	World Economic Forum
WIPO	World Intellectual Property Organization
w/o	without
WTO	World Trade Organization
YoY	year-on-year
yrs.	years
ZEW	Centre for European Economic Research (German: Zentrum für Europäische Wirtschaftsforschung)

Table of variables[2]

α	intercept
β	coefficient
γ	fixed-effect
ε	error term
η	error term
λ	mean and variance parameter of Poisson model
Π	multilateral resistance term of the exporting country
P	multilateral resistance term of the importing country
σ	elasticity of substitution
C_ANY_DP5	existence of C_ANY_E for at least five years
C_ANY_DP10	existence of C_ANY_E for at least ten years
C_ANY_DP15	existence of C_ANY_E for at least fifteen years
C_ANY_E	existence of any of the eleven common policy instruments
C_FIS_D	number of years C_FIS_E has been active
C_FIS_D2	square of C_FIS_D
C_FIS_DP5	existence of C_FIS_E for at least five years
C_FIS_DP10	existence of C_FIS_E for at least ten years
C_FIS_DP15	existence of C_FIS_E for at least fifteen years
C_FIS_E	existence of the fiscal incentives cluster
C_FIT_D	number of years C_FIT_E has been active
C_FIT_D2	square of C_FIT_D
C_FIT_DP5	existence of C_FIT_E for at least five years
C_FIT_DP10	existence of C_FIT_E for at least ten years
C_FIT_DP15	existence of C_FIT_E for at least fifteen years
C_FIT_E	existence of the feed-in tariff cluster
C_GHG_D	number of years C_GHG_E has been active
C_GHG_D2	square of C_GHG_D
C_GHG_DP5	existence of C_GHG_E for at least five years
C_GHG_DP10	existence of C_GHG_E for at least ten years
C_GHG_DP15	existence of C_GHG_E for at least fifteen years

[2] This table lists the variables used throughout this dissertation in alphabetical order and provides brief descriptions. For more extensive descriptions, data sources, and units of measurement, refer to Appendix 10 (variables first introduced in Chapter 3), Appendix 19 (variables first introduced in Chapter 4), and Appendix 26 (variables first introduced in Chapter 5). The variable descriptions provided may contain abbreviations which refer to other, more fundamental variables explained elsewhere in this table.

C_GHG_E	existence of the carbon trading cluster
C_QUO_D	number of years C_QUO_E has been active
C_QUO_D2	square of C_QUO_D
C_QUO_DP5	existence of C_QUO_E for at least five years
C_QUO_DP10	existence of C_QUO_E for at least ten years
C_QUO_DP15	existence of C_QUO_E for at least fifteen years
C_QUO_E	existence of the quotas cluster
C_RDD_D	number of years C_RDD_E has been active
C_RDD_D2	square of C_RDD_D
C_RDD_DP5	existence of C_RDD_E for at least five years
C_RDD_DP10	existence of C_RDD_E for at least ten years
C_RDD_DP15	existence of C_RDD_E for at least fifteen years
C_RDD_E	existence of the RD&D cluster
C_TAR_D	number of years C_TAR_E has been active
C_TAR_D2	square of C_TAR_D
C_TAR_DP5	existence of C_TAR_E for at least five years
C_TAR_DP10	existence of C_TAR_E for at least ten years
C_TAR_DP15	existence of C_TAR_E for at least fifteen years
C_TAR_E	existence of the targets cluster
CPV_E	share of common policy types implemented by the exporter
CPV_E_im	share of common policy types implemented by the importer
d	distance
DKS_FC_S	domestic knowledge stock calculated from FC_S
DKS_FC_SW	domestic knowledge stock calculated from FC_SW
DKS_FC_W	domestic knowledge stock calculated from FC_W
DKS_FCw_S	domestic knowledge stock calculated from FCw_S
DKS_FCw_SW	domestic knowledge stock calculated from FCw_SW
DKS_FCw_W	domestic knowledge stock calculated from FCw_W
DKS_SC_S	domestic knowledge stock calculated from SC_S
DKS_SC_SW	domestic knowledge stock calculated from SC_SW
DKS_SC_SW_im	domestic knowledge stock calculated from SC_SW (of the importing country)

DKS_SC_W	domestic knowledge stock calculated from SC_W
DKS_SCw_S	domestic knowledge stock calculated from SCw_S
DKS_SCw_SW	domestic knowledge stock calculated from SCw_SW
DKS_SCw_W	domestic knowledge stock calculated from SCw_W
DTOPAT	simple count of total domestic patent applications
E()	expected value
exp()	exponential function
EU	joint membership in the EU
EURO	joint membership in the euro area
f()	function
FC_S	family count of solar power patent applications
FC_SW	family count of solar and wind power patent applications
FC_W	family count of wind power patent applications
FCw_S	weighted family count of solar power patent applications
FCw_SW	weighted family count of solar and wind power patent applications
FCw_W	weighted family count of wind power patent applications
FIT_D	number of years FIT_E has been active
FIT_D2	square of FIT_D
FIT_E	existence of fixed or premium rate feed-in tariffs
GHG_D	number of years GHG_E has been active
GHG_D2	square of GHG_D
GHG_E	existence of greenhouse gas certificate trading systems
i (index)	country/exporting country
ITOCAPA_YoY	year-on-year change in total global generation capacity
j (index)	importing country
lnGDP_ex	(natural logarithm of) exporter's gross domestic product
lnGDP_im	(natural logarithm of) importer's gross domestic product
lnREC_SWTW	(natural logarithm of) share of solar and wind in total electricity generation capacity

lnREC_TeH	(natural logarithm of) share of all non-hydro renewables energy technologies in total electricity generation capacity
lnRES_SW	(natural logarithm of) share of solar and wind in total electricity generation
lnRES_TeH	(natural logarithm of) share of all non-hydro renewables energy technologies in total electricity generation
NET_D	number of years NET_E has been active
NET_D2	square of NET_D
NET_E	existence of net metering
P()	probability
PUB_D	number of years PUB_E has been active
PUB_D2	square of PUB_D
PUB_E	existence of public spending, capital subsidies, or low-cost loans
QUO_D	number of years QUO_E has been active
QUO_D2	square of QUO_D
QUO_E	existence of renewable energy quotas (w/o certificate trading)
RDD_D	number of years RDD_E has been active
RDD_D2	square of RDD_D
RDD_E	existence of RD&D programs
REC_D	number of years REC_E has been active
REC_D2	square of REC_D
REC_E	existence of renewable energy quotas (w/ certificate trading)
RES_S	share of solar in total electricity generation
RES_SW	share of solar and wind in total electricity generation
RES_SW_im	share of solar and wind in total electricity generation (of the importing country)
RES_W	share of wind in total electricity generation
SC_S	simple count of solar power patent applications
SC_SW	simple count of solar and wind power patent applications
SC_W	simple count of wind power patent applications
SCw_S	weighted simple count of solar power patent applications
SCw_SW	weighted simple count of solar and wind power patent applications
SCw_W	weighted simple count of wind power patent applications

t	ease of trade between pairs of countries
t (index)	period of observation
TAR_D	number of years TAR_E has been active
TAR_D2	square of TAR_D
TAR_E	existence of renewable energy targets and strategies
TARIFF_SW	effective tariff rate on solar and wind energy equipment
TEN_D	number of years TEN_E has been active
TEN_D2	square of TEN_D
TEN_E	existence of public competitive bidding (tendering)
TXC_D	number of years TXC_E has been active
TXC_D2	square of TXC_D
TXC_E	existence of investment or production tax credits
TXR_D	number of years TXR_E has been active
TXR_D2	square of TXR_D
TXR_E	existence of tax reductions for carbon, energy, sales, VAT, or other taxes
X	bilateral exports (general)
X_ALL	bilateral exports (all commodity classes)
X_SW	bilateral exports of solar and wind energy equipment
Y	economic mass

Executive Summary

Concerns about the consequences of anthropogenic climate change and the binding greenhouse gas reduction targets of the Kyoto Protocol have led to the adoption of more stringent environmental regulation. Many of these policies affect the energy sector, which is traditionally among the largest emitters of greenhouse gases. A common strategy to lower energy-related emissions is to increase the share of renewables in the electricity mix. As these technologies are not yet fully competitive, increasing their share requires considerable regulatory and financial support. Hence, the downside of this strategy is its high cost. The potential upside is, however, that investments in renewables might serve as an industry policy for the renewable energy equipment industry and foster its export competitiveness.

This dissertation takes up that issue and investigates the connection between environmental regulation, technological innovation, and export competitiveness in renewable energy equipment based on a large sample of 225 developed and developing countries from 1990 to 2011; with focus on solar and wind power.

The empirical analysis based on the narrowly strong Porter Hypothesis and the lead market theory consists of two parts. In the first part, I use a patent analysis to explore the connection between environmental regulation intensity and design and innovative output. Hereby, I differentiate between eleven types of renewable energy support policies. Patents are identified based on the novel Y02E system. In the second part, I employ a gravity model of trade to analyze the impact of environmental regulation and regulation-induced innovation on countries' export success. In this context, I also test for policy duration's role as export determinant.

Based on my empirical analysis, I find strong support for the narrowly strong Porter Hypothesis as well as for the lead market theory. The data suggest that environmental regulation drives innovation and export volumes in solar- and wind-power-related goods. This is particularly the case for well-crafted (i.e. market-based, output-oriented, and clear) instruments such carbon trading. Moreover, the data show that early adopters of renewable energy support policies benefit most.

1 Introduction

Over the last decades, climate change has developed from a specialist topic for scientists, dedicated research centers, and non-governmental organizations, to a major item on the political agenda. After a long and heated debate, the international community has arrived at the consensus that anthropogenic climate change is a serious threat which requires a timely and forceful response.

Article 2 of the United Nations Framework Convention on Climate Change (UNFCCC), which was negotiated in Rio de Janerio 1992, states that "[t]he ultimate objective [of the UNFCCC] [...] is to achieve [...] stabilization of greenhouse gas concentrations in the atmosphere at a level that would prevent dangerous anthropogenic interference with the climate system" (UNFCCC, p. 9).

Kyoto 1997 was the next important milestones in climate change negotiations. In this meeting, the parties of the UNFCCC agreed on legally binding reduction targets for developed countries (Annex I countries[3]). Specifically, the Kyoto protocol states that "[e]ach Party included in Annex I [...] shall: Implement and/or further elaborate policies and measures in accordance with its national circumstances" (Kyoto Protocol, pp. 1-2).

The last major breakthrough was made in Cancun 2010, where the conference of parties "[r]ecognizes that warming of the climate system is unequivocal and that most of the observed increase in global average temperatures since the mid-twentieth century is very likely due to the observed increase in anthropogenic greenhouse gas concentrations [and] that deep cuts in global greenhouse gas emissions are required [...] to hold the increase in the global average temperature below 2 °C above pre-industrial levels" (UN, 2011, p. 4).

The progress in international climate change negotiations, especially Kyoto 1997, has encouraged many countries to develop policy measures to address and prevent the negative consequences of climate change through the reduction of greenhouse gas emissions. This trend has far-reaching consequences for the economy. The energy sector, traditionally one of the largest greenhouse gas emitters, is among those who are affected most by changing or additional environmental regulation.

3 The term refers to a list of developed and transitional countries (former centrally planned economies) established in Annex I to the UNFCCC.

To comply with increasingly stringent regulations, utilities have to rethink the way they generate electricity. Their power plant portfolios need to become much more efficient in terms of greenhouse gas emission, especially CO_2 per unit of electricity. In turn, this development implies increasing demand for emission-free renewable energy technologies. Hence, additional regulatory burdens on utilities likewise mean economic stimulus for the renewable energy equipment industry.

Recent data underline the magnitude of the ongoing changes in the energy sector. Back in 2003, 80% of the newly commissioned power generation capacity in the EU-27, Norway, and Switzerland were still powered by fossil fuels. Within a decade, this picture changed dramatically. In 2013, it were renewable energies which accounted for 72% of capacity additions. This development is not limited to Europe, though. In 2014, China also added more renewable energy capacity to the grid than nuclear and fossil power capacities combined (REN21, 2014a).

Inspired by this fundamental change in the composition of the world's energy equipment industry, the objective of my dissertation is to explore how countries can benefits from the boom in renewable energy technologies. Particularly, the research focus is on the impact of design and intensity of countries' environmental regulation on the innovativeness and consequently competitiveness of their domestic renewable energy equipment industries.

The remainder of the introduction is structured as follows. Section 1.1 illustrates the recent progress in the diffusion of renewable energy technologies and the economic importance of this industry sector. Section 1.2 introduces environmental regulation and technological change as driving forces behind these trends. Section 1.3 explores the patterns of trade in renewable energy equipment. Following on the discussion of these indicative economic data, Sections 1.4 and 1.5 present the research question and give an overview on the structure of this dissertation.

1.1 Role of renewables in electricity generation

As briefly indicated in the introduction to this chapter, the importance of renewable energies has increased considerably. This section illustrates the increases in cumulative global capacities and annual capacity additions of selected renewable energy technologies from 2004 to 2013. In addition, it shows the implications of these increases on the composition of the market for power generation equipment.

Part (a) of Figure 1 reveals that the major renewable energy technologies, solar, wind, and hydro power, went through very different growth paths. While hydro power already had a very strong position in 2004 with a global installed capacity of 799 GW, wind power was with 46 GW still a niche technology and solar power with 6 GW not relevant on a global scale[4].

However, an analysis of annual capacity additions presented in Part (b) of Figure 1 shows that installed capacities are just half of the story. Between 2004 and 2013, the share of wind and solar in capacity additions from renewables doubled from one to two thirds. Notably, this change took place in a fast growing market. Annual renewables additions increased fourfold from 30 GW in 2004 to 121 GW in 2013.

Overall, the global renewable energy capacity increased from 923 GW in 2004 to 1,560 GW in 2013. While all technologies added capacities, the growth rates of wind (+23.9% p.a.) and especially solar (+42.8% p.a.) were considerably more dynamic than those of hydro (+2.5% p.a.) and other renewables (+3.8% p.a.).

These data illustrate that the group of renewable energies is very heterogeneous. While hydro power is an established power generation technology with a large installed base and moderate growth rates, wind and solar are newcomers characterized by rather small installed bases but very large growth rates in terms of both cumulative capacity and year-on-year capacity additions.

The recent boom in wind and solar power is not less remarkable when compared with conventional power generation technologies. As Figure 1, Part (c) illustrates, solar power increased its share in the global power plant market from 1% in 2004 to 18% in 2013. Wind power reached with 16% a similar share in 2013, but also started from a larger base. Moreover, all renewables combined accounted for 52% of 2013 capacity additions and were therefore equally important as the group of conventional technologies, which consists of all types of fossil and nuclear power.

---

[4] The other renewable energy technologies mainly consist of modern biomass and geothermal power. These technologies play an important role in heating and alternative fuels. However, their relevance and especially their future potential for electricity generation are small compared to those of solar, wind, and hydro. As this thesis is concerned only with developments in the market for electricity generation equipment, the other renewables are out of scope and therefore not discussed in the remaining part of this document.

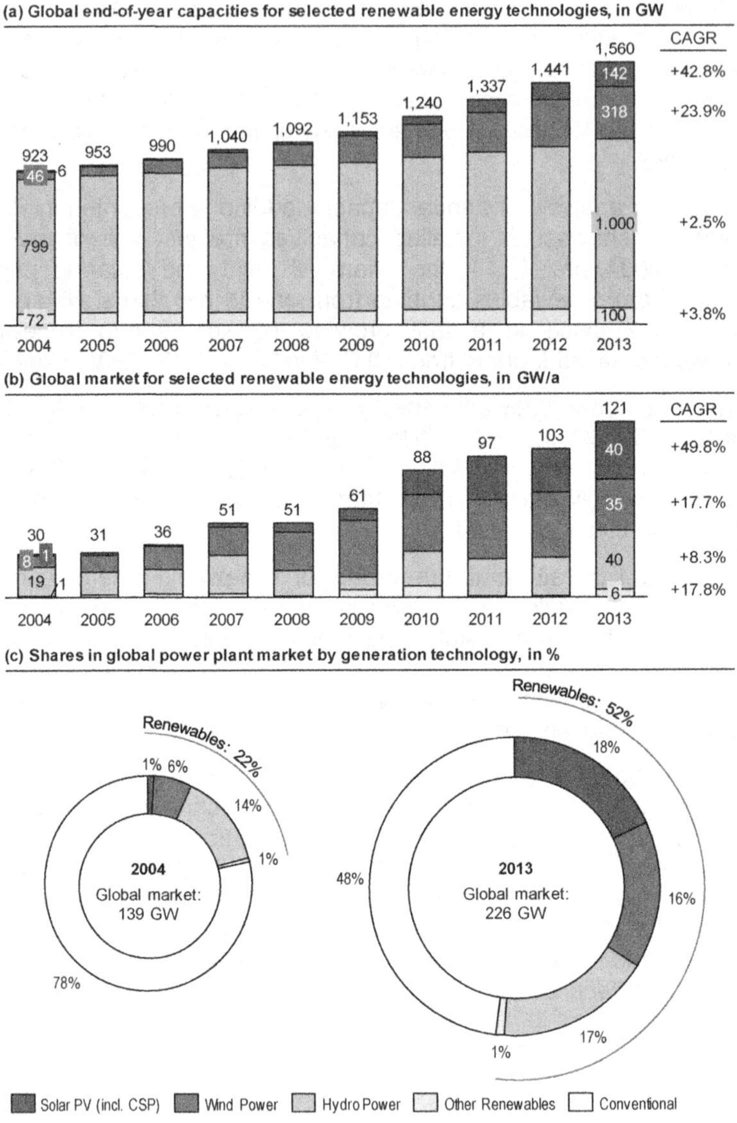

Figure 1 – Market and capacity shares by generation technology[5]
Source: Own illustration based on data from REN21 (2014a), Tables 2 and 12.

[5] For a comprehensive data table containing the values for all individual technology-year-combinations refer to Appendix 1.

Given the size of the global power plant market, the production of renewable energy equipment has clearly developed into an economically very important industry which is observed closely by investors and governments alike.

1.2 Political support and innovation as drivers of renewables

The strong growth of the renewable energy equipment industry raises the question of what has caused this development. The most likely answer is that it has been driven by two interdependent effects. On the one hand, many governments have taken Kyoto and the immediate threat of uncontrolled climate change seriously and adopted more and/or more stringent environmental regulation. On the other hand, technological progress has led to a sharp decrease in the production cost of electricity from wind and solar power.

The trend towards more political support for climate change mitigation is illustrated in Figure 2. The data presented in Part (a) of this figure show that the number of countries with renewable energy support policies in place increased continually between 1990 and 2012. While policy proliferation rates were still quite low in the 1990s, the data nevertheless imply that at least a small group of countries have been active supporters of renewable energies for decades.

Around 2000, shortly after the UNFCCC meeting of Kyoto 1997, policy proliferation gained pace. In the 2000s, the number of countries which have adopted renewable energy support policies doubled about every five years and kept increasing since then to reach 156 countries in 2012. This means that, 15 years after Kyoto, the large majority of countries is engaged in the support of renewable energies.

Part (b) of Figure 2 gives the policy proliferation rates by region. As already expected from the data presented in Part (a), regional proliferation rates increased across the board. But, irrespective of the general trend towards more support for renewable energies, there are also very significant differences between regions in terms of historical adoption rates. The traditional economic hubs of Europe and North America were at the forefront of this development and already had notable adoption rates in the 1990s. With considerable distance, this is also the case for Asia & Oceania and parts of Eurasia. In all other regions, renewable energy support was uncommon until 2000. However, Africa, the Middle East, and South America caught up quickly. As of 2012, the share of countries actively supporting renewable energies reached 60-86% across all regions with Europe and the Middle East being the current leaders.

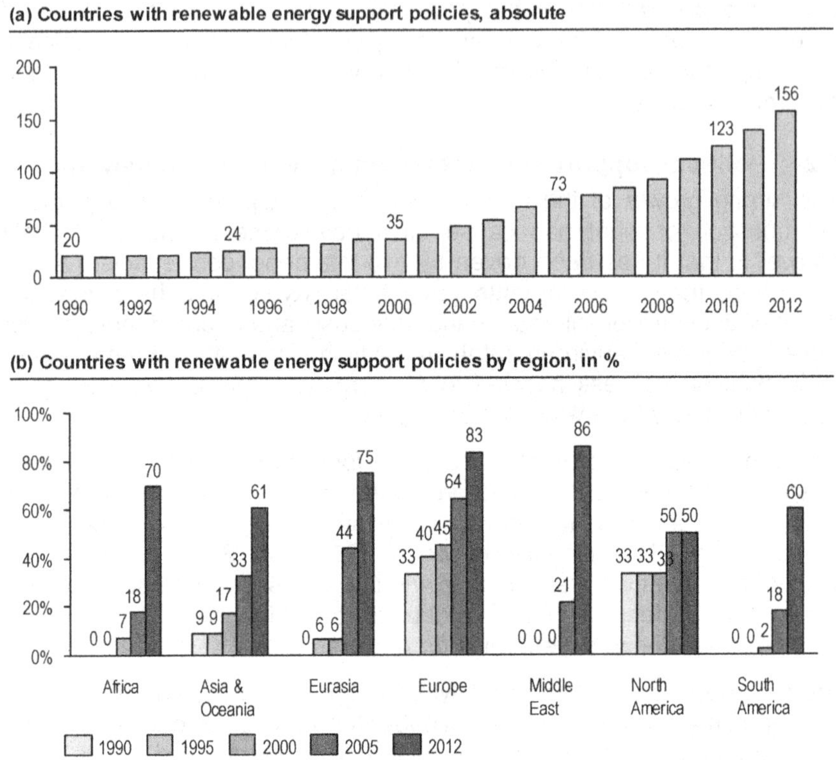

Figure 2 – Number of countries with RE support measures[6]
Source: Own illustration based on data from REN21 (2005, 2006, 2007, 2009, 2010, 2011, 2012, 2013, 2014a, 2014b, 2015), IEA/IRENA (2015), and OECD (2015).

Technological progress, the second driving force behind the boom of renewables installations, can be best illustrated using the case of crystalline-silicon-based photovoltaic (PV) modules. Between 2004 and 2012, the average selling price for such modules dropped from 3 to less than 1 USD/W (IRENA, 2013a). It comes without saying that this very strong decrease in module prices and therefore also generation cost would not have been possible without governmental support.

An analysis of the levelized cost of electricity (LCOE) of different renewable energy technologies compared to energy from fossil fuels presented in Figure 3 suggests that such government support will still be necessary in future. Although, as of 2012, onshore wind and solar power

6 For further details refer to Section 3.3.1 and Appendix 4 to Appendix 8.

installations in prime locations with a strong, constant breeze or high solar radiation are competitive with electricity from fossil-fuel-based power plants, this is certainly not yet the case for all installations.

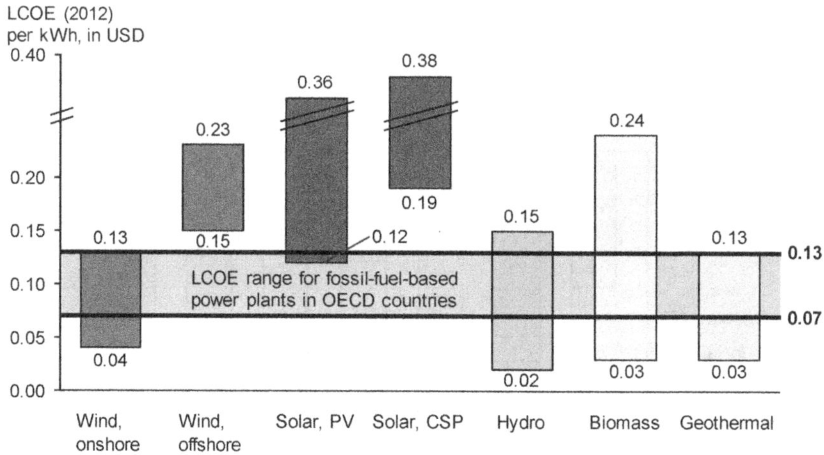

Figure 3 – LCOE for selected RE technologies relative to fossil power
Source: Own illustration, following IRENA (2013a), Figure 10.1, p. 79.

Hence, the bottom line is that the expansion of renewable energy sources can only be expected to continue at the current rate if regulatory support is maintained or even intensified. Therefore the question remains: Why are governments willing to finance renewables to such a large extend?

The most probable reason is immediate economic interest. As illustrated in Part (c) of Figure 1, the production of solar panels and wind turbines has become a very important industry on par with traditional energy equipment. This said it becomes obvious that renewable energy support policies work at the same time as an industry policy for the renewable energy equipment sector. Many governments have apparently recognized the chance to achieve two political goals at a time: a cleaner environment and additional jobs in the renewable energy sector. They hope that, once electricity generated from renewable sources becomes as cheap as or even cheaper than electricity from fossil or nuclear power plants, their initial investment will pay off not only environmentally but also economically.

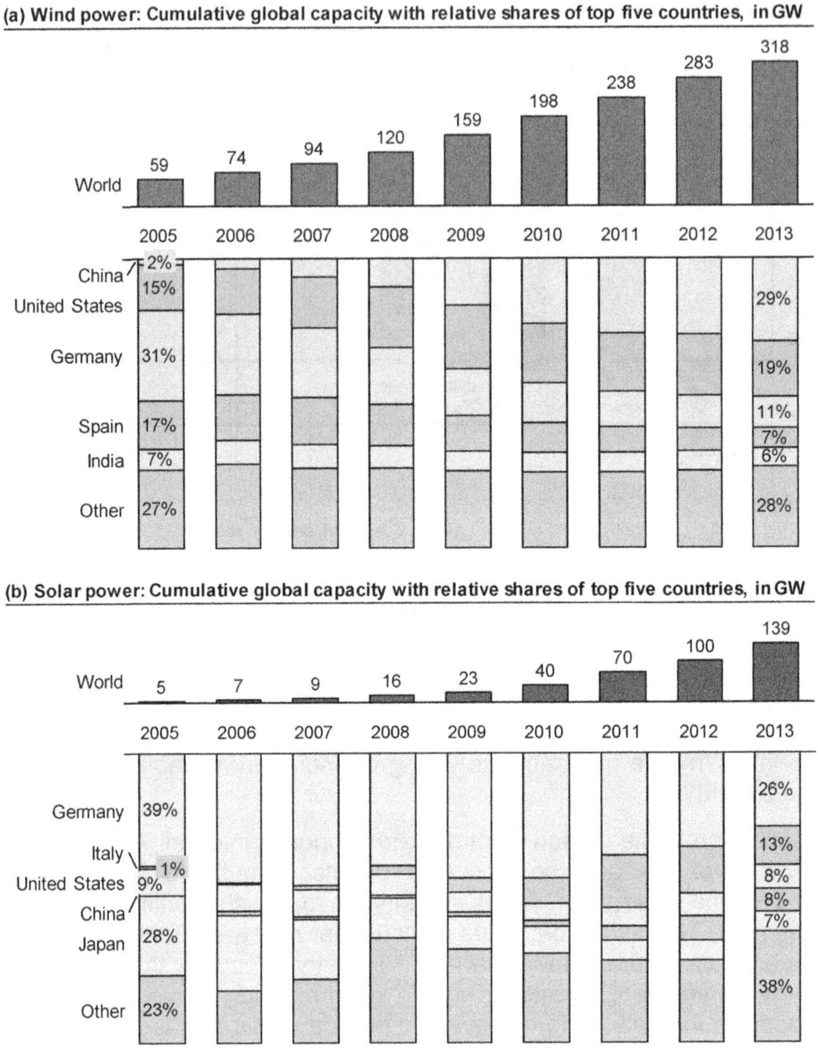

Figure 4 – Global solar and wind capacities with geographic split[7,8]
Source: Own illustration based on data from EPIA (2009, 2011, 2012, 2014) and GWEC (2006, 2008a, 2008b, 2009, 2010, 2011, 2012, 2013).

7 For a comprehensive data table containing the values for all individual country-year-combinations refer to Appendix 2.

8 Top five countries are selected based on installed capacities in 2013.

The data presented in Figure 4 show that a small group of countries has been very active in ramping up renewables installations and is, therefore, likely to follow a dual strategy of environmental protection and industrial support. Between 2005 and 2013, Germany, China, the US, and some others have dominated the market and jointly accounted for about two thirds of global demand. However, the data also show that some early adopters (e.g. Germany and Spain for wind power and Germany and Japan for solar power) continuously lose market share while China and others gain. With respect to solar, the market is also getting more fragmented.

Against the background of the efforts which these countries' made to create their own national renewable energy sectors, it would be interesting to see what implications shifts on the demand side of the energy equipment market have for the supply side. Do early investments in renewable energy capacities lead to the development of a domestic renewable energy equipment industry? If so, is this industry competitive enough to benefit from the emergence of new demand markets? These and other questions will be addressed in the following section based on an analysis of trade flows in renewables.

1.3 Patterns of trade in renewable energy equipment

The data presented in the previous sections highlight the simultaneous growth of renewable energy installations and respective support policies around the world. Based on these data and the summary of the political discussion on international climate change, it is reasonable to assume that these two developments are highly interrelated. In short, the expansion in green energy seems to depend strongly on the intensity of regulatory support and public funding.

Hence, governments have a strong incentive to develop not only renewable energy installations but also a domestic equipment industry including the related manufacturing jobs. This approach ensures that renewable energy subsidies stay local and are not used to prop up foreign suppliers. A recent case highlights governments' desire to support green energies and green jobs at the same time. In the so called 'Canada – Renewable energy' dispute the settlement bodies of the WTO ruled that a feed-in tariff of the province Ontario which contains local content requirements for the equipment is not in line with WTO's anti-discrimination principle (Bougette & Charlier, 2014; Charnovitz & Fischer, 2014; Lewis, 2014).

This section employs descriptive statistics on trade flows to find first indications for the existence of a positive relationship between government-induced renewable energy demand and export competitiveness of the domestic equipment industry.

The discussion starts with an analysis of the development of export and import volumes and shares by country and power generation technology for the years 1998, 2005 and 2012: Part (a) of Table 1 gives the results for the development of trade volumes; Part (b) shows changes in the distribution of world import and export market shares. Afterwards, the discussion turns to commonly used trade indicators which facilitate the comparison of countries' relative competitiveness.

In general, the results presented in Table 1 show that global trade volumes increased across all power generation technologies. However, while exports in conventional and hydro power equipment tripled between 1998 and 2012, exports in solar and wind increased more than 12- to 18-fold. These strong differences in technology-wise growth rates match the development of market shares (Figure 1).

One result that clearly stands out on the country level is the development of China into a major exporter of energy equipment. Even though China also increased its imports, the much stronger growth in exports more than compensated this development. By 2012, China is one of the largest exporters in all equipment classes. What is especially interesting with respect to China is the strong increase in imports of wind equipment between 1998 and 2005 followed by an even stronger drop between 2005 and 2012. Imports fell even below 1998 values. At the same time, exports in wind power equipment increased more than 100-times. This dramatic change in trade flows coincides with a strong increase in China's domestic wind energy capacities (see Figure 4). These developments indicate that China successfully managed to develop an internationally competitive domestic wind power industry.

Another interesting case is Denmark which has been a pioneer in wind power with first industrial-scale capacities in the 1970s/1980s. Table 1 shows that the early adoption of wind power in Denmark has translated into a very strong export performance which is maintained until today. Its import volumes, on the contrary, have always been marginal. Worth mentioning, Denmark has historically not been a relevant exporter of energy equipment and does not export significant volumes of any other electricity generation technology.

	Conventional			Renewables								
				Solar			Wind			Hydro		
	1998	2005	2012	1998	2005	2012	1998	2005	2012	1998	2005	2012
(a.1) Export volumes (1998 = 100)												
China[1)]	100	1,138	4,952	100	1,354	18,820		100	14,646	100	394	4,326
Denmark	100	98	120	100	103	153	100	336	551	100	58	997
Germany	100	174	320	100	384	1,321	100	3,044	11,215	100	191	331
Italy	100	206	295	100	458	1,913	100	145	4,889	100	87	318
Japan	100	150	256	100	402	489	100	40	363	100	154	112
Malaysia	100	173	334	100	241	720						
Spain	100	321	532	100	1,111	1,679	100	1,346	8,788	100	178	668
UK	100	136	204	100	326	372				100	124	82
US	100	172	256	100	164	228	100	17	1,847	100	68	146
World	**100**	**181**	**323**	**100**	**357**	**1,259**	**100**	**525**	**1,831**	**100**	**137**	**311**
(a.2) Imports volumes (1998 = 100)												
China	100	309	401	100	1,190	3,240	100	2,033	32	100	189	39
Denmark	100	80	95	100	158	1,448						
Germany	100	161	167	100	599	1,255	100	523	269	100	192	355
Italy	100	164	289	100	340	3,645	100	40	1,303	100	200	522
Japan	100	110	167	100	462	1,260	100	458	437	100	554	757
Malaysia	100	227	419	100	218	320						
Spain	100	502	299	100	630	1,181	100	78	412	100	108	385
UK	100	109	130	100	192	519	100	9,269	35,649	100	304	61
US	100	177	369	100	141	738	100	1,136	2,234	100	216	391
World	**100**	**181**	**325**	**100**	**383**	**1,312**	**100**	**874**	**2,523**	**100**	**119**	**309**
(b.1) Share in export volumes												
China	1%	3%	8%	3%	10%	38%	*	*	7%	2%	6%	27%
Denmark	*	*	*	1%	*	*	82%	52%	25%	*	*	1%
Germany	12%	11%	12%	9%	10%	10%	5%	31%	33%	8%	12%	9%
Italy	5%	6%	5%	1%	1%	1%	2%	1%	6%	4%	3%	4%
Japan	12%	10%	9%	33%	37%	13%	6%	*	1%	4%	5%	1%
Malaysia	*	*	*	10%	7%	6%	*	*	*	1%	*	*
Spain	*	1%	*	1%	2%	1%	4%	10%	18%	2%	3%	5%
UK	13%	10%	8%	3%	3%	1%	*	*	*	4%	3%	1%
US	30%	28%	23%	22%	10%	4%	6%	*	6%	9%	4%	4%
(b.2) Share in import volumes												
China	5%	8%	6%	5%	16%	12%	4%	10%	*	10%	16%	1%
Denmark	1%	*	*	1%	*	1%	4%	*	*	*	*	*
Germany	8%	7%	4%	14%	21%	13%	29%	17%	3%	3%	6%	4%
Italy	3%	3%	3%	2%	2%	6%	10%	*	5%	1%	2%	2%
Japan	5%	3%	2%	6%	7%	6%	4%	2%	1%	1%	3%	1%
Malaysia	1%	1%	2%	3%	2%	1%	*	*	*	1%	*	4%
Spain	1%	3%	1%	1%	2%	1%	5%	*	1%	1%	1%	1%
UK	11%	6%	4%	5%	2%	2%	1%	11%	15%	1%	2%	*
US	10%	10%	11%	25%	9%	14%	18%	24%	16%	3%	6%	4%

Notes: Data are taken from Comtrade database (UN, 2015). For details on the commodity classes used, see Appendix 3. Asterisks (*) indicate trade shares below 0.5%. Exports (Imports) are measured as FOB (CIF). Different reporting practices lead to mismatches between national and global data. | (1) Base year is 2006. Earlier data are not available.

Table 1 – Development of trade in power generation equipment

Source: Own illustration based on data from UN (2015); table structure following Groba & Kemfert (2011), Table 1, p. 25.

Germany is the third very interesting country case. It has traditionally been a leading exporter of conventional and hydro power equipment and even strengthened this position between 1998 and 2012. In addition, Germany has historically been one of the most important markets for solar and wind energy equipment. Similar to Denmark, Germany could leverage its large-scale and early investments in domestic wind power capacities and now claims very large and increasing shares in global exports. For solar power, however, the results are mixed. Although Germany has been the by far largest solar power market for decades, the country is still a net importer of such equipment (see also Table 2).

However, Germany is not the only country which has struggled to fully leverage its position as early adopter. Until the 2000s, Japan was leading in solar power equipment and continuously lost this position. The United States went through a similar development with its wind power industry during the 2000s.

In sum, these observations indicate that early adoption and large-scale development often lead to increasing export volumes and increasing market shares. However, as the cases of solar in Japan and Germany and wind in the United States show, there are also prominent exceptions to this pattern. It will be interesting to explore what the reasons for these exceptions might be and what role environmental regulation plays.

So far the discussion of changes in trade patterns of energy equipment was based on absolute figures, which do not take into account country-specific factors such as the trade openness or market size. Although the analysis of absolute indicators was helpful to examine volume changes and market shares, relative trade indicators are better suited to compare countries' competitiveness. Table 2 gives the values of widely used relative trade indicators. These indicators are first relative world market share, values > 1 indicate that a country's export success in a specific good is above country average, second relative trade position, values > 0 represent net exports, and third revealed comparative advantage, values > 1 indicate that the ratio of a good's exports over its imports exceed the average ratio of exports over imports for all goods traded by this country. In combination, these indicators allows for a profound evaluation of countries' export competitiveness (Groba & Kemfert, 2011).

The relative world market shares confirm the results of Table 1. The data in Part (a) of Table 2 show above average world market shares for Denmark and Spain in wind and for China and Japan in solar power equipment, which is perfectly in line with these countries' high (absolute) market shares discussed before. However, the data presented in Table 2 also suggest that absolute world market shares should generally be interpreted with care. Although Germany is the largest exporter of wind turbines by volume, the relative indicator reveals that this is partly due to economic size and trade openness. While Germany is competitive in wind power, it is not as competitive as Spain and Denmark.

The results for the relative trade position and the revealed comparative advantage, presented in Parts (b) and (c) of Table 2, likewise confirm the outcome of the previous discussion. However, it is worthwhile to highlight some additional observations. Between 1998 and 2012, China and Spain developed from near pure importers to near pure exporters of wind energy equipment. A similar effect can be observed for Germany. As all three countries have also large domestic wind power markets, this observation again supports the notion that some countries have been successful in combining environmental and industrial policies.

Moreover, the data suggest that export success in wind and solar power equipment does not depend on existing competencies in the production of conventional energy equipment. The cases of Denmark and Spain demonstrate that very high levels of export competitiveness in wind turbines can be achieved without access to existing knowledge or industrial infrastructures from the production of gas- and steam-powered turbines used in conventional power plants (fossil and nuclear). Similarly, the data also indicate that export successes in wind and solar power are largely independent from each other. As of 2012, only China and Japan manage to maintain competitive advantages in both technologies.

Generally, the analyses show increasing numbers of net exporters in renewable energy equipment and highly volatile trade positions, especially compared to conventional technologies. Both are strong signs of an ongoing competition for market leadership in one of the key industry sectors for the decades to come.

Overall, the three main findings of the analysis of trade flows in renewable energy equipment can be summarized as follows: First and most important, there seems to be a positive relationship between early and large-scale adoption of renewables and exports of the same. This means that there might be an opportunity to use environmental regulation as industry policy. Second, early adoption and large domestic installations do not per se guarantee export success as the examples of the United States and others show. Third, competitiveness in wind and solar power equipment seems to be rather independent from each other as well as from competitiveness in conventional power generation technologies.

	Conventional			Renewables								
				Solar			Wind			Hydro		
	'98	'05	'12	'98	'05	'12	'98	'05	'12	'98	'05	'12
(a) Relative world market share[1)]												
China	0.1	0.4	0.6	0.7	1.2	3.1	0.0	0.0	0.6	0.5	0.7	2.2
Denmark	0.2	*	*	0.6	*	0.1	84.9	60.9	37.9	*	*	2.0
Germany	1.1	1.1	1.3	0.9	1.0	1.1	0.5	3.0	3.8	0.8	1.2	1.0
Italy	1.1	1.6	1.7	0.1	0.2	0.3	0.0	0.2	2.2	0.8	0.6	1.4
Japan	1.5	1.5	1.9	4.2	5.9	2.6	0.7	0.1	0.2	0.5	0.7	0.3
Malaysia	0.2	0.2	0.2	6.5	4.4	4.0	*	*	*	0.5	*	0.1
Spain	0.1	0.2	0.3	0.3	1.0	0.5	0.0	4.7	10.2	1.1	1.5	2.9
UK	2.4	2.4	2.9	0.6	0.7	0.3	0.0	0.0	0.0	0.6	0.8	0.3
US	2.3	3.3	2.8	1.7	1.2	0.5	0.5	0.0	0.7	0.7	0.5	0.5
(b) Relative trade position[2)]												
China	-0.8	-0.4	0.2	-0.4	-0.3	0.5	-1.0	-1.0	1.0	-0.7	-0.4	0.9
Denmark	-0.4	*	*	0.0	*	-0.8	0.9	1.0	1.0	*	*	1.0
Germany	0.2	0.2	0.5	-0.2	-0.4	-0.2	-0.6	0.2	0.8	0.4	0.4	0.4
Italy	0.3	0.4	0.3	-0.6	-0.5	-0.8	-1.0	0.2	0.2	0.5	0.1	0.3
Japan	0.4	0.5	0.6	0.7	0.6	0.3	0.4	-0.7	0.3	0.8	0.3	0.0
Malaysia	-0.6	-0.7	-0.7	0.5	0.5	0.7	*	*	*	-0.0	*	-0.9
Spain	-0.6	-0.7	-0.4	-0.2	0.0	-0.1	-1.0	0.9	0.9	0.4	0.6	0.6
UK	0.1	0.2	0.3	-0.2	0.0	-0.4	-1.0	-1.0	-1.0	0.6	0.3	0.7
US	0.5	0.5	0.4	-0.1	-0.0	-0.6	-0.4	-1.0	-0.4	0.5	-0.1	0.0
(c) Revealed comparative advantage[3)]												
China	0.1	0.3	1.1	0.4	0.4	2.2	0.0	0.0	116	0.2	0.3	18.1
Denmark	0.5	*	*	1.0	*	0.1	27.5	++	++	*	*	++
Germany	1.3	1.3	2.3	0.5	0.3	0.6	0.2	1.3	9.6	2.1	1.9	1.9
Italy	1.5	2.2	1.8	0.2	0.4	0.1	0.0	1.4	1.4	2.5	1.2	1.7
Japan	1.8	3.0	4.3	3.5	3.7	2.1	1.6	0.2	2.0	5.3	1.8	1.2
Malaysia	0.2	0.1	0.2	2.4	2.6	5.8	*	*	*	0.7	*	0.0
Spain	0.3	0.2	0.5	0.7	1.6	1.0	0.0	29.1	27.3	2.8	5.6	4.5
UK	1.5	2.1	2.9	0.7	1.4	0.6	0.0	0.0	0.0	4.9	2.3	8.2
US	4.7	6.6	3.8	1.2	2.0	0.4	0.7	0.0	0.7	4.0	1.8	1.8

Notes: Trade data are taken from the Comtrade database (UN, 2015). For details on the commodity classes used (Harmonized System), refer to Appendix 3. Asterisks (*) indicate that trade flows are too low to calculate meaningful trade indicators. Double pluses (++) indicate high positive values. | (1) The relative world market share is calculated as the ratio of a country's share in the total world exports in a specific commodity class (e.g. solar power equipment) and the country's average share in total world exports. Values above 1 (highlighted in gray) indicate an above average world market share compared to other commodities exported by the same country. (2) The relative trade position is calculated as the ratio of a country's exports minus its imports and the sum of a country's exports and imports. Values above 0 (highlighted in gray) indicate that a country's exports exceed its imports in the given commodity class. (3) The revealed comparative advantage is calculated as the ratio of a country's exports in a specific commodity class (e.g. solar power equipment) over its imports in the same commodity class and the country's overall exports over its overall imports. Values above 1 (highlighted in gray) indicate a comparative advantage in a given commodity class.

Table 2 – Indicators of trade in electricity generation equipment
Source: Own illustration based on data from UN (2015); table structure following Groba & Kemfert (2011), Table 4, p. 28.

1.4 Research question

The discussion of the previous sections highlights the extent and the pace at which renewable energies have changed the composition of the electricity mix and the market for new power plants. Within little more than a decade, renewable energies developed from niche into mainstream technologies, which are now close to becoming fully competitive with conventional electricity sources. This fundamental change in the structure of a major industry such as energy equipment would most certainly not have been possible without regulatory interference.

However, governments' enormous support for renewable energies is probably not driven by environmental considerations alone. The prospect of creating an internationally competitive, domestic renewable energy equipment industry seems to play an important role in the definition of national policies as well. The analysis of trade flows conducted in Section 1.3 supports this notion and shows that early investments in renewable energy and export success often come together.

In sum, these observations suggest the existence of a relationship between environmental regulation, technological progress in and diffusion of renewable energy technologies, and the development of a comparative advantage in these product groups. The objective of this dissertation is to investigate this relationship and to determine the impact of countries' environmental regulation on the export competitiveness of their domestic renewable energy equipment industries[9].

The first step will be to investigate the connection between environmental regulation and technological innovation in the field of renewable energy equipment. This part of my research project is based on Hicks' (1932) theory of induced innovation.

In a second step, I will explore the connection between these regulation-induced technological innovations and the export competitiveness of manufacturers of renewable energy equipment. On the one hand, this part of the thesis builds on the theory of lead markets for environmental products (Beise, 2001, 2004; Beise & Rennings, 2005), and, on the other hand, it contains elements of Porter's diamond model to analyze the competitive advantage of nations (Porter, 1990).

---

9 Due to data availability and economic relevance, the analysis is limited to wind and solar power.

The theoretical foundations of these two parts of the research model are combined in the so called narrowly strong Porter Hypothesis[10] (Porter, 1991; Porter & van der Linde, 1995). This specific version of the Porter Hypothesis entails that well-crafted environmental regulation induces innovation which ultimately leads to a comparative advantage of the domestic environmental technology industry. This effect is assumed to increase in regulation intensity (Jaffe & Palmer, 1997).

The research approach used in this thesis builds on previous empirical work by Costantini & Crespi (2008), Johnstone, Haščič, & Popp (2008), Costantini & Mazzanti (2012), Cao & Groba (2013), and Groba (2014). Taken together, these studies find that countries which have adopted stringent environmental regulation are more innovative and more competitive in renewable energy technologies.

My dissertation advances the existing empirical research on the narrowly strong Porter Hypothesis in four ways. First, it builds on the most recent data, what is a decisive aspect given the fast-paced development in the renewable energy technologies sector (REN21, 2014a). Second, it is exclusively concerned with renewable power generation technologies. Existing publications either cover the entire green sector or restrict their analyses to one specific technology like solar power. Third, it uses a two-step approach and tests both parts of the Porter Hypothesis separately. Recent research projects on the narrowly strong Porter Hypothesis combine both parts and focus on the competitiveness effect alone. Fourth and most important, this thesis takes carefully into consideration the impact of multiple different types of environmental regulation. This novelty is of particular importance for research on the narrowly strong Porter Hypothesis. Porter & van der Linde (1995) clearly stress that both the innovation inducement and the export effect are conditional to the existence of well-crafted regulation. Nevertheless, as to the best of my knowledge, none of the existing studies on the narrowly strong Porter Hypothesis measured regulation design at sufficient levels of detail.

1.5 Structure of the thesis

The thesis is subdivided into six chapters. Figure 5 gives an overview of the chapter structure and the connections between individual chapters.

In this chapter, I have established the rationale for the assumed relationship between the intensity and design of countries' renewable energy support policies, and their export competitiveness in wind and solar power equipment. Based on this discussion, I have formulated my

10 For a discussion on the different types of the Porter Hypothesis refer to Section 2.1.

research question and have introduced the narrowly strong Porter Hypothesis (Porter, 1991; Porter & van der Linde, 1995) and, to a lesser extent, the lead market theory for environmental goods and services (Beise & Rennings, 2005) as the theoretical underpinnings of my research project.

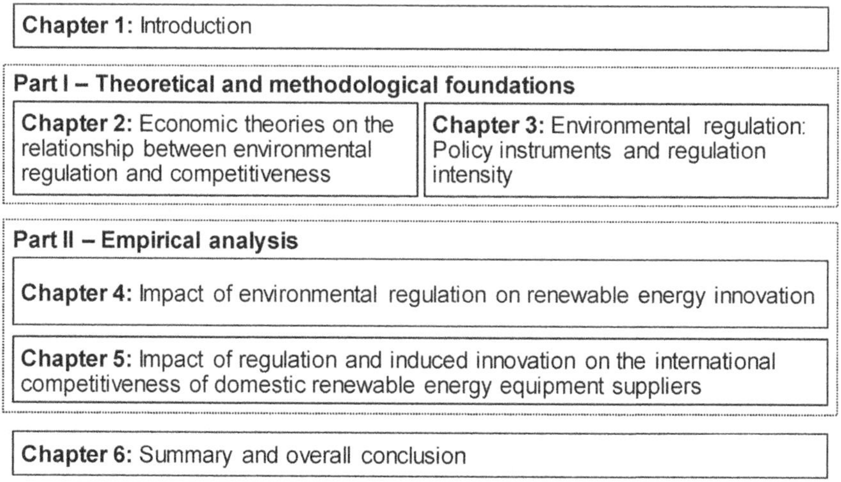

Figure 5 – Overview of the chapter structure
Source: Own illustration.

Part I, which follows directly on the introduction, deals with the thesis' theoretical and methodological foundations and consists of two separate chapters. Chapter 2 summarizes the established economic theories on the relationship between environmental regulation and competitiveness. The focus of the theoretical discussion is on the concepts of induced innovation and the Porter Hypothesis in its different manifestations. A special emphasis is on the question what Porter & van der Linde (1995) meant by well-crafted environmental regulation. The following literature review concentrates on the most recent empirical research.

Chapter 3 has a more methodological focus. It starts with an overview of common instruments of environmental policy and an evaluation of these instruments against Porter & van der Linde's (1995) criteria for well-crafted environmental regulation. After a brief discussion on the relevance of these instruments for the demand and supply of renewable energy technologies, the emphasis shifts from policy design to regulation intensity. The section on regulation intensity covers measurement challenges and compares alternative intensity indicators. Finally, the section contains a comprehensive analysis of the dissemination patterns and rates of different renewable energy support policies as well as an analysis of the contribution of specific policy instruments to countries' overall regulation intensity.

The second part of the thesis contains the empirical test of the narrowly strong Porter Hypothesis. As previously mentioned in the discussion of the research question, the Porter Hypothesis can be disentangled into two steps. Consequently, Part II of the thesis consists of two dedicated chapters as well, one for each step of the Porter Hypothesis. The analysis starts with Chapter 4 and the empirical test of the relationship between intensity and design of environmental regulation and innovation in renewable energy technologies. Similarly, Chapter 5 covers the second step of the empirical analysis and tests the impact of regulation and regulation-induced innovation on the export competitiveness of countries' domestic renewable energy equipment industries. Each chapter contains a critical review of the methodological approaches and data collection processes applied in the existing empirical research, as well as a detailed comparison of results between this and previous studies.

Chapter 6 summarizes the results of the empirical analysis and discusses the implications for researchers and policy makers.

2 Review of the Porter Hypothesis and the related literature

Beginning in the 1970s and 1980s, interested citizen, non-governmental organizations and policy makers became increasingly aware of the potentially negative consequences of ever growing economic activity and resource demand. The notion of finite resources, the unsustainability of prevailing consumption levels in the industrialized world, and accordingly the need to preserve these natural resources spread very quickly. Prominent hallmarks of the developing modern environmental movement are the celebration of the first Earth Day in 1970, the foundation of Greenpeace in 1971 and the presentation of the Limits to Growth report by the Club of Rome in 1972 (Jaffe, Peterson, Portney, & Stavins, 1995).

Not surprisingly, these substantial changes in common thinking on economic activity soon triggered an intensive debate in academia. This discussion ultimately led to the creation of an entirely new, specialized field of research: environmental economics (Mäler & Vincent, 2005). Amongst others, environmental economics is concerned with research on the relationship between countries' level of environmental regulation and their international competitiveness – the research area of this doctoral thesis.

Until the emergence of the revisionist view in the early 1990s, the conventional view was the uncontested standard theory in trade and environment research. Although the proponents of the conventional view do not question the effectiveness of environmental regulation in fighting pollution, they argue that environmental protection comes at considerable economic cost (Jaffe et al., 1995).

Their line of argumentation is based on classical trade theory which suggests that any constraint imposed on a firm's production function restricts its choice set and therefore forces it to move away from the efficient frontier. On an abstract level, the environment is a regular factor of production such as capital or labor. A clean environment allows firms to dispose of pollutants which they generate as by-products in their production processes. However, if a government decides to restrict firms' access to the production factor environment by limiting the discharge volume or charging a fine per unit of pollution, it imposes an additional restriction on their production functions. Hence, the adoption of more or more stringent environmental policies inevitably leaves domestic firms at a comparative disadvantage relative to competitors operating in jurisdictions without such restrictions (Copeland & Taylor, 2003).

Irrespective of the presumed negative effects on countries' international competitiveness, many governments were ready to increase the requirements of existing environmental standards or even adopt additional policy measures. In other words, policy makers were willing to trade off the private interests of domestic export-oriented corporations against the public's interest of a clean and healthy environment (Jaffe et al., 1995). It is not surprising that this notion of the environment-competitiveness relationship as an arm's length distribution battle between energy-intensive and trade-exposed industries and the general public resulted in political conflicts between business and environmentalists.

The revisionist view, established by Porter (1991) and others[11] around 1990, offers a way out of this deadlock between the two political camps. It takes issue with the idea of a fixed trade-off between environmental protection and international competitiveness, a central pillar of the conventional view. It suggests instead that these two objectives are not necessarily competing ends but can be achieved at the same time.

According to the Porter Hypothesis, the proponents of the conventional view incorrectly assume a static competition framework which implies that ceteris paribus changes in environmental regulation inevitably result in cost changes and corresponding competitiveness effects. In reality however, competition is not a static but highly dynamic game. Competitive positions are subject to frequent change and are constantly re-determined through innovation and entrepreneurial activity in a broader sense. This entails that changes in regulatory stringency can result in win-win situations where both firms and the environment are left better off. The key to these win-win situations are regulation-induced innovations which are completely neglected under the static competition framework of the conventional view (Porter, 1991; Porter & van der Linde, 1995).

Irrespective of the undisputed importance of the conventional view for research on the trade and environment relationship in general, the scope of this literature review is restricted to the concepts of the revisionist view and most importantly the Porter Hypothesis. As this research project is concerned with the effect of environmental regulation on the renewable energy equipment industry, it can certainly be assumed that the positive effects of regulation proposed by Porter and his followers by far outweigh the negative effects stressed by the proponents of the conventional view.

---

11 Barrett (1991) is a good example for another early publication questioning the conventional view on competitiveness and the environment.

For other industries[12], such as oil and gas or basic materials, this scope limitation would indeed not be possible.

This literature review starts in Section 2.1 with a detailed presentation of the Porter Hypothesis, its different manifestations, and frequent criticism on its underlying assumptions. Section 2.2 follows with the discussion of the related empirical research. Hereby, it lays a special emphasis on recent publications and contributions related to the narrowly strong version of the Porter Hypothesis. Afterwards, Section 2.3 establishes the connections between Porter Hypothesis, induced innovation, and lead market theory. Finally, Section 2.4 outlines the thesis' contribution to research on the relationship between environmental regulation and countries' competitiveness in renewable energy equipment.

2.1 Porter Hypothesis: Main arguments, types and criticism

As mentioned before, the fundamental argument of the Porter Hypothesis is that well-crafted environmental regulation fosters innovations which frequently lead to win-win situations where the regulated firm and the environment are left with a benefit. In order to convince the scientific community of their hypothesis, Porter & van der Linde (1995) address three main topics. First, how can environmental regulation induce innovation? Second, how common are the associated innovation offsets[13]? Third, what are the characteristics of well-crafted environmental regulation? I will briefly discuss these questions in the following.

According to Porter & van der Linde (1995), innovation inducement is possible as the Panglossian belief of optimal decision making does not hold under a dynamic model which is characterized by imperfect information. Top management of corporations is concerned with a wide range of topics and environmental protection is usually not a top priority. Hence, profound knowledge on profit-enhancing environmental investments is rare. The authors argue further that under such circumstances, well-crafted environmental regulation promotes innovation in six distinct ways. Two out of these six ways are particularly relevant for the renewable energy sector. First, regulation reduces uncertainty and thereby encourages firms to increase their investments into research and development. Second, regulation ensures a level

12 This is especially true for energy-intensive and export-exposed industries.

13 Innovation offsets occur when the benefits from induced eco-innovations exceed the costs of complying with more stringent environmental regulation.

playing field in the transitional phase from established to new technologies[14].

The second point addressed by Porter & van der Linde (1995) is the frequency at which innovation offsets occur. Although critics of the revisionist view usually do not question the overall concept of innovation offsets, they do insist that such offsets are not the general rule but the rare exception. In order to convince critics of their point, Porter & van der Linde (1995) draw back on the concept of resource productivity. According to their arguments, pollution "is a manifestation of economic waste and involves unnecessary, inefficient or incomplete utilization of resources" (p. 105). Hence, as pollution and waste exist in almost all economic processes, opportunities for productivity improvements and therefore innovation should be plentiful. However, the article leaves open the nature of the connection between resource productivity and profitability which is necessary for an end-to-end explanation of economic offsets measured in monetary terms.

The third and probably most important aspect for the research scope of this thesis are the characteristics of well-crafted environmental regulation. Porter & van der Linde (1995) are very clear on this point and stress repeatedly that only well-crafted regulation leads to their postulated universally desirable win-win situations. According to the Porter Hypothesis, well-crafted "[e]nvironmental regulation should focus on outcomes, not technologies [...] [and] include the use of market incentives" (pp. 110-111). Moreover, "[a]n appropriate regulatory process is one in which regulations themselves are clear, who must meet them is clear and industry accepts regulation and begins innovating to address them" (p. 113).

Although all three main features of well-designed environmental policy are individually important, the role of market incentives stands out. Tradable emission permits or comparable instruments help to determine a fair price for pollution based on supply and demand. Hence, they ensure that the costs of emission are internalized at source. This feature is especially important in the energy sector where conventional electricity generation technologies traditionally benefit from the fact that operators of power plants do not or only partially bear the cost of pollution. This entails that conventional technologies have a natural advantage over renewables. Well-crafted environmental regulation which captures the

[14] As discussed in more detail in Section 2.3.1, new technologies are usually not competitive with established solutions from the very beginning. Their competitiveness improves gradually through learning curve effects in development, production, and operation as well as through network effects.

cost of emitting carbon dioxide and other pollutants nullifies this unfair advantage and thereby ensures that conventional and renewable power generation technologies compete on equal terms.

Clearly, the ideas of the Porter Hypothesis stand in stark contrast to the conventional view of a fixed trade-off between environmental regulation and competitiveness. Consequently, the publication of the Porter Hypothesis triggered a wave of criticism by the proponents of the conventional view. The most cited critical publication on the Porter Hypothesis is Palmer, Oates, & Portney (1995).

In their response to Porter & van der Linde (1995), Palmer, Oates, & Portney (1995) state that they are strictly opposed to some aspects of the Porter Hypothesis while they well agree to others. They fully agree, for instance, to the notion that market-based instruments are preferable to traditional command-and-control measures which prescribe a specific technology and thereby reduce degrees of freedom. They also acknowledge that regulation sometimes promotes eco-innovations which in turn lead to improved product quality or lower cost. However, they are strictly opposed to the idea that "enlightened" regulators systematically direct firms towards profit-enhancing investment opportunities, which they would not have pursued in the absence of environmental regulation. In other words, they take issue with the view that regulators are better in identifying opportunities for profit-enhancing innovations than private sector managers.

Besides Porter & van der Linde's (1995) line of argumentation, Palmer, Oates, & Portney (1995) also question the validity of their case-study-based approach. They argue that anecdotal evidence is not sufficiently reliable and representative to support an idea which is as broadly applicable as the Porter Hypothesis. They bring forward the argument that "[i]t would be an easy matter [...] to assemble a matching list where firms have found their costs increased and profits reduced as a result of (even enlightened) environmental regulations, not to mention cases where regulation has pushed firms over the brink into bankruptcy" (pp. 120-121). Moreover, they refer to the Commerce Department's Bureau of Economic Analysis' annual report on pollution abatement and control expenditures. According to the 1992 version of this report, US corporations' pollution abatement and control expenditures (PACE) accumulated to USD 102 bn while documented innovation offsets just summed up to USD 1.7 bn, i.e. US corporations' 1992 net expenditures exceeded USD 100 bn. They argue further that although expenditures are much easier to measure and therefore much more reliable than offsets, even large errors in offset estimation would not change the overall picture that environmental regulation had a large and negative effect on profitability and therefore international competitiveness.

On the initial publication of the Porter Hypothesis and the critical response by Palmer, Oates, & Portney (1995), followed an intensive academic discussion among the proponents of the conventional and the revisionist view. In order to structure the discussion for and against the revisionist view, Jaffe & Palmer (1997) disentangle the original Porter Hypothesis into four distinct types. Each of these types highlights specific aspects of the Porter Hypothesis and therefore allows for a much more focused discussion.

First, the weak version of the Porter Hypothesis states that environmental regulation induces product and/or process innovations by introducing additional restrictions into the competitive framework. As for any change in framework conditions, firms are expected to adjust their offerings and operations in order to reach a new optimum. The weak version of the Porter Hypothesis does not require that these adjustments are profit-enhancing, i.e. complete innovation offsets are not expected to be the rule.

Second, the narrow version of the Porter Hypothesis suggests that only well-crafted environmental regulation induces eco-innovations. Therefore, the narrow version is a special case of the weak Porter Hypothesis.

Third, the strong version of the Porter Hypothesis goes beyond pure innovation inducement and predicts the frequent occurrence of complete innovation offsets. Hence, it requires that without environmental regulation firms do not realize all profit-maximizing investment opportunities. As discussed before, this assumption is sharply criticized by opponents of the revisionist view. Jaffe & Palmer (1997) point out that this version of the Porter Hypothesis implies "that environmental regulation is a free lunch (or even a 'paid lunch')" (p. 611).

Fourth and final, the narrowly strong version of the Porter Hypothesis entails that complete innovation offsets are most likely in the environmental goods and services industry. The reason is that this industry naturally benefits from the need of other (polluting) industries to comply with more stringent regulatory requirements. It follows that "government can garner dynamic comparative advantage for its domestic environmental technology industry by inducing early innovation in environmental technologies" (Jaffe & Palmer, 1997, p. 610). Therefore, the narrowly strong version of the Porter Hypothesis is most closely related to the research focus of this thesis due to its focus on the renewable energy equipment sector.

2.2 Empirical research on the Porter Hypothesis

This section presents the empirical literature on the weak, narrow, strong and narrowly strong Porter Hypothesis and discusses its main results, common shortcomings and limitations, and highlights areas of future research.

The discussion builds on but is not limited to the literature reviews of Ambec, Cohen, Elgie, & Lanoie (2011, 2013), Ambec & Barla (2006), Ambec & Lanoie (2008), and Brännlund & Lundgren (2009)[15]. In addition to the literature presented in these reviews, I introduce the most recent studies and working papers to ensure a comprehensive and up-to-date picture on research on the Porter Hypothesis. Moreover, I include some older publications which have not been covered previously but which I deem relevant for the discussion. Most importantly, I extend the scope of the previous literature reviews to include research on the narrowly strong Porter Hypothesis, which is of highest relevance for this thesis. None of the above-mentioned literature reviews covers this specific version of the Porter Hypothesis.

2.2.1 The weak Porter Hypothesis

The weak Porter Hypothesis is certainly among the versions which get most attention by researchers. This is probably due to the fact that the question whether environmental regulation induces innovation is essential for the Porter Hypothesis as a whole. If regulation fails to induce innovation in the first place, chances are very low that it leads to Pareto-optimal outcomes where both the environment and the economy are better off.

Research on the weak Porter Hypothesis can be classified in three categories based on how it measures innovation. The first group of studies proxies innovation by plant age. The authors argue that decreases in plant age imply that older, less efficient equipment has been replaced my more modern and efficient installations. The second group of studies measures innovation as research and development (R&D) expenditures. It is argued that changes in input measures, such

[15] For additional literature reviews on the Porter Hypothesis refer to Pasurka (2008) who discusses the relationship between environmental regulation and pollution abatement in general and covers the conventional as well as the revisionist view, and to a report by the OECD (2010) which reviews the literature on the relationship between environmental policy and competitiveness.

as R&D expenditures, are well suited to test if regulation has a positive impact on research activity. Put differently, a change in regulation followed by a sudden increase in R&D expenditures would indicate that firms invest in research in order to find more efficient production methods and reduce pollution (or resource demand) per unit of output. The third group of studies goes one step further and tests whether environmental regulation has a positive impact on the inventiveness of regulated firms. While measuring innovation by R&D expenditures is a good approach to test whether firms respond to regulation, measuring innovation by the inventive output is a good approach to test whether regulation actually leads to technological advancement which is a necessary precondition for the win-win situations predicted by the Porter Hypothesis.

In the following, I will introduce studies from all three categories of research on the weak Porter Hypothesis and discuss their results as well as the methodologies and data samples employed. An overview of the studies covered in this section is given in Table 3.

The discussion starts with publications that proxy innovation by plant age. Nelson, Tietenberg, & Donihue (1993) are first to examine this relationship. Using a simultaneous equation model with three equations for regulatory stringency, emission levels and plant age, they find that average plant age of US steam power plants increased by more than three years between 1969 and 1983. A more recent study by Hamamoto (2006) finds for a sample of Japanese manufacturing firms in the 1960s and 1970s that regulation had a negative impact on plant age. In contrast to Nelson et al. (1993), Hamamoto (2006) uses a reduced form linear regression model and is only interested in the effect of regulation, measured by PACE or R&D grants, on plant age. Overall, the empirical results appear to be mixed. However, Burtraw (2000) points out that until 1990 clean air regulation in the US was not in line with the criteria for well-crafted regulation in the sense of the Porter Hypothesis. Hence, the results of Nelson et al. (1993) should be interpreted carefully, as their entire data sample represents the situation in the US before 1990.

The second approach to empirically test the weak Porter Hypothesis is based on R&D expenditures and provides more consistent results than the plant age approach discussed previously. Jaffe & Palmer (1997) are among the first to adopt this approach. They find for their panel of 24 US manufacturing industries from 1973 to 1991 that environmental regulation, measured by pollution abatement and control expenditures and government R&D support, has a positive impact on R&D expenditures in the private sector. However, maybe more important than the actual results, is a methodological novelty introduced in this study.

Jaffe & Palmer (1997) use a lag of one year to model the impact of their regulation indicators on research activity. Many researchers have successfully applied this approach in later empirical studies.

Kneller & Manderson (2012) and Rubashkina, Galeotti, & Verdolini (2015) are among those more recent empirical studies on the weak Porter Hypothesis which apply the lag structure proposed by Jaffe & Palmer (1997). Kneller & Manderson (2012) use a dynamic linear regression model with fixed effects for industry affiliation and time to estimate the impact of lagged PACE and lagged R&D investments on current R&D investments. Their panel includes UK manufacturing firms between 2000 and 2006. They find that while regulation has a positive impact on environment-related R&D investments it has no impact on R&D investments in general. Hence, they conclude that innovation-induced green R&D investments crowd out other (more profitable) research projects. Rubashkina et al. (2015) find similar results for their panel of European manufacturing firms between 1997 and 2009. Their study shows that the innovation-inducement-effect can be demonstrated for multi-country samples and for different time lags[16].

Another recent study is Lanoie et al. (2011) who employ a questionnaire-based approach to explore the impact of environmental regulation on R&D expenditures. Their questionnaire database contains information on 4,200 manufacturing facilities from seven OECD countries in 2003. The outcome of their probit estimation confirms the results of other studies: regulation induces environment-related R&D expenditures.

The third class of publications, empirical studies on the impact of environmental regulation on innovativeness which is mostly measured by patent applications, finds on balance a positive relationship as well. While early studies on US manufacturing firms by Jaffe & Palmer (1997) and Brunnermeier & Cohen (2003) only find a quite small and partly insignificant positive effect of environmental regulation on patent applications, later studies with more recent samples all find positive effects which are statistically significant.

Popp (2006) finds in his study on a panel of electrical utilities in the US, Japan and Germany between 1967 and 2001 that environmental regulation has a positive effect on domestic patent applications. Interestingly, he also finds that regulation has no impact on foreign patents. This finding implies that suppliers of pollution abatement and control technologies do not respond to demand changes in foreign

---

16 Rubashkina et al. (2015) use time lags of one, two and three years to demonstrate the robustness of their results.

markets. In other words, only domestic regulation changes are found to induce environment-related innovation in electricity generation technologies. Similarly, Calel & Dechezleprêtre (2012) show in their economy-wide study on the impact of the European Emission Trading Systems (EU ETS) on patent applications by European firms in the years 2000 to 2009 that regulated firms reacted to the EU ETS introduction by a 10% increase in low-carbon innovations. Unregulated firms, which were not affected by the EU ETS introduction, did not change their innovation patterns. Hence, Popp (2006) and Calel & Dechezleprêtre (2012) both demonstrate that the innovation effect of increases in regulatory stringency is limited to those countries and industries which are directly affected by the change in regulation.

A study of Johnstone, Haščič, Poirier, & Hemar (2012) unveils an additional facet of the relationship between environmental regulation and new patent application in the green sector. The study shows based on a panel of 77 countries over the period from 2001 to 2007 that policy stringency (derived from WEF survey data) has a positive impact on the number of environment-related patent applications. In addition, they show that this effect of environmental regulation is amplified by a country's general innovation capacity. Under the assumption that economically advanced countries generally have high or even very high innovation capacities, this means that leading industrialized countries have the greatest potential to use environmental regulation as means to induce green-sector innovations.

Finally, a recent publication by Nesta, Vona, & Nicolli (2014) explores whether the intensity of industry competition has an additional effect on regulation-induced innovativeness in the respective sector. Based on a pre-sample mean Poisson model and generalized method of moments estimation, they find for their panel of 27 countries between 1976 and 2007 that environmental regulation generally has a positive impact on innovativeness and that this effect is pronounced in sectors which are characterized by a high level of intra-industry competition. Moreover, they find that higher quality patents are associated with regulation-inducement, while lower quality patents are mostly related to high levels of industry competition. Nesta et al. (2014) define high quality patents, as patents which have been filed to multiple patent offices in different jurisdictions. In this context, the so-called triadic patent families signal especially high value and quality. The attribute triadic applies to patent families which have been registered with the patent offices in the US, Japan, and Europe.

In sum, all three approaches to explore the relationship between environmental regulation and innovation unveil positive and statically significant effects and therefore provide empirical support for the weak Porter Hypothesis. Although many of these studies are based on data from the United States, the number of non-US and international studies is high enough to conclude that the discovered effects are valid on a global level. Only two of the studies reviewed report insignificant or contradictory results. However, as discussed previously, the data sample of these studies are already quite dated and do no longer represent the current state of the world. From a methodological perspective, it becomes apparent that studies with use a lag structure to model the effect of regulation on innovation yield comparably strong and highly significant results.

Study	Sample	Dependent var.	Explanatory var. (selected)	Methodology	Results (selected)	
(a) Impact of environmental regulation on plant age						
Nelson, Tietenberg, & Donihue (1993)	> Utilities > United States > 1969 to 1983 (panel data)	> Plant age > Emission > Env. regulation	> Env. regulation (PACE (total and related to air pollution))	> Simultaneous equation model with 3 equations > Three-stage least squares estimation	> Env. regulation has positive impact on plant age	+
Hamamoto (2006)	> Manufacturing > Japan > 1960s to 1970s (panel data)	> Innovation (plant age)	> Env. regulation (PACE, R&D subsidies)	> Reduced form linear regression with fixed effects (industry, time)	> PACE have negative impact on plant age	-
(b) Impact of environmental regulation on R&D expenditures						
Jaffe & Palmer (1997)	> Manufacturing (24 industries) > United States > 1973 to 1991 (panel data)	> Innovation (R&D expenditures)	> Env. regulation (PACE, government R&D)	> Linear regression model with(out) fixed effects (industry, time) > Lag for env. reg. indicator (1 year)	> Env. regulation has positive impact on R&D expenditures	+
Hamamoto (2006)	> Manufacturing > Japan > 1960s to 1970s (panel data)	> Innovation (R&D expenditures)	> Env. regulation (PACE, R&D subsidies)	> Reduced form linear regression with fixed effects (industry, time)	> PACE have positive impact on R&D expenditures	+
Lanoie, Laurent-Lucchetti, Johnstone, & Ambec (2011)	> Manufacturing (4,200 facilities) > 7 countries (all OECD) > 2003 (cross-section)	> Env.-related R&D expenditures (response to questionnaire (binary))	> Env. regulation (stringency dummies (low, medium, high); policy dummies (technology-standards, performance-standards, environmental taxes))	> Questionnaire > Linear regression model with fixed effects (country, sector) > Estimation of the model using the probit approach	> Env. regulation has positive impact on innovation	+

Table 3 – Literature on the weak Porter Hypothesis
Source: Own illustration.

Study	Sample	Dependent var.	Explanatory var. (selected)	Methodology	Results (selected)	
(b) Impact of environmental regulation on R&D expenditures						
Kneller & Manderson (2012)	> Manufacturing > United Kingdom > 2000 to 2006 (panel data)	> Innovation (env. and total R&D expenditures; env. and total CAPEX)	> Env. regulation (PACE (investment in end-of-pipe technology and operating costs) > Innovation (env. and total R&D expenditures, env. and total CAPEX)	> Dynamic linear regression model with fixed effects (industry, time) > Generalized method of moments estimation > Lag structure for env. regulation (2 years)	> Env. regulation has positive impact on investments in env. R&D and equipment for pollution abatement > Env. regulation has no impact on overall R&D and capital investments > Green investments may crowd out other investments	+
Rubashkina, Galeotti, & Verdolini (2015)	> Manufacturing > Europe > 1997 to 2009 (panel data)	> Innovation (R&D expenditures)	> Env. regulation (PACE)	> Linear regression model with fixed effects (sector-country, time) > Lag structure for env. regulation (1-3 years)	> Env. regulation has positive impact on innovation	+
(c) Impact of environmental regulation on inventiveness						
Jaffe & Palmer (1997)	> Manufacturing (24 industries) > United States > 1973 to 1991 (panel data)	> Innovation (patent applications)	> Env. regulation (PACE) > Innovation (foreign patents)	> Linear regression model with(out) fixed effects (industry, time) > Lag structure for env. regulation (1 year)	> Impact on patent applications is positive but not significant	o

Table 3 – Literature on the weak Porter Hypothesis (cont'd)
Source: Own illustration.

Study	Sample	Dependent var.	Explanatory var. (selected)	Methodology	Results (selected)	
(c) Impact of environmental regulation on inventiveness						
Brunner-meier & Cohen (2003)	> Manufacturing (146 industries) > United States > 1983 to 1992 (panel data)	> Innovation (env.-related patents)	> Env. regulation (PACE, number of visits by government inspectors) > Export intensity (export share)	> Linear model with fixed effects (industry, time) > No lags	> PACE has a small positive effect on patent applications > Enforcement efforts have no impact on innovation > Innovation effect is strongest in industries which are exposed to domestic and international competition	+
Vries & Withagen (2005)	> All sectors > Europe, United States, Canada > 1970 to 2000 (panel data)	> Innovation (patent applications related to SO_2 reductions)	> Env. regulation (emissions level (high emission levels indicate stringent regulation))	> Linear model with fixed effects (country)	> Env. regulation has positive impact on innovation	+
Popp (2006)	> Utilities > US, Japan, Germany > 1967 to 2001 (panel data)	> Likelihood of patent citation	> Env. regulation (time dummy (Japan, the US and Germany adopted regulation at different points in time))	> Non-linear model > NLS approach	> Env. regulation induces domestic patenting, but has no impact on foreign patents	+
Horbach (2008)	> Green-tech > Germany > 2001, 2004 (2 cross-sections)	> Suppliers with/without product innovation (binary)	> Env. regulation (env. mgmt. systems (binary), R&D activities (binary); regulatory standards (binary)) > Other indicators (e.g. firm age; business outlook)	> Questionnaire > Random-effects probit regression	> R&D expenditures, env. regulation and env. management tools have positive impact on green-tech innovations	+
Calel & Dechezle-prêtre (2012)	> All sectors > Europe > 2000 to 2009 (panel data)	> n/a	> n/a	> Matched difference-in-differences approach	> EU ETS increased patenting of low-carbon innovations by regulated firms by 10% > EU ETS had no impact of low-carbon innovations by unregulated firms	+

Table 3 – Literature on the weak Porter Hypothesis (cont'd)
Source: Own illustration.

Study	Sample	Dependent var.	Explanatory var. (selected)	Methodology	Results (selected)	
(c) Impact of environmental regulation on inventiveness						
Johnstone, Haščič, Poirier, & Hemar (2012)	> All sectors > 77 countries > 2001 to 2007 (panel data)	> Innovation (env.-related patents)	> Env. regulation (index of policy stringency based on WEF survey)	> Linear regression model with/without fixed effects (time) > 2-step approach: (i) innovation in general (ii) env. innovation (with fitted values)	> Env. regulation has positive impact on innovation > Effect is supported by a high general innovation capacity	+
Crespi (2013)	> All sectors > 8 countries (all Europe) > 1994 to 1996, 1998 to 2000, 2002 to 2004 (3 sets of panel data)	> Innovation (firms genera-ting energy and resource efficiency inno-ations)	> Env. regulation (share of firms which introduce innovations to comply with regulation; change in carbon/acid intensity)	> Linear regression model > Lag structure for env. regulation indicator (1 year) and external knowledge indicator (1 year)	> Env. regulation has positive effect on innovations in energy and resource efficiency	+
Nesta, Vona, & Nicolli (2014)	> All sectors > 27 countries (all OECD) > 1976 to 2007 (panel data)	> Innovation (env.-related patents)	> Env. regulation (index of renewables support policies; R&D expenditures on renewables per capita) > Competition intensity (index of market reg.)	> Pre-sample mean Poisson model > Generalized method of moments estimation	> Env. regulation has positive impact on innovation > Effect is more pronounced in countries with competitive electricity markets	+
Rubashkina, Galeotti, & Verdolini (2015)	> Manufacturing > Europe > 1997 to 2009 (panel data)	> Innovation (patents)	> Env. regulation (PACE)	> Linear regression model with fixed effects (sector-country, time) > Env. regulation time lag (1-3 yrs.)	> Env. regulation has positive impact on innovation	+

Table 3 – Literature on the weak Porter Hypothesis (cont'd)
Source: Own illustration.

2.2.2 *The narrow Porter Hypothesis*

Compared to all other types of the Porter Hypothesis, empirical research on the narrow type is rare. As to the best of my knowledge, only four studies exist which generate at least some insights on this version of the Porter Hypothesis[17]. Table 4 provides an overview of these studies.

The first study which finds empirical support for the narrow Porter Hypothesis is Popp (2003) who uses a linear regression model to analyze the impact of changes in environmental regulation on total factor productivity and operating costs of special equipment to control SO_2 emissions. Hereby, Popp (2003) makes use of a fundamental change in US air pollution regulation in 1990. At this time, the rigid technology-standards of the Clean Air Act were replaced by a flexible emission trading system. Hence, this amendment serves as a natural experiment for the effect of a large scale shift from command-and-control to market-based instruments, which are more in line with the concept of well-crafted environmental regulation. Based on this natural experiment, Popp (2003) finds for a panel of utility companies in the US between 1972 and 1997 that the 1990 amendment of the Clean Air Act led to a considerable increase in SO_2 removal rates, which in turn led to significant improvements in technical efficiency and operating costs. An essay of Burtraw (2000) supports Popp's (2003) assessment of clean air regulation in the United States. Burtraw (2000) concludes that the shift in regulation from technology standard to emission trading caused a strong reduction in compliance costs which happened to be considerably stronger than projected.

Two studies confirm the results of Burtraw (2000) and Popp (2003) for non-US countries. Isaksson (2005) shows for her panel of Swedish firms between 1990 and 1996 that technological innovations enabled by a flexible emission trading program allowed firms to meet their emission targets at very low or even negative cost. Unlike other studies, Isaksson (2005) does not rely on reported PACE but uses a (marginal) cost function approach to estimate abatement costs directly.

Similarly, Lanoie et al. (2011) show for their sample of 4,200 manufacturing firms in seven OECD countries that performance-based regulation has a considerably stronger impact on R&D investments than technology-based measures. However, the true contribution of this study is a methodological one. While previous studies tested the narrow Porter

---

[17] The literature review section of Lanoie et al. (2011) supports this notion: "Because market instruments have not been widely used so far, no study has been able to conduct a direct test of the 'narrow' version of PH" (Lanoie et al., 2011, p. 808).

Hypothesis indirectly based on natural experiments or single case studies, Lanoie et al. (2011) are first to conduct a direct test of the impact of alternative regulation designs on a large multi-country sample. The approach is based on a set of dummy variables which allow them to identify the discrete impact of technology-standards, performance-standards and environmental taxes as well as low, medium and high regulatory stringency.

In summary, empirical research on the narrow Porter Hypothesis demonstrates that the type of regulation matters. All reviewed studies consistently show that flexible, market-based regulatory instruments are better suited than command-and-control measures to induce innovation and to enable countries to reach environmental targets at very little or even negative economic cost. However, given the small number of studies in this field, these results should be interpreted with care until they are confirmed by additional empirical research. Overall, the widespread negligence of policy design in empirical research is very surprising against the background that Porter (1991) and especially Porter & van der Linde (1995) stress the importance of this point very forcefully.

Study	Sample	Dependent var.	Explanatory var. (selected)	Methodology	Results (selected)	
(a) Impact of regulation type on cost						
Burtraw (2000)	> United States	> n/a	> n/a	> Essay	> Change from technological standard to emission trading improved compliance costs (25-50% below projections) > Many cost savings have been realized outside of the formal allowance market	+
Popp (2003)	> Utilities > United States > 1972 to 1997 (panel data)	Model (a) > Total factor productivity Model (b) > Operating cost	Model (a) > Innovation (patent stock) > Env. regulation (policy indicators (binary and continuous); time dummy (reg. changes in 1990)) Model (b) > Innovation (patent stock) > Env. reg.(time dummy (reg.changes in 1990))	Models (a) and (b) > Linear regression model	> Env. regulation has positive impact of technical efficiency > Env. regulation has negative impact on operating cost > Under technology standards (prior to 1990) R&D focus was on reducing cost to meet minimum requirements > Under emission trading (since 1990) R&D focus was on increasing removal rates	+
Isaksson (2005)	> Utilities, pulp & paper, chemicals > Sweden > 1990 to 1996	> Pollution abatement cost	> Env. regulation (plant-specific discharge limits)	> (Marginal abatement) cost function approach	> Due to technological innovation and process changes emission targets were achieved at very low, zero or even negative cost	+
(b) Impact of regulation type on R&D expenditures						
Lanoie, Laurent-Lucchetti, Johnstone, & Ambec (2011)	> Manufacturing (4,200 facilities) > 7 countries (all OECD) > 2003 (cross-section)	> Env.-related R&D expenditures	> Env. regulation (stringency dummies (low, medium, high); policy dummies (technology-standards, performance-standards, environmental taxes))	> Questionnaire > Linear model with fixed effects (country, sector)	> Type of regulation has some positive impact on innovation	+

Table 4 – Literature on the narrow Porter Hypothesis
Source: Own illustration.

2.2.3 *The strong Porter Hypothesis*

Empirical research on the relationship between environmental regulation and firm or industry performance is a central area of environmental economics (Rauscher, 2005). Although most of these studies do not explicitly test the Porter Hypothesis, their results provide valuable insights for the discussion of this section.

Research on or related to the strong Porter Hypothesis can be classified in two major streams, namely studies which either focus on regulation's effect on productivity or its effect on profitability (Brännlund & Lundgren, 2009). Within these two streams, researchers might take a macroeconomic perspective and analyze the effect on an aggregated industry or country level, or take a microeconomic perspective and analyze regulation's impact on individual firms.

I will first discuss those studies which examine the productivity effect of regulation within the US, followed by corresponding studies with a non-US or multinational focus. Afterwards I will turn to research on the relationship between environmental regulation and profitability. An overview of all studies covered in this section is presented in Table 5.

As discussed in Section 2.2.2 on the narrow version of the Porter Hypothesis, the 1990 amendment to the Clean Air Act marked a fundamental change in the US' approach towards air pollution regulation. Under the 1990 amendment the government replaced the old technology-standards by an emission trading system. Hence, it is only since 1990 that air pollution regulation in the United States is in line with the characteristics of well-crafted regulation defined by Porter & van der Linde (1995).

This change in regulation is also apparent in the results of empirical studies on the productivity effect of environmental regulation in the US. Studies using data samples which reflect the situation prior to the changes in regulation univocally report negative effects of environmental regulation on productivity. Barbera & McConnell (1990) for instance use a cost function approach to estimate the effect of pollution abatement and control expenditures on total factor productivity for certain energy- and pollution-intensive industries in the US between 1960 and 1980. They find that increasing regulatory pressure driven by public concerns about the state of the environment had a significantly negative impact on productivity growth. Boyd & McClelland (1999) confirm these results using a distance function approach. They find that 25% of the productivity losses in their sample are attributable to increasingly stringent pollution abatement requirements.

This effect is, however, not limited to older studies. Even quite recent publications using pre-1990 samples show the same pattern. A very comprehensive work by Greenstone, List, & Syverson (2012), which analyzes regulation's productivity effect based on a sample with 1,185,000 observations from the US manufacturing industry, arrives at the usual result that stringent environmental regulation slows down productivity progress. Interestingly, the authors also find that productivity impacts vary considerable between different air pollutants. As these pollutants are also subject to different regulatory schemes, this finding once more indicates that policy design plays a role in determining the overall impact that regulation has on business.

In contrast, those studies which use data samples from the period after 1990 show exactly the opposite results and conclude that environmental regulation has a positive effect on productivity progress. Berman & Bui (2001), for instance, use a cost function approach to analyze the impact of regulation on oil refineries in the Los Angeles basin, an area which is associated with especially stringent air pollution requirements. The authors measure environmental regulation in great detail and consider plant-specific data on capital expenditures and operating costs related to pollution abatement. Moreover, they take into account the exact dates at which regulations are adopted, compliance is required, or stringency levels change. Berman & Bui (2001) conclude that in the case of Los Angeles oil refineries environmental regulation has a positive impact on compliance costs (cost reductions) and total factor productivity alike. These results are also confirmed by a study of Popp (2003), which was already discussed in the previous two sections on the weak and narrow Porter Hypothesis. Popp (2003) concludes that, since the 1990 amendment of the Clean Air Act, air pollution regulation is associated with considerable technological advancement in exhaust gas treatment which ultimately led to higher technical efficiency and therefore resource productivity.

Other than the publications on the United States, non-US studies find positive links between environmental regulation and total factor productivity regardless of the observation period. Alpay, Buccola, & Kerkvliet (2002) show for a sample of Mexican firms between 1962 and 1994 that environmental regulation, proxied by pollution abatement and control expenditures and monitoring efforts by government agencies, has a positive impact on productivity. Murty & Kumar (2003), Hamamoto (2006), and Vlist, Withagen, & Folmer (2007) present comparable results for the Indian sugar industry between 1996 and 1999, the Japanese manufacturing industry in the 1960s and 1970s, and the Dutch horticulture industry between 1991 and 1999.

Of special interest from a methodological perspective is a pair of studies on manufacturing industries in Quebec, Canada. While the earlier study of Dufour, Lanoie, & Patry (1998) concludes that environmental regulation is detrimental to total factor productivity, the recent study by Lanoie, Patry, & Lajeunesse (2008) concludes that stringent regulation is beneficial for productivity growth, especially in industries which are exposed to international competition. Both studies regress total factor productivity against environmental regulation measured by changes in pollution abatement and control expenditures. The later study by Lanoie et al. (2008), however, uses a dynamic model while the earlier study relies on a static one. Hence, the comparison of these two studies is another example which illustrates the importance of modelling the relationship between regulation and the corresponding innovation and competitiveness effects in a dynamic fashion.

The earliest publication from the second stream of literature on the strong Porter Hypothesis, which I discuss in this section, is Brännlund, Färe, & Grosskopf (1995). The authors of this study use a profit function approach to estimate the impact of plant-specific discharge limits on profitability. Based on their sample of Swedish firms from the pulp and paper industry in 1989 and 1990, they find that regulation's average impact on profitability is negative. However, they also find that profitability of two-thirds of the firms is unaffected by regulation. It remains unclear whether these results are caused by unobserved heterogeneity in the sample or other reasons.

Two other studies which use plant-specific data and therefore a rather microeconomic perspective arrive at similar conclusions. Rassier & Earnhart (2010) find a negative impact of water pollution regulation on the profitability of 73 US chemical firms in the years 1995 to 2001. Similarly, Lanoie et al. (2011) find in their previously cited study on 4,200 manufacturing facilities in seven OECD countries that environmental regulation has no significant effect on profitability.

Studies with a more macroeconomic and therefore less industry-focused perspective, however, tend to find positive relationships between environmental regulation and profitability. Hart & Abuja (1996), for example, show in their study on S&P 500 corporations between 1989 and 1992 that year-on-year emission reductions translate into return on sales increases with a time lag of one to two years.

In summary, the findings of the empirical literature tend to support the strong Porter Hypothesis. However, there are also critical publications which point in the opposite direction and suggest that regulation is costly and leaves firms at a competitive disadvantage compared to their unregulated competitors.

Two things become clear from the discussion of alternative methodological approaches. First, the selection of policy instruments matters and it is therefore essential to control for differences in regulation design between countries and over time. The discussion around the 1990 amendment of the US Clean Air Act illustrates this point very well. Second, econometric models which attempt to test the Porter Hypothesis have to consider its dynamic nature. A central element of the Porter Hypothesis is the innovation inducement process which requires time to unfold. Common approaches to account for the dynamics of this effect are time lags and the use of panel data. Empirical research on any version of the Porter Hypothesis should take these two aspects into account in order to generate meaningful results.

Study	Sample	Dependent var.	Explanatory var. (selected)	Methodology	Results (selected)	
(a) Impact of environmental regulation on productivity						
Barbera & McConnell (1990)	> Pulp and paper, chemicals, iron and steel, metal, stone and glass > United States > 1960 to 1980 (panel data)	> Total factor productivity	> Env. regulation (PACE)	> Cost function approach	> Env. regulation has negative impact on factor productivity	-
Dufour, Lanoie, & Patry (1998)	> Manufacturing (19 industries) > Canada > 1985 to 1988 (panel data)	> Total factor productivity	> Env. regulation (change in PACE)	> Linear regression model with fixed effects (industry, time) > Generalized least squares estimation	> Env. regulation has negative impact on factor productivity	-
Boyd & McClelland (1999)	> Pulp and paper > United States > 1988 to 1992 (panel data)	> Total factor productivity	> Multiple factors of production incl. emissions	> Distance function approach	> Env. regulation reduces factor productivity > 25% of productivity loss due to additional pollution abatement equipment	-
Berman & Bui (2001)	> Oil refineries > United States (Los Angeles > 1987 to 1995 (panel data)	> Total factor productivity	> Env. regulation (PACE (investments and operating costs); regulation adoption and compliance dates; increased stringency dates)	> Cost function approach	> Env. reg. reduces compliance costs > Env. reg. increases factor productivity	+
Popp (2003)	> Utilities > United States > 1972 to 1997 (panel data)	> Total factor productivity	> Innovation (patent stock) > Env. regulation (policy indicators (binary and continuous); time dummy (reg. changes in 1990))	> Linear regression model	> Env. regulation has positive impact of technical efficiency	+

Table 5 – Literature on the strong Porter Hypothesis
Source: Own illustration.

Study	Sample	Dependent var.	Explanatory var. (selected)	Methodology	Results (selected)	
(a) Impact of environmental regulation on productivity						
Alpay, Buccola, & Kerkvliet (2002)	> Food processing > United States, Mexico > 1962 to 1994 (panel data)	> Total factor productivity	> Env. regulation (PACE; monitoring efforts of government agencies)	> Profit function approach	> US: Env. regulation has no significant effect on productivity and profitability > Mexico: Negative effect for profits, positive effect for productivity	o
Gray & Shadbegian (2003)	> Pulp & paper (116 firms) > United States > 1979 to 1990 (panel data)	> Total factor productivity > Output (sanity check)	> Env. regulation (PACE (operating costs); plant vintage (binary); plant technology (binary))	> Linear model with fixed effects (industry, state, time) > Cobb-Douglas production function	> Env. regulation has negative impact on productivity	-
Marklund (2003)	> Pulp & paper > Sweden > 1983 to 1990 (panel data)	> Total factor productivity	> Env. regulation (limits for waste water discharge)	> Distance function approach	> Env. regulation has no significant impact on productivity	o
Murty & Kumar (2003)	> Sugar (92 firms) > India > 1996 to 1999 (panel data)	> Total factor productivity	> Env. regulation (regulation index (geometric mean of scaled emission levels for three pollutants); conservation index (waste water discharge to turnover))	> Distance function approach > Maximum likelihood estimation	> Env. regulation has positive impact on productivity	+
Hamamoto (2006)	> Manufacturing > Japan > 1960s to 1970s (panel data)	> Total factor productivity	> Innovation (R&D expenditures; plant age)	> Reduced form linear regression with fixed effects (industry, time) > Cobb-Douglas function	> Regulation induced innovation has positive impact on factor productivity	+

Table 5 – Literature on the strong Porter Hypothesis (cont'd)
Source: Own illustration.

Study	Sample	Dependent var.	Explanatory var. (selected)	Methodology	Results (selected)	
(a) Impact of environmental regulation on productivity						
Vlist, Withagen, & Folmer (2007)	> Horticulture > Netherlands > 1991 to 1999 (panel data)	> Total factor productivity	> Env. regulation (time dummy (regulation changes in 1997))	> Cobb-Douglas production function (stochastic frontier approach)	> Increased stringency of env. regulation has positive impact on factor productivity	+
Lanoie, Patry, & Lajeunesse (2008)	> Manufacturing (17 industries) > Canada (Quebec) > 1985 to 1994 (panel data)	> Total factor productivity	> Env. regulation (change in PACE to total cost ratio)	> Dynamic linear regression model with fixed effects (industry, time) > Interaction terms to capture effect of pollution intensity and trade exposure	> Env. regulation has positive impact on total factor productivity > Effect is amplified in trade exposed industries	+
Greenstone, List, & Syverson (2012)	> Manufacturing > United States > 1972 to 1993 (panel data)	> Total factor productivity	> Env. regulation (location of production plant in counties that attain/do not attain pollution limits; classification of industries as heavy or regular polluters)	> (Dynamic) linear regression model with fixed effects (plant) > Lag structure for attainment status (1 or 2 years)	> Env. regulation had negative impact on productivity > Ozone regulation had the strongest negative impact on productivity > CO regulation had positive effect on productivity, esp. for refineries	-
Rubashkina, Galeotti, & Verdolini (2015)	> Manufacturing > Europe > 1997 to 2009 (panel data)	> Total factor productivity	> Env. regulation (PACE)	> Linear regression with fixed effects (sector-country, time) > Env. regulation time lag (1-3 yrs.) > Estimation of productivity based on Cobb-Douglas function	> Env. regulation has no impact on productivity	o

Table 5 – Literature on the strong Porter Hypothesis (cont'd)
Source: Own illustration.

Study	Sample	Dependent var.	Explanatory var. (selected)	Methodology	Results (selected)	
(b) Impact of environmental regulation on financial performance						
Brännlund, Färe, & Grosskopf (1995)	> Pulp and paper > Sweden > 1989 to 1990 (panel data)	> Profitability	> Env. regulation (plant-specific discharge limits)	> Profit function approach > Non-linear programming approach (maximization problem)	> Env. regulation has on average a negative impact on profitability > Two-thirds of the firms are unaffected by regulation	o
Hart & Ahuja (1996)	> All sectors (S&P 500) > United States > 1989 to 1992 (4 cross-sections)	> Return on sales	> Env. regulation: (YoY emission reductions)	> Linear model	> Emission reduction results in a net benefit (with a time lag of 1 or 2 years) > Firms with the initially highest emission levels are found to benefit the most	+
Popp (2003)	> Utilities > United States > 1972 to 1997 (panel data)	> Operating cost	> Innovation (patent stock) > Env. regulation (time dummy (regulation changes in 1990))	> Linear model	> Env. regulation has negative impact on operating cost	+
Rassier & Earnhart (2010)	> Chemicals > United States > 1995 to 2001 (panel data)	> Profitability	> Env. regulation (limits for waste water discharge)	> Linear model	> Env. reg. has negative impact on profitability (due to cost increases for given levels of sales)	-
Lanoie, Laurent-Lucchetti, Johnstone, & Ambec (2011)	> Manufacturing (4,200 facilities) > 7 countries (all OECD) > 2003 (cross-section)	> Profitability (responses to questionnaire (binary))	> Env. regulation (stringency dummies (low, medium, high); policy dummies (technology-standards, performance-standards, environmental taxes))	> Questionnaire > Linear model with fixed effects (country, sector) > Estimation based on probit approach for instrumental variables	> Env. regulation has no impact on profitability	o

Table 5 – Literature on the strong Porter Hypothesis (cont'd)
Source: Own illustration.

Study	Sample	Dependent var.	Explanatory var. (selected)	Methodology	Results (selected)	
(b) Impact of environmental regulation on financial performance						
Rexhäuser & Rammer (2013)	> All sectors > Germany > 2009 (cross-section)	> Profitability	> Innovation (innovations improving resource efficiency (binary); innovations reducing externalities (binary)) > Study distinguishes between regulation-induced and voluntary innovations	> Questionnaire > Profit function model > Maximum likelihood estimation	> Induced-innovations have a stronger positive impact on profitability than regular innovations > Induced innovations which only reduce externalities without improving resource efficiency have a negative impact of profitability (this is not the case for voluntary investments in pollution abatement)	+

Table 5 – Literature on the strong Porter Hypothesis (cont'd)
Source: Own illustration.

2.2.4 *The narrowly strong Porter Hypothesis*

Unlike the other three versions, the scope of the narrowly strong Porter Hypothesis is restricted to the environmental goods and services sector. Historically, the narrowly strong Porter Hypothesis has received little attention. As to the best of my knowledge[18], there are so far just eight relevant publications, which are discussed in the following. Table 6 provides a structured overview.

The earliest publication in this field[19] is Shrivastava (1995) which introduces different channels through which firms can turn increasing environmental regulation into a competitive advantage. As this publication rather focusses on business than economic aspects, I will spare a detailed discussion.

Costantini & Crespi (2008) analyze the impact of countries' level of environmental regulation stringency and the capacity of their national innovation systems on these countries' export performance in environmental goods and services. In other words, the study aims to demonstrate that "countries that are subject to more stringent regulation may become net exporters of environmental technology" (p. 447). Therefore, this is the first publication to explicitly conduct research on the narrowly strong Porter Hypothesis.

The authors' definition of environmental technologies restricts the analysis to the energy sector, specifically to "technologies to exploit renewable energies and enhance energy efficiency" (p. 450). Hence, the sample covers trade in renewable energy equipment for all common technology types including wind, solar PV (incl. CSP), solar thermal, biomass and biofuels, as well as trade in equipment for energy saving and management including for instance catalysts, heat pumps, fuel cells, multi-walled insulating glass and thermostats.

To empirically test their hypothesis, Costantini & Crespi (2008) examine the bilateral trade flows between 20 exporting and 148 importing countries from 1996 to 2005 in a gravity model of trade. All exporting countries are also OECD countries, while the importing countries include developing countries as well. Building on their basic model specification, the authors run multiple regressions with different indicators of

---

18 The literature review sections of the cited publications on the narrowly strong Porter Hypothesis support this view.

19 The research question of Shrivastava (1995) fits quite well with the narrowly strong Porter Hypothesis. However, as the development of the typology for the different versions of the Porter Hypothesis was only developed after his publication (Jaffe & Palmer, 1997), Shrivastava (1995) does not explicit refer to this specific version of the Porter Hypothesis.

environmental policy stringency and innovation capacity. Their stringency indicators include importers' and exporters' CO_2 emissions, private and public environmental protection expenditures, environmental tax revenues, and public environmental investments. The national innovation capacity is proxied by patents in the energy sector, overall patents, R&D expenditures relative to GDP, and a measure of technology diffusion.

Based on their empirical model, Costantini & Crespi (2008) find that stringent environmental standards and advanced innovation capabilities have a positive impact on countries' export success in energy-related environmental technologies.

In a related study, Costantini & Mazzanti (2012) analyze the impact of environmental regulation and innovation on the export competitiveness of EU countries. The study contains a set of three research hypotheses to test for the strong as well as for the narrowly strong version of the Porter Hypothesis. Based on the strong version, the first research hypothesis predicts a positive connection between energy and environmental taxes and the export competitiveness of the manufacturing sector as a whole. The remaining two hypotheses relate to the narrowly strong Porter Hypothesis. The authors' second hypothesis postulates that public environmental policy has a positive impact on export performance in the green sector. The third hypothesis is concerned with the difference between the export effect of voluntary and compulsory investments in pollution prevention and abatement.

Again, Costantini & Mazzanti (2012) use a gravity model of trade as basic structure in their econometric model. With respect to countries covered, their data sample is slightly smaller than that of Costantini & Crespi (2008) and only includes bilateral trade flows between 14 exporting countries (all EU) and 145 importing countries from 1996 to 2007. According to the authors, the restriction to exporters from the European Union was necessary due to limited data available at the time of publication. In terms of commodities covered, Costantini & Mazzanti's (2012) sample is much broader. In order to estimate the strong Porter effect, they include goods from all manufacturing industries which they divide into four groups (low, medium-low, medium-high and high) according to their technological content. For their analysis on the narrowly strong Porter Hypothesis, they use a different sample which consists of all goods associated with the green sector. According to their definition, the green sector is not limited to renewable energy equipment but includes 158 different commodity classes which contain products as diverse as equipment to treat waste water, recycling machinery, air filters, building insulation, environmentally-friendly heating systems, and batteries for hybrid vehicles.

In their study on countries from the European Union, Costantini & Mazzanti (2012) find some support for the strong Porter Hypothesis in so far that environmental regulation does not harm the export competitiveness of low- and medium-tech industries while it fosters competitiveness of high-tech industries. Their results on the narrowly strong Porter Hypothesis indicate that environmental regulation but especially regulation-induced innovation efforts in the private sector significantly improve the export competitiveness of the green manufacturing sector.

Another empirical test of the narrowly strong Porter Hypothesis is Groba (2013, 2014)[20], which is of particular interest for this research project due to two reasons. First, Groba (2014) is exclusively concerned with trade in solar energy equipment, one of the renewable energy technologies covered in this thesis. Therefore, the study is considerably more focused than the previous work by Costantini & Crespi (2008) and Costantini & Mazzanti (2012). Second, this study is first in research on the narrowly strong Porter Hypothesis to go beyond pure stringency measurement and take into account regulation design as well.

Groba (2014) structures his research along three distinct hypotheses. Building on the Porter Hypothesis, he postulates that more stringent regulation results in an export advantage in solar power equipment. His second hypothesis brings in aspects of the lead market theory[21] and predicts that countries which introduce stringent environmental regulation early on will experience an even stronger export advantage in solar power equipment. Finally, hypothesis three is concerned with features of the import markets and contains that countries which have support policies as well as low import tariffs on solar power equipment in place import more than other countries with less favorable market conditions.

Same as all earlier studies, Groba's (2014) econometric estimation strategy builds on the gravity model of trade. His sample includes 21 exporting countries from North America, Europe and Asia (all OECD) and 118 importing countries. Commodity-wise he covers solar PV and solar thermal equipment.

---

[20] For the sake of shortness, I will in the following just refer to Groba (2014). Groba (2014) is an individual publication which is (nearly) identical to the corresponding chapter of the doctoral thesis Groba (2013).

[21] A detailed introduction to the lead market theory follows in Section 2.3.2.

As mentioned previously, the novelty of Groba's (2014) estimation approach is the consideration of policy design as an important determinant of export competitiveness. In addition to classical stringency measures, renewable energy shares and an index of CO_2 emission reduction, he tests for the particular effects from the implementation of common policy instruments. Moreover, he tests if the effect from specific policy measures increases in their duration. In other words, he tests whether policies which have been in place for several years have a stronger effect than newly adopted policies.

The estimation results confirm all three hypotheses. Therefore, Groba (2014) does not only find empirical support for the narrowly strong Porter Hypothesis and the lead market theory for environmental goods and services, but is also the first to successfully employ policy-based stringency measures which are in-line with the original idea of Porter (1991).

Another publication, Cao & Groba (2013), which emerged out of the same research project as Groba (2014), focusses exclusively on one particular export country and examines the determinants of China's export performance in solar PV and wind power equipment. As none of the other studies on the narrowly strong Porter Hypothesis covers China as an exporter of environmental goods and services, the findings of Cao & Groba (2013) are of particular interest. This is especially true against the background of the discussion in Section 1.3 which showed that China developed into a leading exporter of renewable energy equipment.

Following the example of others, Cao & Groba (2013) also use a gravity model to analyze the determinants of trade in solar and wind equipment between China and 43 importing countries over the period ranging from 1996 to 2008. The set of potential determinants of trade included in the regression model contains environmental policy, patent applications related to wind and solar power, tariffs and other trading costs, and import market characteristics such as support policies and market size. Similar to Groba (2014), Cao & Groba (2013) distinguish between different forms of support regimes for renewable energies, namely incentive tariffs, obligations, and tax-related measures.

Cao & Groba (2013) find that Chinese export flows in wind power and solar PV equipment are determined by support policies of import markets and public R&D support in China. Technological knowledge, measured as patent applications in China, is not found to have a positive impact on exports. Generally, the results for solar PV are much larger and also more significant than those for wind power equipment. The authors suggest that this effect is due to restrictions in the data sample, as Chinese wind energy exports only took off after the end of the observation period.

The last two publications which I introduce in this section are two closely related studies by Sung & Song (2013, 2014). Sung & Song (2013) attempt to analyze the causal relationships between exports in renewable energy equipment, R&D investments, and domestic renewable energy shares. Their econometric model consists of a system of three equations, which models the interactions between the three before-mentioned variables. The authors use a vector error correction model with fixed effects for im- and exporting country and time.

The estimation results for their panel of 18 OECD countries between 1991 and 2007 indicate that the effect of environmental regulation on exports is mixed. On the one hand, Sung & Song (2013) find that government R&D expenditures, their proxy for market-push instruments, have a positive impact on countries' exports in renewable energy equipment; on the other hand, they find that renewable energy shares, their proxy for market-pull instruments, have a negative impact.

On first sight, the second finding that renewable energy shares have a negative impact on export performance is inconsistent with the results of previous studies (Jha, 2009; Groba, 2014). However, these results might have been caused by differences in the specification of key variables or the model itself. First, Sung & Song (2013) use exports instead of trade flows (i.e. net exports) as depending variable in their model. Second, they use year-on-year changes in renewable shares (i.e. capacity additions) as stringency measures, while other studies use absolute shares (i.e. installed base). Third and most importantly, Sung & Song (2013) do not control for business cycle effects. Hence, the documented negative effect of renewable energy capacity additions on exports might just be an artefact of changes over the business cycle. For instance, if constant production and import levels are assumed, GDP increases, which are usually associated with growing domestic demand for renewable energy installation, lead to ceteris paribus decreases in exports, because a larger share of the domestic production is consumed locally.

Sung & Song (2014), a second study which builds on Sung & Song (2013), corrects for this short coming and includes GDP growth as additional variable into the model. As Sung & Song (2013), Sung & Song (2014) also use a vector error correction model[22] with time- and country-

[22] The results for the solar PV sector are estimated using a vector auto-regression model.

fixed effects and generalized methods of moments to estimate their system of four equations. Like the previous study, their sample includes data from 18 OECD countries. However, in contrast to Sung & Song (2013), Sung & Song (2014) cover a slightly different time period, 1992 to 2008, and distinguish between different types of renewable energy technologies, namely biomass, solar, and wind.

Sung & Song's (2014) decision to include GDP into the system of equations leads to results which support the hypothesis that the findings of Sung & Song (2013) suffer from an omitted variable bias. The results of their revised model are consistent with the finding of previous studies (Jha, 2009; Groba, 2014) which show that high renewable energy shares (or additions) go hand in hand with strong export performance.

In summary, the empirical results support the narrowly strong Porter Hypothesis that more stringent environmental regulation induces eco-innovations which in turn increase the export competitiveness of the green sector. However, as Jaffe et al. (1995) point out, it is not surprising that environmental regulation has a positive effect on the environmental goods and services sector because it directly increases the demand for its offerings.

But, regardless of the common sense character of the overall outcome, research on the narrowly strong Porter Hypothesis is still important. As I have discussed throughout Chapter 0, an increasingly large number of countries has adopted measures to support electricity generation from renewable energies. Leaving aside the, from today's perspective, abstract and uncertain future public benefits, these measures come at an economic cost as renewables are currently not generally competitive with conventional power generation technologies. However, only some countries such as Denmark managed to turn these current costs into a current economic benefit, namely a strong wind power equipment industry. Research on the narrowly strong Porter Hypothesis aims to reveal the mechanism underlying this process and helps to explain why some countries successfully turn renewable energy investments into homegrown innovations and consequently export success while others fail to achieve this goal[23].

[23] See also Jaffe, Newell, & Stavins (2002), who argue that the debate around Porter's win-win hypothesis would benefit from a shift towards the question how policies and private-sector institutions can enable the development of low-cost solutions for pressing environmental problems. The pure ideological/political debate on whether or not environmental regulation is generally beneficial for countries' competitiveness is considered to be of little help.

Study	Sample	Dependent var.	Explanatory var. (selected)	Methodology	Results (selected)	
Shrivastava (1995)	> 3M case study	> n/a	> n/a	> Essay	> Environmental technologies offer great opportunities to differentiate and develop sustainable competitive advantages	+
Costantini & Crespi (2008)	> Renewables; green-tech > 148 countries (incl. OECD) > 1996 to 2005 (panel data)	> Trade flows (ex- and imports)	> Env. regulation (CO_2 emissions; env. protection expenditures; env. tax revenues) > Innovation (patents per capita (energy sector and total); R&D expenditures per unit of GDP)	> Gravity model of trade > Static linear regression model	> Env. regulation has a positive impact on net exports in renewable energy equipment and energy saving technologies > Strong national innovations systems increase this effect further	+
Jha (2009)	> Renewables > 34 countries > 1996 (cross-section)	> Export flows	> Env. regulation (RE share; renewable energy support policies (binary)) > Innovation (country's share in global patents on renewables) > Import tariffs	> Linear regression model	> Renewable energy patents and national renewable energy shares have a positive impact on exports > Import tariffs and feed-in tariffs have no impact on exports	+
Costantini & Mazzanti (2012)	> Manufacturing > 145 countries (14 exporting countries, all EU) > 1996 to 2007 (panel data)	> Trade flows (ex- and imports)	> Env. regulation (energy and env. tax revenues; PACE in % of GDP; private sector env. management and audit schemes) > Innovation (patent stock of exporting countries)	> Gravity model of trade > Dynamic linear regr. with fixed effects (im- and exporting country; pair of countries)	> Env. regulation in general seems to have no effect on exports > Some tax and innovation support policies have a positive effect on exports > Env. policies and innovation efforts have a positive impact on green sector exports	+

Table 6 – Literature on the narrowly strong Porter Hypothesis
Source: Own illustration.

Study	Sample	Dependent var.	Explanatory var. (selected)	Methodology	Results (selected)	
Cao & Groba (2013)	> Renewables (solar and wind) > 44 countries (1 exporting country: China) > 1996 to 2008 (panel data)	> Export flows	> Env. regulation (renewable energy support policies in importing countries (binary); electricity generated from wind and solar) > Innovation (patent stock of green-tech sector)	> Gravity model of trade > Linear regression model with fixes effects (importing country)	> Export flows are determined by support policies of import markets and public R&D support in China > Technological knowledge is not found to have a positive impact on exports	+
Sung & Song (2013)	> Renewables (5 types) > 18 countries (all OECD) > 1991 to 2007 (panel data)	> Export flows > R&D investments > RE shares	> Export flows > R&D investments > Renewable energy shares	> Vector error correction model with fixed effects (country)	> Gov. R&D has positive impact on exports in renewable energy equipment > Renewables additions have negative impact on exports > Exports have positive impact on RE shares	o
Groba (2014)	> Renewables (solar) > 118 countries (21 exporting countries, all OECD) > 1999 to 2007 (panel data)	> Export flows	> Env. reg. (index; electricity from solar power; existence/duration of incentive tariffs, obligations and tax measures) > Innovation (R&D exp.) > Import tariffs	> Gravity model of trade > Linear regression model with fixes effects (im- and exporting country, time)	> Env. regulation has positive impact on export flows in solar energy equipment > Duration of policy schemes is more important than its mere existence	+
Sung & Song (2014)	> Renewables (biomass, solar, wind) > 18 countries (all OECD) > 1992 to 2008 (panel data)	> Env. regulation (R&D spending; feed-in tariffs (proxied by RE share)) > Export flows > GDP	> Env. regulation (R&D investments; feed-in tariffs (proxied by renewables share)) > Export flows > GDP	> Vector error correction model with fixed effects (country) for biomass and wind > Vector auto-reg. model for solar	> Gov. R&D has positive impact on exports in renewable energy equipment > Renewables additions have positive impact on exports	+

Table 6 – Literature on the narrowly strong Porter Hypothesis (cont'd)
Source: Own illustration.

2.3 Theories related to the narrowly strong Porter Hypothesis

The discussion of the empirical literature shows that the Porter Hypothesis is still far away from being generally accepted. This is, however, not the case for its narrowly strong formulation. This special case is well-founded on economic theory. In this section, I briefly introduce two theoretical concepts which support the ideas behind the narrowly strong Porter Hypothesis. These concepts are induced innovation and the overall technological change process, and the lead market theory for environmental goods and services.

2.3.1 Induced innovation and technological change[24]

The commonly used framework concept for research on technological change is the so called Schumpeter trichotomy. According to the Schumpeter trichotomy the process of technological change consists of three steps: invention, innovation, and diffusion. The first step, invention, refers to the original development of a technology or a process. Hereby, it is irrelevant whether or not this invention is patented. The second step, innovation, describes the commercialization of the newly developed product. In other words, the invention is made available on the regular product market. Interestingly, by distinguishing between the first two steps of the technological change process, Schumpeter highlights that inventor and innovator might be completely unrelated. This means that firms (or countries) might benefit from the successful marketing of a new, innovative product which was originally developed elsewhere. Finally, the third step in the technological change process is diffusion, the adoption of successfully marketed innovations by a growing number of users.

The interesting question for this thesis is: What triggers the process described by Schumpeter? According to Jaffe, Newell, & Stavins (2003) there are two competing schools of thought which attempt to answer this question, namely the evolutionary approach, a rather new idea, and the induced innovation approach, which dates back to Hicks (1932). The proponents of the evolutionary view argue that firms' R&D investments are to a great extend arbitrary rather than systematically determined. In contrast, the proponents of the induced innovation approach suggest that firms set their R&D budgets in a deterministic fashion. Their idea is that R&D expenditures and therefore invention and innovation are driven by changes in factor prices. According to their view, firms consciously invest in R&D to reduce consumption of relatively more expensive input factors.

---

[24] This section builds on Jaffe, Newell, & Stavins (2003).

However, reality shows that firms often deviate from the optimal level of R&D investments, suggested by Hicks and his followers, by investing less than the theoretically optimal amount. This effect is explained by two market failures. On the one hand, investments in R&D are risky and outcomes highly uncertain. However, this is also the case for investments in production equipment or other tangible assets. The specific problem of R&D investments is the skewed distribution of potential outcomes. Especially early research is associated with very large potential returns and a very low likelihood of success. Therefore, firms face difficulties to secure outside financing and have to draw back on equity. Hence, the opportunity costs of R&D investments increase and firms tend to underinvest. On the other hand, the outcomes of R&D projects are intangible in nature. Therefore, firms can expect knowledge spillovers to other firms, irrespective of patenting. The inability to appropriate the full returns of successful research projects is seen as the second major reason for underinvestments in this area.

According to empirical research on R&D budgeting, firms' actual research investments are mainly driven by the after-tax cost of the R&D project, the size of the target market, the technical feasibility, and the ability of appropriate returns on research. If firms actually make their R&D investment decisions based on these criteria, this gives regulators the opportunity to counter the presumably wealth-reducing underinvestments in R&D. Suitable policy instruments to reduce after-tax cost are, for instance, tax incentives or direct research subsidies. Common policy instruments to increase the size of the market for new technologies are direct government purchases, demand side subsidies, or, similarly, fees on competing technologies. As the discussion of Chapter 0 shows, many governments make use of such measures to promote research on renewable energy equipment[25].

Regardless the importance of invention and innovation, diffusion is not less critical for a successful completion of any technology change process such as the transition from conventional to renewable forms of electricity generation. However, the process of technology diffusion is often perceived as slow and cumbersome, even for apparently superior technologies. If we assume that users only switch technologies if their perceived benefits outweigh the costs, there are at least two reasons for the usually rather slow diffusion of new technologies: The group of potential users is heterogeneous and their perceived benefits differ

[25] For a detailed discussion on the role of policy-induced innovation in the energy sector refer to Chapter 4.

considerably; and the early adoption of new technologies is risky as reliable information on operational performance is still very scarce.

Over time, the diffusion process gains pace as both manufacturers and users slide down the learning curve. In many cases, network effects play an important role as well, i.e. the benefits of a particular technology increase in the number of users. To stress an example from the renewable energy sector, improvements in product design and manufacturing processes led to a significant decrease in the costs of wind turbines (learning-by-doing). At the same time, operators gained experience as well. They developed more efficient maintenance routines and thereby reduced operating costs (learning-by-using). In addition, the growing number of wind farms triggered the development of support industries such as specialized wind forecasting agencies or third party maintenance contractors. The availability of these support services made wind power generally more attractive for all users (network effect).

As the previous discussion shows, government support was and continues to be essential to the diffusion of renewable energy equipment. Without demand side measures like quotas, feed-in tariffs, or production premiums, renewables installations would certainly not have reached their current levels, and the considerable technological and economical improvements through learning and network effects would not have been possible.

This observation suggests that manufacturers of renewable energy equipment directly benefit from an increasing number of renewables installations in their home market. This idea links the discussion to the lead market theory for environmental goods and services, which is introduced in the following section.

2.3.2 Lead market theory

Beise & Rennings (2005)[26] extend the original lead market theory of Beise (2001, 2004) to environmental innovations and consider the special role of regulation in this context. According to their theory, lead markets for environmental goods and services are defined as countries which are first to adopt a future global design standard and lead the international diffusion. Hence, green sector firms from these countries experience a classical first mover advantage as described by Porter (1990).

The extended lead market framework of Beise & Rennings (2005) lists five market characteristics which can individually or collective explain the

[26] An independent publication of Jänicke & Jacob (2004) developed a similar idea.

development of countries into lead markets for a specific technology. The first market factor is what they call price advantage. Beise & Rennings (2005) argue that environmental innovations which are developed in countries with large or strongly growing domestic markets will develop a price advantage relative to similar innovations developed in countries with smaller local markets. Hence, the price effect is equivalent to the learning-curve or the economies-of-scale effect.

The second factor described by the authors is the demand advantage. This effect occurs if a country develops a future global standard first thanks to special features of its domestic market. Put differently, the benefits of the future global standard are especially high for users located in the lead market country.

Factor three is the transfer advantage. The early adoption of the future global standards in the lead market provides a convincing showcase for potential users in other countries. This prove-of-concept serves as a strong marketing instrument for the lead market's domestic standards and increases the likelihood that other countries follow their example and continuously advance the standard of the lead market into a global standard.

The fourth market factor is the export advantage which in itself consists of three individual aspects. The export advantage arises for countries which either take into account the local design preference of future export markets from the very beginning (the development of global design standards is their clear target), for countries which are generally strong exporters and can build on their export experience, or for countries which have just by coincidence similar market conditions than follower countries.

The fifth and final factor is the Porter effect. This factor is special to the extended lead market framework and cannot be found in its original formulation by Beise (2001). According to the Porter effect, countries can create a competitive advantage for their local environmental goods and services industry if they are first to adopt a future global regulatory standard (Porter & van der Linde, 1995; Beise & Rennings, 2005). It is important to note here that the export success critically depends on other countries to follow the example of the potential lead market. Without international diffusion of the novel environmental regulation, export opportunities will most likely not occur, and the market for the formerly promising eco-innovation remains local. However, if other countries follow and enact similar regulations, innovators from the lead market have a good chance to maintain their first mover advantage in the long-run (Nehrt, 1998).

Rennings & Beise (2005) present two case studies to provide empirical evidence for their extended lead market theory. They find that the lead market framework explains the development of Denmark and Germany into the global lead markets for wind turbines and fuel-efficient passenger cars respectively. Furthermore, they conclude that the Porter effect is especially strong if it is complemented by favorable trends in environmental regulation and global demand. Hence, the findings of Rennings & Beise (2005) are consistent with the majority view in environment and trade research which is that "[f]irst-mover advantages may result from domestic regulation that correctly anticipates world-wide trends" (Jaffe et al., 2003, p. 488).

Two studies on countries' wind turbine industries provide further empirical evidence. Klinge Jacobson (1999) finds that regulation had a positive impact on the competitiveness of the Danish wind industry. Lacerda & Bergh (2014) find that the lead market framework and especially the Porter effect explain the success of the wind power equipment industries in China, Germany, and the US.

2.4 Research contribution of this thesis

The previous discussion clearly shows that research on the determinants of trade in renewable energy equipment is important. Thanks to the support mechanisms that have been implemented by regulators around the world, renewable energies grew from niche to mainstream technologies which now compete head-on-head with conventional sources of electricity. However, even though more and more countries benefit from an increasing share of renewables in their electricity mix and therefore lower emission levels, the number of countries which reap the additional economic benefits of a meaningful domestic renewable energy equipment industry remains limited.

So far only a small body of literature sets out to resolve this puzzle. First empirical publications on the narrowly strong Porter Hypothesis and the related lead market theory for environmental goods and services provide answers to the question why some countries benefit more strongly from increasingly stringent environmental regulation than others. However, as discussed throughout Section 2.2, the existing literature on the narrowly strong Porter Hypothesis and the Porter Hypothesis in general has limitations and would benefit from further research in this field.

This doctoral thesis contributes to the research on the narrowly strong Porter Hypothesis in four ways. First, it builds on the most recent data which is critical given the fast pace at which the renewable energy industry develops (REN21, 2014a).

Second, it has a clear focus on renewable power generation equipment represented by the two main technologies from this field, wind and solar power. Previous studies either focused on the whole environmental goods and services industry (Costantini & Mazzanti, 2012) or mixed renewable energy equipment with energy efficiency technology (Costantini & Crespi, 2008). Similarly, Groba (2014) combined the trade flows of solar PV and solar thermal equipment.

Third, it examines both steps of the Porter Hypothesis individually. In the first step I test for the impact of environmental regulation on technological innovation in renewable energy equipment. In the second step, I test for the impact of both, countries' environmental regulation and the innovation which it induced, on the export competitiveness of their respective renewable energy equipment industries. All previous studies on the narrowly strong Porter Hypothesis integrate these two steps and estimate the innovation and the competitiveness effect simultaneously. Therefore, they do not explicitly demonstrate that the export-enhancing innovations, which serve as explanatory variables in their models, were actually induced by environmental regulation. This causal chain, however, is a key feature of the Porter Hypothesis.

Fourth and most important, this doctoral thesis clearly differentiates between two aspects of environmental regulation: regulation design and regulation intensity. The failure of many studies on the Porter Hypothesis to differentiate between these two dimensions has often been criticized by commentators (Jaffe, Newell, & Stavins, 2002; Brännlund & Lundgren, 2009). As discussed before, Porter (1991) and Porter & van der Linde (1995) explicitly stress the importance of regulation design and state repeatedly that only well-crafted environmental regulation leads to their famous win-win situations where both environment and businesses are better off. Within the body of literature on the narrowly strong Porter Hypothesis only Groba (2014) and to a lesser extend also Cao & Groba (2013) consider differences in regulation design. All other studies rely on intensity measures alone.

3 Measurement of environmental regulation

As discussed in the previous section, a main contribution of this research project is the differentiation between policy instruments and regulation intensity as the two main dimensions of environmental regulation.

This chapter develops the respective tools and methods. The development process is structured as follows. Section 3.1 introduces the most common policy instruments in environmental regulation, discusses their underlying economic rationales, and presents the scope and taxonomy of renewable energy support policies covered in this thesis. Section 3.2 is dedicated to the measurement of regulation intensity. After a discussion and evaluation of intensity measures used in research on the narrowly strong Porter Hypothesis and in trade and environment research in general, the section also includes the selection of the most suitable intensity measures for the specific research questions of this thesis. The center piece of this chapter is Section 3.3, which carefully analyzes the policy instrument types and regulation intensity measures defined in the previous two sections. Besides a separate analysis of the development of instrument types and intensity measures over time, the section also evaluates the contribution of individual instrument types to the overall intensity of environmental regulation.

3.1 Common policy instruments in environmental regulation

The analysis of renewable energy installations and the related discussion presented in Chapter 0 shows that policymakers in many countries from around the world have the political will to promote renewables and increase their share in power generation. The further discussion throughout Chapter 0 revealed that governments have at least three reasons to support the transition from conventional to renewable sources of electricity.

First, policymakers promote renewable energies as a primary mean to reduce pollution and counter climate change through reduction of greenhouse gas emissions. Thereby the dissemination of renewable energies enables countries to fulfill their Kyoto obligations or other non-binding climate change targets. Second, renewables can help countries to reduce their dependency on energy imports or simply meet their growing domestic electricity demand. Third, many governments also view renewable energy support as an effective industry policy. They believe that government support for renewable energies creates new manufacturing jobs in the booming green sector (REN 21, 2014a).

In order to increase the share of renewable energies in the electricity mix and to reach their underlying objectives in environmental, energy, and industry policy, governments need to adopt the right regulatory instruments. The challenge for these instruments is to resolve the double externality problem associated with technological change processes related to environmental goods such as renewable power generation technologies (Jaffe, Newell, & Stavins, 2005).

As all other technological change processes, the transition from conventional to renewable sources of electricity is hampered by knowledge externalities. These knowledge externalities occur if firms are not able to reap the full benefits of their inventions. Due to the public good nature of knowledge, competitors inevitably benefit from the inventor's newly created technical knowledge. Even in the presence of advanced patent protection, the effort and the financial risk to develop a similar technology is certainly lower for a competitor than it was for the original inventor. The same logic applies to early adopters of new technologies and the operational know-how they create. The early adopter is usually not able to keep all know-how completely proprietary. Therefore, followers can adopt new technologies at lower cost and at a lower risk than the early adopter. In summary, knowledge externalities related to the invention and early adoption of new technologies decrease the incentives for first movers and therefore slow down the development and deployment of new technologies (Jaffe et al., 2005).

However, unlike most technological change processes, the transition from conventional to renewable energies is complicated further by a second externality problem – the negative externalities associated with environmental pollution. Conventional power plants dump large amounts of greenhouse gases and other harmful substances into the atmosphere at no cost. The public good nature of a clean environment clearly leaves emission-free renewable energies at a comparative disadvantage. Therefore, the demand for renewable energy equipment remains low. In other words, there is no market for the in terms of levelized cost of electricity more expensive renewables. As a consequence, firms are neither willing to invest in the development nor in the deployment of these technologies. In sum, the double externality problem leads to a situation in which technological change becomes highly unlikely. The lack of a sufficiently large market reduces the already low attractiveness of R&D investments in completely new technologies even further (Jaffe et al., 2005).

In the following parts of this section, I will introduce three groups[27] of policy instruments (Bahar, Egeland, & Steenblik, 2013) which address one or both components of the double externality problem associated with technological change in the energy sector. The discussion starts with technology-push policies. This group of policies is designed to counter the knowledge externality problem and to increase the attractiveness of private R&D investments. It also contains measures to foster knowledge generation in the public sector (Bahar et al., 2013).

The second group of polices creates a market-pull by addressing the pollution externality problem. It contains measures which create financial incentives for renewable energy investments. These incentives are meant to compensate utilities for avoiding socially undesirable CO_2 emissions and for carrying the (initially) higher costs of electricity generation from renewables (Bahar et al., 2013).

Finally, a third group of policies supports renewables indirectly through partial or full internalization of the cost of environmental pollution at source. Hence, these measures increase the demand for renewables by lowering the attractiveness of its traditional substitutes which do no longer benefit from the possibility to dispose of harmful substance into the atmosphere free of charge (Bahar et al., 2013).

3.1.1 Renewable energy support policies: Technology-push[28]

Within the category of technology-push policies, Bahar et al. (2013) distinguish between three types of instruments. The first instrument type is public support for research, development, and demonstration (RD&D) of early stage renewable energy technologies. Depending on the country, governments might either directly fund their own public research institutions and universities, or team up with private sector corporations to conduct joint research programs. In the case of public-private research partnerships, funding is mostly provided in form of grants, subsidies, or tax credits. Public RD&D support is quite common in advanced countries such as the member states of OECD (Jaffe et al.,

[27] While a general differentiation between renewable energy support policies on the one hand and policies restricting the use of conventional technologies on the other hand is straightforward, the more detailed differentiation between technology-push and market-pull policies for renewables is less clear. As technological progress and market demand often coincide, most renewable energy support polices have both a technology-push and a market-pull effect. Hence, the allocation of policies to either group is done based on the stronger of the two effects. Therefore, an instruments allocation to a specific policy group does not mean that the instrument has no effect in other areas.

[28] This section builds on Bahar, Egeland, & Steenblik (2013), Appendix I, pp. 24-50.

2005). However, also emerging countries increasingly adopt RD&D programs to support their local renewable energy equipment industries. China for instance increased their public R&D investments in renewable energy technologies from USD 2.5 bn in 1996 to USD 15.2 bn in 2008 (Cao & Groba, 2013).

The second type of technology-push policies is government support for the development of commercial products and the following industrialization. Most governments clearly differentiate between these later stage R&D programs and the early stage measures discussed before. Due to the significantly lower uncertainty in this phase, private sector firms are expected to carry a greater portion of the investment risk. Depending on the national context, such support measures usually include tax incentives, subsidized loans, or loan guarantees.

Finally, technology-push policies can take the form of export support. In this case, governments support the dissemination of technologies developed by their domestic industry into foreign markets. The most common form of export support is the provision of low-cost loans to international customers by dedicated export credit agencies or development banks. Moreover, countries might use their diplomatic relationships to convince others of the benefits of a certain technology.

Overall, technology-push policies are mostly associated with the earlier stages of the technology introduction process and are phased out as technologies mature.

3.1.2 Renewable energy support policies: Market-pull[29]

The largest group of renewable energy support policies is market-pull measures. These measures have been designed to correct for the inherent disadvantage that renewable energies have compared to conventional sources of electricity by providing financial compensations for not emitting pollutants into the atmosphere. Moreover, market-pull policies are meant to equalize the non-externality-related differences in production cost between renewable and conventional technologies.

Figure 6 illustrates how market-pull policies foster the technological change process from conventional to renewable power generation technologies. With an increasing share of renewables in the electricity mix, equipment manufacturers slide down the learning curve as they accumulate experiences and upgrade their knowledge in engineering and producing renewable energy equipment. These learning curve effects lead in turn to equipment cost reductions, quality improvements,

[29] This section builds on Bahar, Egeland, & Steenblik (2013), Appendix I, pp. 24-50.

or both. Hence, renewable energies gain competitiveness versus conventional technologies, and their share in the energy mix increases further to trigger the next round of learning-based improvements.

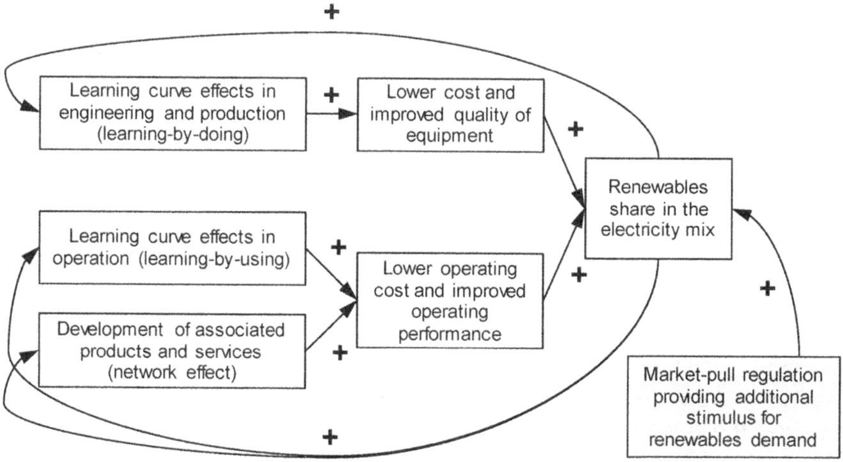

Figure 6 – Principle of market-pull policies
Source: Own illustration based on written ideas from Jaffe et al. (2003, 2005).

The learning-by-doing effect associated with manufacturers of renewable energy equipment is complemented by the learning-by-using effect associated with operators of renewable power plants. The more experience an operator has with renewable energies the more efficient his processes and therefore the lower the operating cost and the higher the operating performance of his power plant. In addition to the learning-by-using effect, operators benefit from the so called network effect. This effect entails that the number and quality of complementary products and services increases in the share of renewables in the electricity mix. These products and services commonly translate into additional operational improvements which make renewables even more competitive relative to conventional power generation technologies.

Market-pull policies work as a catalyst for the self-enforcing relationship between higher renewable energy shares, downward movements on the learning curve, and increased competitiveness. In order to reach higher shares of renewable energies faster, these policies provide additional incentives for electrical utilities or independent operators to add renewables installations to their portfolio. Hence, market-pull policies aim to accelerate the knowledge accumulation process and thereby the movement of renewable energy technologies towards cost competitiveness with fossil and nuclear power[30].

Market-pull policies are a central element of many portfolios of renewable energy support policies. Hence, it doesn't surprise much that the spectrum of different policy instruments is quite broad. Researchers usually distinguish between three groups of market-pull policies: quantity-based, price-based, and fiscal instruments (Bahar et al., 2013; Groba & Breitschopf, 2013).

Quantity-based instruments usually take the form of quota systems which are also referred to as Renewable Portfolio Standards in the US or Renewable Energy Targets in Australia. Under a quota system, regulators define minimum shares or amounts of electricity generated from renewable sources which have to be met in predefined time periods. Depending on the jurisdiction, these minimum quotas are either imposed on suppliers or consumers of electricity. Due to administrative reasons, most jurisdictions hold the electricity producers liable for meeting the quotas. If they are imposed on consumers, these schemes are mostly limited to specific industries and do not apply to smaller companies or private households. In addition, some countries differentiate between quotas for large- and small-scale installations or types of renewable energies to ensure that also currently less advanced technologies benefit from higher deployment rates. In any case, utilities or consumers which do not meet their obligations face a fine depending on the gap between actual and required renewables quota.

In many cases, renewable quotas are supplemented with trading systems for renewable energy certificates, which are also referred to as tradable green certificates or renewable energy credits. These trading systems are meant to increase flexibility by leaving the decision to buy renewable energy certificates on the market or to invest in own installations to individual market participants. A key advantage of trading systems is that renewables are installed by operators or at locations which guarantee highest efficiency and therefore lowest generation cost. An electrical utility provider in a sunny, coastal area might be able to increase the renewables share in its portfolio at a considerably lower cost than a utility provider in an urban area with less beneficial deployment conditions for wind turbines or solar PV modules. Hence, utility providers which produce more green electricity than required can

---

[30] For further detail on the process of technological change in environmental goods and services, refer to Section 2.3.1.

trade their excess certificates and thereby create a second revenue stream besides the sale of electricity.

The second large group of market-pull policies is price-based instruments. The oldest and most widely applied representative from this group of instruments is the feed-in tariff. Unlike renewable energy quotas, feed-in tariffs overcome the problems associated with the negative externalities of environmental pollution and the prevailing differences in terms of levelized cost of electricity by financially incentivizing electricity generation form renewable energy sources. Feed-in tariffs are usually designed as a system of cross-subsidies. Renewable energy producers receive a fixed price or a price premium per unit of electricity. These incentive payments are financed through surcharges on the price of electricity paid by private and industrial customers. Therefore, renewables become competitive with conventional technologies as the feed-in tariff systems artificially decreases the cost of green and increases the cost of conventional power.

The attractiveness of investments in green energy and therefore the market-pull is often increased further through guaranteed connection and preferred access to the gird. Hence, investors can calculate the future revenues of potential renewable energy projects upfront and keep their financial risk at a minimum.

Although the basic mechanism of feed-in tariff schemes is similar worldwide, national systems are quite different in detail. As mentioned previously, some countries grant fixed rates while others prefer premium payments on the market price of electricity. Moreover, some countries have set different rates for different types of technologies. In some cases, feed-in tariffs decrease over time while in again other cases they are adjusted for inflation. In addition, a recent trend is to link feed-in tariff payments with local content requirements for the energy equipment employed (Bougette & Charlier, 2014; Charnovitz & Fischer, 2014).

Another instrument from the group of market-pull policies is net metering. Net metering is essentially a simplified feed-in tariff for small-scale installations, mostly photovoltaics. In contrast to traditional feed-in tariff schemes, incentives are only granted for the amount of electricity which is not immediately self-consumed by the owner of the renewable energy installation. Hereby, the amount of electricity which can be fed into the grid is often limited by contract. The classic example is a private house with roof-top PV system. In summer, the electricity provided by the PV modules often exceeds the household's demand, and electricity is fed into the grid. In winter or at night, however, the PV modules do not meet the household's electricity demand, and additional power is purchased from the grid. Depending on the specific net metering scheme, the amount of electricity fed into the grid is either compensate at market rates or at higher feed-in tariff rates for renewables.

The third price-based policy instrument defined by Bahar et al. (2013) is public competitive bidding or tendering. The only difference between tendering and traditional feed-in tariff systems is that the fixed or premium rate at which operators can feed electricity into the grid is not predefined by regulators but is determined in an auctioning process. The regulator or utility provider puts out renewable energy projects for tender and awards the contract to the bidder with the lowest fixed or premium rate requirements.

The third and last large group of market-pull instruments is fiscal policy measures. Unlike the quantity- and price-based measures discussed previously, fiscal policy instruments are financed through tax money. The most common fiscal policy measures are tax credits, tax reductions, accelerated depreciation schemes, low-cost loans or public loan guarantees, and energy production payments. All of these measures have in common that they attempt to stimulate the demand for renewable energies by decreasing the investment risk or increasing the expected return on investment.

Tax credits come in two different versions: production tax credits and investment tax credits. The former awards tax credits for the production of renewable energy and is coupled to the amount of electricity generated by a given power plant. The payment period is usually shorter than for feed-in tariffs. The latter is granted for investments in new renewable energy installations and usually depends on the investment amount. Tax credits are traditionally very common in the United States. In a broader sense, accelerated depreciation schemes fall into this category as well because of their direct effect on income tax payments.

Tax reduction or tax exemption programs come in different forms and may cover carbon, energy, sales, VAT, or other taxes. Depending on the specific taxes selected for reduction or exemption schemes, governments can either incentivize the investment in or the production of renewable energies.

Another very common instrument is the provision of low-cost loans or public loan guarantees for investments in renewable energy projects. These measures are again meant to make investments in renewables cheaper and less risky and thereby increase the expected return.

Finally, energy production payments are a quite rare policy instrument which is basically the same as a feed-in tariff. The only difference is that energy production payments are financed with tax money and not with cross-subsidies from other generation technologies.

3.1.3 Policies restricting conventional technologies

Out of the group of emission control policies, carbon taxes have the strongest positive effect on the development and dissemination of pollution-free power generation technologies (Denicolo, 1999; Jaffe et al., 2002). Under a carbon tax regime, governments set a price per unit of greenhouse gas emission and thereby internalize the cost of anthropogenic climate change at its source. Hence, operators of conventional power plants are charged for the air pollution associated with the combustion of fossil fuels and therefore lose a key cost advantage compared to renewable energies.

Cap-and-trade-systems, which restrict the amount of greenhouse gases to a certain level, are another approach to counter climate change. For each unit of pollution, a company emits it needs to hold emission rights. Similar to the renewable energy certificates discussed before, firms can either buy certificates on the market or launch own pollution abatement or control programs. The benefit compared to pollution taxes is that cap-and-trade-systems help to reduce emissions where the marginal costs are lowest. Hence, cap-and-trade-systems achieve certain pollution levels at lower economic costs than tax systems. But, this means also that from the perspective of renewable energy support, the less efficient carbon tax system generates a stronger market-pull effect even though at higher economic costs (Jaffe et al., 2002; Stavins, 2003).

Prominent examples for pollution taxes and trading systems are the US cap-and-trade system for SO_2 and the EU Emission Trading System for greenhouse gases. However, such examples are still rare. It is due to political reasons that governments mostly prefer second best policies like RD&D support, renewable energy quotas, or feed-in tariffs to promote development and diffusion of renewable energies (Jaffe et al., 2005).

3.1.4 Policy instruments covered in this thesis

In order to analyze the impact of environmental policy design on countries' innovativeness and export competitiveness in renewable energy equipment, I have compiled a comprehensive database of renewables support policies from data of the REN21's annual Renewables Global Status Reports, the OECD's statistics on research and development expenditures in the energy sector, and the Global

Renewable Energy Policies and Measures database of IEA and IRENA[31]. My consolidated policy database reports the implementation status of eleven different policy instruments in 225 countries and territories between 1974 and 2013. The typology of policy instruments used in the database is consistent with the classification of Bahar et al. (2013), which has been followed to structure the discussion on common policy instruments throughout this section.

Table 7 maps the eleven individual instruments reported in my policy database to the classification scheme of Bahar et al. (2013). Especially for the category of market-pull policies, the information level is very detailed and allows differentiating between specific policy instruments. With respect to technology-push policies and policies constraining conventional technologies, the level of detail is much lower.

For the sake of meaningful econometric analyses, the eleven individual measures are grouped into six policy clusters: targets, RD&D support, quotas, feed-in tariffs, fiscal incentives, and carbon trading. The grouping was conducted based on similarities in the underlying mechanisms of the different policy instruments as discussed throughout the previous sections of this chapter.

The quotas cluster consists of all quantity-based renewable energy support policies. Besides feed-in tariffs and premiums, the feed-in tariff cluster includes net metering, public competitive bidding, and energy-production payments. Although energy production payments are a tax-financed instrument while the other three are not, this measure certainly belongs into this cluster because the underlying support mechanism is exactly the same as for regular feed-in tariffs financed through cross-subsidies. Given the very high degree of similarity, feed-in tariffs and energy production payments are grouped together on instrument level, too. The fiscal incentives cluster consists of all tax funded measures[32] which increase the attractive of investments in renewable energy installation by reducing the financial risk or increasing the return on investment. The clusters targets, RD&D support, and carbon trading are not aggregated and just contain one individual policy instrument each.

---

[31] For details on the policy database and the underlying sources, refer to Section 3.3.1.

[32] Except for energy production payments.

Policy clusters for subsequent analysis	Renewable support policies: Technology-push	Renewable support policies: Market-pull	Policies restricting conventional technologies	Other policies
Targets				Renewable energy targets or strategies
RD&D support	Research, development and deployment programs			
Quotas		Renewable energy quotas with certificate trading Renewable energy quotas without certificate trading		
Feed-in tariffs		Feed-in tariff (fixed rate or premium) (incl. energy production payments) Net metering Public competitive bidding (tendering)		
Fiscal incentives		Tax credits (investment of production) Tax reduction (carbon, energy, sales, VAT, or other taxes) Public spending, capital subsidies, and low-cost loans		
Carbon trading			Greenhouse gas certificate trading systems	

Notes: Differentiation into technology-push and market-pull policies is based on policy instruments' primary mode of operation. For details, see discussion in the introductory part of Section 3.1.

Table 7 – Taxonomy of types and clusters of RE support policies
Source: Own illustration.

3.2 Measures of regulation intensity

Following on the discussion and classification of different policy instruments, this section covers regulation intensity, the second main dimension along which countries' environmental policy schemes are compared and evaluated. Adding regulation intensity as second dimension to the overall evaluation framework is essential to understand how serious countries' efforts to protect the environment and to promote renewable energies actually are.

Hence, generally applicable and reliable indicators are required to make regulation intensity measurable, to compare intensities between countries, and to track its changes over time. Moreover, if designed properly, these indicators should also be suitable to determine which instruments of environmental policy are effective and which fail to achieve their objectives.

However, the question of how to reliably measure the intensity of environmental regulation has traditionally been one of the greatest challenges in environmental economics. Although multiple alternative approaches have been applied in empirical research, there is no one single standard tool for intensity measurement. The tools applied in empirical studies vary considerably depending on factors like research question and data availability. The latter being a critical issue as it appears to be strongly dependent on industry context, national context, and time period covered in the data sample (Jaffe et al., 2002, 2003).

The objective of this section is to systematically review and evaluate commonly used indicators of regulation intensity and to identify those measures which are best suited for the research focus of this thesis. Suitability is determined based on two criteria. First, the intensity indicators shall measure as directly as possible the impact that environmental regulation has on the domestic demand for renewable energy equipment. Second, the intensity indicators shall be available for as many countries and time periods as possible.

In the remaining part of this section, I first review and discuss intensity indicators which have been applied in the broader field of empirical research on trade and environment. Afterwards, I take a closer look on the intensity measures applied in research on the Porter Hypothesis in general and the narrowly strong version specifically. Finally, I introduce the intensity measures which have been selected for application throughout this research project.

3.2.1 Intensity measures in trade and environment research

Before the discussion of alternative policy indicators, I need to introduce an important difference in terminology between this thesis and other publications in trade and environment research in order to avoid misinterpretations.

Traditionally, indicators which measure firms' difficulty to comply with environmental regulation have been called *stringency* measures (Brunel & Levinson, 2013); a terminology which paints a rather dull picture of environmental regulation and highlights the negative aspects such as additional burdens and restrictions. This notion is consistent with both the conventional view that high regulatory standards compromise the competitiveness of domestic firms and with the revisionist view that stricter regulation induces innovation and requires firms to rethink their business models. Both schools of thought interpret environmental regulation as additional burden for business, at least in the first step[33].

In research on the narrowly strong Porter Hypothesis however, regulation is expected to have a positive effect from the very beginning. Firms operating in the environmental goods and services sector directly benefit from (additional) regulatory burdens imposed on their customers. Moreover, they are expected to benefit regardless whether the overall policy effect on regulated industries is positive or negative (Jaffe & Palmer, 1997). Due to this change in perspectives, the original terminology, *regulatory stringency,* is misleading and too negative. Therefore, I have introduced an alternative term, *regulation intensity*, for the discussion on the narrowly strong Porter Hypothesis. This term illustrates that strong renewable energy support policies accelerate the transition towards renewable sources of electricity and thus create business opportunities for the renewable energy equipment industry.

As mentioned in the introduction to this section, developing meaningful measures of environmental regulation is a key challenge in research on trade and the environment. Based on their review of stringency indicators used in the empirical literature, Brunel & Levinson (2013) identify four inherent obstacles of commonly used measures of regulatory stringency.

The first obstacle, multidimensionality, contains that "environmental regulations cannot easily be captured by one measure of 'stringency' "

---

33 While the proponents of the conventional view expect an overall negative effect of environmental regulation, the proponents of the revisionist view expect that firms can turn the initially negative effects positive as soon as their innovation efforts bear fruit. See also discussion Section 2.1.

(Brunel & Levinson, 2013, p. 5). Countries' environmental policy portfolio usually consists of several different policy instruments some of which might apply to all businesses while others only apply to specific subsets. Hence, different measures of regulatory stringency are required depending on the industry under investigation. However, the problem of multidimensionality does not only arise from differences in the composition of countries' policy portfolios but also from differences between like policy instruments. For instance, even though two countries have adopted regulation limiting pollution from coal-fired power plants, these regulations might differ considerably in terms of pollution limits, exceptions granted, fines for non-compliance, etc. Hence, it is not an easy task to determine which country has the more stringent regulation scheme in place. In sum, multidimensionality describes researchers' challenge to reliably measure the size of the regulatory burden and to compare stringency levels between jurisdictions.

The second obstacle, simultaneity, is deemed even more serious and describes the puzzle that both "countries with strong economies or [countries with] bad pollution problems may impose more stringent regulations" (Brunel & Levinson, 2013, pp. 5-6). Put differently, simultaneity means that while regulation has an impact on economic performance, economic performance does also have an impact on regulation. Advanced economies with strong and differentiated competitive advantages might be able to adopt environmental regulation at lower economic cost than developing countries, whose competitiveness is more dependent on simple production cost advantages also including the cost of pollution[34]. Hence, the challenge is to develop stringency measures which isolate regulation's effect on economic performance from the opposite effect of economic performance on governments' willingness to adopt stringent regulation.

Brunel & Levinson's (2013) remaining two obstacles, industrial composition and capital vintage, are described as special cases of simultaneity. Analogous to the interaction between regulation and its impact on economic performance, similar interdependencies exists between environmental regulation and industrial composition, and between environmental regulation and capital vintage.

According to Brunel & Levinson (2013), the only viable approaches to correct for the simultaneity effects are natural experiments, instrumental variables, or panel approaches with fixed effects. While natural experiments, such as the 1990 amendment to the US Clean Air Act, and

---

[34] Refer to the introduction of Chapter 2 for a brief overview on the pollution haven effect.

meaningful instrumental variables are rare, panels with fixed country or industry effects only correct for time-invariant differences. Hence, all intensity measurement approaches reviewed by the two authors are to some extent subject to the different manifestations of simultaneity.

Table 8 gives an overview of common measures regulatory stringency applied in research on trade and the environment. Generally, researchers used two approaches to measure environmental stringency. On the one hand, they have estimated the impact which regulation has on the economy using direct, output-oriented measures such as private sector compliance costs and changes in emission intensity. On the other hand, researchers made attempts to measure stringency directly using more input-oriented indicators such as the enactment status of certain policies, aggregated regulation intensity indices, or public expenditures on environmental protection and policy enforcement.

The most widely used group of indicators of regulatory stringency is private-sector pollution abatement and control expenditures, a measure of regulation's impact on private businesses (e.g. Levinson, 1996; Brunnermeier & Cohen, 2003; Millimet & Roy, 2011). The benefits of this indicator are good comparability between industries and jurisdictions. Moreover, indicator values are mostly in line with intuition in terms of variations between countries, industries, and over time. The main drawback, besides the ubiquitous simultaneity issue, is its reliance of self-reported data from industry questionnaires. Hence, data reliability depends on the ability of management to correctly value the isolated impact of regulation on operating costs and capital expenditures.

The second group of indicators is also output-oriented and measures the impact of regulation on changes in emission levels and energy usage. Prominent studies applying such indicators are Beers & Bergh (1997) and Harris, Kónya, & Mátyás (2002). These indicators have the advantage that, at least on a high level, emission data are available for more countries than compliance costs data. However, compared to compliance cost measures, the interpretation of emission and energy intensities is less intuitive.

The most direct approach is to assess stringency based on the existence or even the detailed characteristics of specific policies (e.g. McConnell & Schwab, 1990). Due to the complexity of policy portfolios and the instruments themselves, multidimensionality is the main drawback of this approach. This is especially the case for measures of policy strictness which attempt to compare the stringency of alternative policy instruments based on their actual wording and provisions. One approach to reduce the problem of multidimensionality is to restrict the analysis to a clearly defined industry scope such as Berman & Bui (2001) do in their study on oil refineries in the Los Angeles basin.

Aggregated policy indices are another solution for the multidimensionality issue. The idea is to summarize the estimated stringency levels of all relevant provisions in one aggregated measure. This approach has a great appeal with researchers and has been applied amongst others by Dasgupta, Mody, Roy, & Wheeler (2001), Cagatay & Mihci (2006), Johnstone et al. (2012), and Sauvage (2014). However, a key shortcoming is the indices' lack of robustness. Even slight changes in the aggregation process might significantly change the overall results (Brunel & Levinson, 2013).

The last group of policy-based stringency indicators is public expenditures on pollution abatement and policy enforcement (e.g. Gray, 1997). The benefit of measuring regulation based on expenditures is the relatively high data availability and quality, at least for developed countries, and the good comparability among jurisdictions. However, there are also two major drawbacks to this approach. First, all regulatory instruments which require no or only small direct government expenditures, such as emission restrictions, are not adequately captured under this approach. Second, it is not clear whether high government expenditures indicate high or low stringency levels. High expenditures could on the one hand be caused by high enforcement efforts which increase compliance costs, or on the other hand by high subsidies for energy-intensive and export-oriented industries which decrease compliance costs.

Measurement approach	Common obstacles in application: Multidimen-sionality[1)]	Simulta-neity[2)]	Further comments	Intensity measures (selection)	Application frequency[3)]
(a) Indicators measuring the (economic) effect of environmental regulation (indirect, output-oriented approach)					
Private sector compliance costs		x	(+) Good comparability (continuous measure) (–) Subjectivity and reliability issues of self-reported figures (PACE only) (–) Subject to distortions through industry composition and capital vintage effects (–) Ambiguity: depending on interpretation high values might indicate high/low intensity	Private pollution abatement expenditures	++
				Shadow prices of pollution	o
Emission levels and energy usage	x	x	(+) Good comparability (continuous measure) (–) Subject to distortions through industry composition and capital vintage effects (–) Ambiguity: depending on interpretation high values might indicate high/low intensity	Emissions	o
				Ambient pollution	o
				Energy consumption	+
(b) Indicators measuring environmental regulation (direct, input-oriented approach)					
Regulation-based measures	x	x	(+) Multidimensionality issue becomes manageable for narrow industry focus (–) Heterogeneity of regulation hinders international comparability	Ratification status	o
				Policy enactment status	o
				Policy attainment status	+
				Policy strictness	+
Policy indices and surveys		x	(+) Multidimensionality issue of regulation-based approaches compressed to one figure (–) Index aggregation often lacks robustness (–) Subjectivity of surveys: perceived intensity	Composite indices	++
				Surveys of regulated firms	+
Public exp-enditures and enforcement	x	x	(+) Good comparability (continuous measure) (–) Env. regulation only partly covered (–) Ambiguity: depending on interpretation high values might indicate high/low intensity	Public pollution abatement	+
				Monitoring expenditures	+

Notes: (1) Multidimensionality: Overall intensity of all policies which are relevant for a sample is difficult to represent in one number. (2) Simultaneity: Regulation intensity and impact are determined simultaneously through the political process. (3) ++, +, and o indicate application in more than 10, 3 to 10, or less than 3 of the studies reviewed by Brunel & Levinson (2013).

Table 8 – Common intensity measures in environmental economics
Source: Own illustration based on data from Brunel and Levinson (2013), Table 1, pp. 36-41.

3.2.2 Intensity measurement in Porter Hypothesis research

As discussed in the previous section, the same stringency measures developed for tests on the pollution haven hypothesis or the conventional view in general, have also been applied in research on the Porter Hypothesis. Table 9 shows how often certain stringency measures have been used in empirical research on the different versions of the Porter Hypothesis. The analysis is based on the selection of Porter studies presented in the literature review and on the classification of stringency measures developed by Brunel & Levinson (2013). For easier comparison, Table 9 also gives approximated application frequencies of the different indicators in the broader area of trade and environment research[35].

In a comparison of application frequencies between research on the Porter Hypothesis and environment and trade research in general three aspects stand out. First, based on the studies covered in the literature review, research on the Porter Hypothesis draws back on stringency measures from each of the five indicator categories introduced by Brunel & Levinson (2013).

Second, studies on the Porter Hypothesis often apply indicators using absolute, continuous scales such private and public pollution abatement and control expenditures. One explanation might be that indicators measured in absolute terms can be easily compared among jurisdictions and over time. This is an important aspect for empirical test of the Porter Hypothesis such as studies on the impact of changes in regulatory stringency on innovation activity.

Third, research on the Porter Hypothesis often applies direct measures of regulation. Especially the impact of the implementation status of specific policies has been applied much more frequently than in other fields of trade and environment research. This finding is consistent with the fact that policy design, i.e. the existence of instruments which are in line with criteria of well-crafted environmental regulation, is highly relevant in the Porter context.

A closer look on publications from the immediate research area of this doctoral thesis reveals that studies on the narrowly strong Porter Hypothesis also rely on stringency measures – or, in this context, better intensity measures – which are well known from the previous discussion on research on trade and the environment and the Porter Hypothesis in general.

---

[35] The application frequencies were already presented in Table 8 (page 77).

Measurement approach	Intensity measures (selection)	Application frequency in research on Porter Hypothesis: weak	narrow	strong	narrowly strong	Total	Application frequency in research on trade and environment[1)2)]
Private-sector compliance costs	Private pollution abatement expenditures	3		6	2	**11**	++
	Shadow prices of pollution						o
Emission levels and energy usage	Emission	1		2	1	**4**	o
	Ambient pollution						o
	Energy consumption						+
Regulation-based measures	Ratification status of international treaties						o
	Policy implementation status	1	1	3	2	**7**	o
	Industry attainment status	1		1		**2**	+
	Strictness of regulation		1	3		**4**	+
Policy indices and surveys	Composite indices	2		1	1	**4**	++
	Surveys of regulated firms	2	1	2		**5**	+
Public expenditures and enforcement	Public pollution abatement expenditures	5			2	**7**	+
	Monitoring and inspection expenditures	1		1		**2**	+

Notes: (1) Column repeats the results presented in Table 8. (2) ++, +, and o indicate application in more than 10, 3 to 10, or less than 3 of the studies reviewed by Brunel & Levinson (2013).

Table 9 – Common intensity measures in Porter Hypothesis research
Source: Own illustration (partially) based on data from Brunel & Levinson (2013).

Table 10 lists all proxies of overall regulation intensity applied in the existing empirical studies on the narrowly Porter Hypothesis. Besides measures from the framework of Brunel & Levinson (2013), the list also contains quite a few indicators which have not been covered before.

Costantini & Crespi (2008) and Costantini & Mazzanti (2012), for instance, both use revenues from environmental taxes as an indicator of regulation intensity. They argue that high tax revenues indicate intensive market interference by governments trying to influence consumption patterns and shift demand away from goods which are known to have a negative impact on the environment.

Moreover, Costantini & Crespi (2008) introduce a measure to assess voluntary conservation efforts of the private sector by tracking the number of corporations which have environment management systems in place. Increases in the number of these management systems indicate that firms are willing to act proactively in order to prepare for future regulations or for increasing requirements of customers, investors, or other stakeholders.

Most interesting, however, is a finding based on the subset of studies which are directly focused on renewable energies. All of these five studies use countries' share of electricity generated from renewable energies as indicator of regulation intensity. While two studies, Jha (2009) and Cao & Groba (2013), exclusively rely on renewables shares as intensity indicator, the remaining three, Groba (2014), Sung & Song (2013), and Sung & Song (2014), use renewables shares in combination with public R&D expenditures on renewable energies. The combination of these two regulation intensity indicators ensures that the intensities of both technology-push and market-pull instruments are covered.

Study	Industry	Period	Countries	Measures of overall regulation intensity
Costantini & Crespi (2008)	> Renewables > Green-tech	1996 - 2005	148 countries, thereof: 20 exporting (OECD) 148 importing	> CO_2 emissions > Pollution abatement and control expenditures > Environmental taxation
Jha (2009)	> Renewables	2006	34 countries, thereof 34 exporting	> Share of renewables
Costantini & Mazzanti (2012)	> Manufacturing: 5 sectors classified by technological content	1996 - 2007	145 countries, thereof: 14 exporting (EU) 145 importing	> Pollution abatement and control expenditures > Environmental taxation > Environmental management systems > EU Emission Trading Scheme Robustness checks (unreported): > CO_2 emissions > Energy intensity > Institutional quality
Cao & Groba (2013)	> Renewables: Solar and wind	1996 - 2008	44 countries, thereof: 1 exporting (China) 43 importing	> RE share (wind and solar)
Sung & Song (2013)	> Renewables: 5 technologies	1991 - 2007	18 countries, thereof 18 exporting (OECD)	> RE share > RE R&D expenditures
Groba (2014)	> Renewables: Solar	1999 - 2007	118 countries, thereof: 21 exporting 118 importing	General indicator > Carbon intensity index based on current rate and trend since 1990 Sector-specific indicators > RE share > Duration of renewable energy support policies > Public R&D expenditures on renewables
Sung & Song (2014)	> Renewables: 3 technologies	1992 - 2008	18 countries, thereof 18 exporting (OECD)	> RE share > RE R&D expenditures

Table 10 – Policy types and intensity measures of related publications
Source: Own illustration.

3.2.3 *Intensity measures applied in this thesis*

The objective of this section is to discuss, evaluate, and select measures of regulation intensity. As defined before, the selected measure shall directly reflect demand for renewable energy equipment, and it shall be available for as many countries and as long periods of time as possible.

In contrast to many earlier publications, the empirical models used throughout this thesis always distinguish between two dimensions of environmental regulation, namely regulation design and regulation intensity. As discussed in Section 3.1.4, I control for eleven policy instruments or six policy clusters to capture the effects of different regulation designs. Given that all known, existing policy instruments have been included in this classification process, the design dimension of environmental regulation is sufficiently covered. Therefore, all intensity indicators from Brunel and Levinson's (2013) framework, which fall into category (b), i.e. direct or input-based measures, are out of scope[36]. Hence, measures of private sector compliance costs and measures of changes in energy consumption and pollutant emission remain.

Pollution abatement and compliance expenditures can be ruled out, due to the limited data availability, esp. beyond the group of OECD countries, and due to the lack of a close relationship to the renewable energy equipment industry. In other words, high abatement expenditures do not necessarily mean high domestic demand for additional renewable energy capacities.

Changes in emission levels and energy consumption are not suitable either. Although data availability is not an issue here, it is actually quite good for the required level of granularity, it remains unclear what emission levels and energy consumption tell about regulation intensity. Previous studies have interpreted high indicator values likewise as signs of high and low intensity levels.

The only indicator of regulation intensity which seems to be well suited for research on the renewable energy equipment industry are renewable energies' shares in countries' total electricity generation.

Using renewable energy shares as single indicator to measure the intensity of renewable energy support policies has five distinct advantages. First, the indicator fulfills both of the previously specified selection criteria. Renewable energy shares in power generation are

---

[36] This applies to all measures from the categories, regulation-based measures, policy indices and surveys, as well as public expenditures and enforcement. See Table 8 (page 77) for details.

most directly related to the renewable energy equipment industry because they represent the strength of domestic demand for the products of this very industry. Regarding the availability criterion, renewable energy shares are readily available in great detail for literally all countries and territories over the last couple of decades.

Second, renewable energy shares are as one of few regulation intensity indicators, not affected by issues of multidimensionality. The aggregated effects of all demand-oriented renewable energy support policies is correctly captured by this measures regardless how many policy instruments are in place and how these instruments interact. In addition, multidimensionality issues related to design characteristics of the policy portfolio are addressed by the eleven policy instruments and six policy clusters introduced earlier.

Third, although simultaneity issues can't be ruled out with certainty, they seem manageable. Arguments against the existence of simultaneity problems are the considerable time lag between regulation changes and corresponding changes in countries' portfolio of power plants, and the commitment of many countries to considerably increase their renewable energy shares in the long run. However, for the presence of simultaneity issues speaks that governments might feel the urge to rebalance their policies if the ramp-up of renewables capacities turns out to happen too fast or to become too costly. In these cases policies and their outcome would be interdependent and therefore determined simultaneously. However, as renewable energy shares remain quite low in most, but not all, countries, the overall impact of simultaneity is assumed to be moderate.

Fourth, thanks to globally similar calculation approaches, indicator values of different countries can be compared very easily. Moreover, most countries report renewables shares for each of the major technologies separately and therefore enable the calculation of intensity indicators either for all renewables in aggregation or individually for specific technologies.

Fifth and final, renewable energy shares have been applied in all other studies on the narrowly strong Porter Hypothesis. Hence, applying this indicator facilitates the comparison of the results of this thesis with those of earlier publications.

In summary, the share of renewables in countries' electricity mix is the ideal intensity measure for this research project. The indicator is directly related to the renewable energy equipment industry, available for most countries and at great levels of detail, not or only partially affected by multidimensionality and simultaneity, easy to interpret and compare, and widely applied in research on the narrowly strong Porter Hypothesis.

3.3 Dissemination and intensity of common policy instruments

The objective of the previous two sections was to develop, first, a system to categorize renewable energy support policies according to their underlying mechanisms of action and, second, a suitable measure for the overall intensity of countries' renewable energy support policies.

In the following, I will build on the results of these sections to explore the relationship between regulation design, i.e. the presence of certain policy instruments in a given country, and regulation intensity using a strictly balanced panel of 225 countries and territories between 1990 and 2013. The discussion starts with an in-depth analysis of the design and intensity data. Afterwards, I will conduct multiple regression analyses in order to test for the contribution of individual policy instruments to overall regulation intensity.

3.3.1 Dissemination status of common support policies

One major finding of the literature review presented in Chapter 2 was that most studies on the narrowly strong Porter Hypothesis do not control for differences in policy design with Cao & Groba (2013) and Groba (2014) being the only exceptions. Given the importance that the seminal contributions of Porter (1991) and Porter & van der Linde (1995) assign to regulation design, it was concluded that research on the narrowly strong Porter Hypothesis would certainly benefit from more detailed data on policy design.

In order to advance the existing research in this area, I have compiled a comprehensive database of renewable energy support policies covering 225 countries and territories from 1990 to 2012. The sources of policy information used for this dissertation are the REN21's Renewable Energy Status Reports (REN21, 2005, 2006, 2007, 2009, 2010, 2011, 2012, 2013, 2014a, 2014b), the REN21's Renewables Interactive Map (REN21, 2015), IEA/IRENA's Global Renewable Energy: Joint Policies and Measures Database (IEA/IRENA, 2015), and the OECD's IEA Energy Technology RD&D Statistics (OECD, 2015). The data were matched and consolidated in a single database. This database contains the annual policy implementation status for each of the eleven instruments types and six clusters of renewable energy support policies.

Figure 7 shows the cumulative number of countries which have implemented certain types of policy instruments by 1990, 2002, 2008, and 2013. It becomes apparent from the data that policy implementation rates vary considerably between instruments and instrument clusters. Renewable energy targets and strategies are the single policy with the highest implementation rate as of 2013. 146 governments use this type of policy to promote renewable energies in their countries. However, implementation rates have not always been this high. The relatively low values for 2002 and 1990 indicate that coordinated support for renewables is a quite recent phenomenon. Other wide-spread policy instruments are the different types of feed-in tariffs and fiscal incentives.

Besides the general differences in policy dissemination rates, the data presented in Figure 7 also reveal considerable differences in the speed at which policy instruments proliferate. While implementation rates traditional policy instruments like classic feed-in tariffs (fixed rate or premium) or research, development, and demonstration programs increase quite constantly, implementation rates innovative instruments such as net metering and tendering seem to explode. As discussed in Section 3.1.2, net metering and tendering are innovative ways to promote renewables at relatively low cost. Hence, the fast proliferation of these instruments indicates that regulators learn from each other.

A third finding based on the data from Figure 7 is that adoption rates for measures from the targets, feed-in tariffs, and fiscal incentives clusters appear to be much higher than those for measure from the quotas and carbon trading clusters[37]. This effect might be due to two reasons. On the one hand, trading systems for greenhouse and renewable energy certificates are quite complex regulatory measure which are less easily implemented compared to, for instance, capital subsidies. On the other hand, quotas and carbon trading promote renewables by imposing binding requirements on utility providers or by restricting the usage of conventional technologies. Hence, governments might be more careful to implement such measures compared to more positivistic, incentive-based support instruments such as tax reductions or feed-in tariffs.

Overall the development of policy implementation rates presented in Figure 7 indicates that countries are quite heterogeneous with respect to their approach towards renewables promotion. Some countries take the lead and adopt renewable energy support policies early on while others are more cautious and prefer to wait a bit longer before they take action.

---

[37] The RD&D cluster is excluded from this discussion as its implementation rates cannot be directly compared to the other five clusters due to limited data availability.

Furthermore, some countries adopt only a single policy while again others decide to implement several support policies at the same time[38].

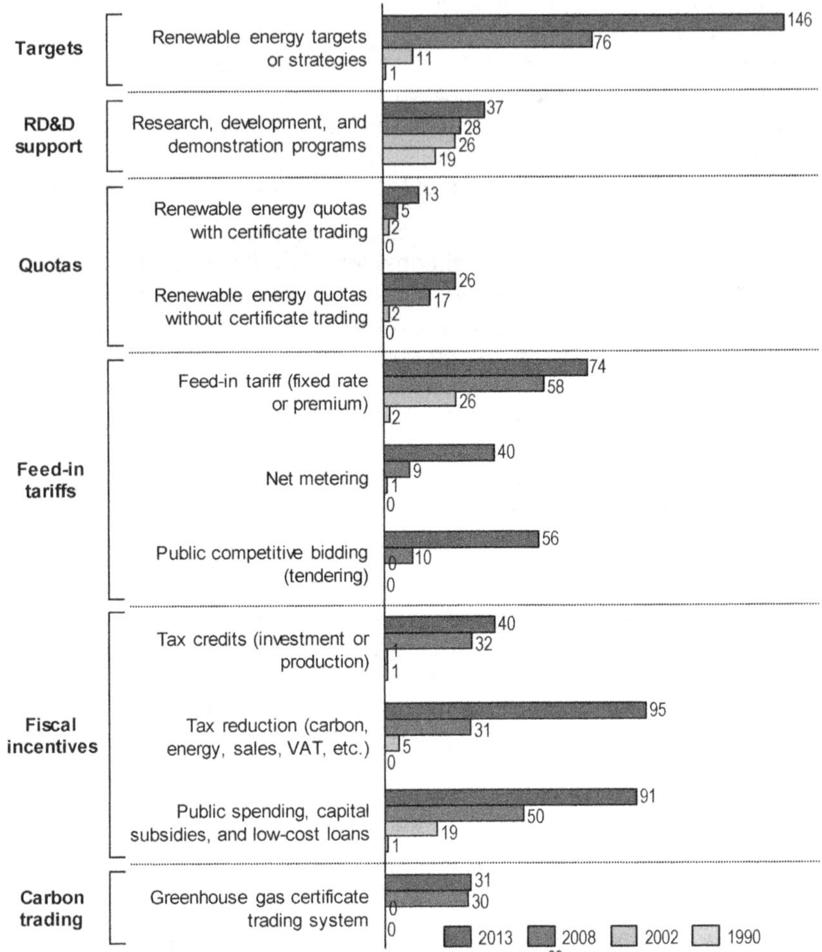

Figure 7 – Proliferation of renewable energy support policies[39]
Source: Own illustration based on data from IEA/IRENA (2015), OECD (2015), REN21 (2005, 2006, 2007, 2009, 2010, 2011, 2012, 2013, 2014a, 2014b, 2015).

[38] In 2008 and 2013, the cumulative number of adopted policies exceeds the number of countries. Hence, some countries have adopted more than one policy. For a detailed representation of the policy instruments adopted by certain countries, refer to Appendix 4 to Appendix 8.

[39] Data on RD&D programs are mostly limited to OECD countries; figures might understate actual dissemination rate. For details refer to Appendix 4 to Appendix 8.

In the following, I will explore potential determinates of these country-to-country differences along four dimensions, namely countries' regional association, GDP per capita, energy intensity per capita, and primary energy balance. In order to facilitate the discussion, countries are grouped together into clusters. On the geographic dimension, countries are clustered into the regions North America, Central and South America, Europe, Eurasia, Middle East, Africa, and Asia and Oceania. In terms of GDP per capita, countries are grouped based on quantiles. Those 25% of countries with the lowest GDP per capita make up cluster 1, the next 25% make up cluster 2, and so on. The same logic is applied for energy intensity per capita. In the fourth dimension, primary energy balance, countries are categorized as primary energy exports if their primary energy production exceeds their consumption and as primary energy importers if otherwise.

Table 11 gives the average values of the GDP per capita, energy intensity per capita, and primary energy indicators by region for the years 1990, 2000, and 2010. As expected, the results of Table 11 indicate that per capita income and energy consumption are highest for North American and European countries, and lowest for African and Asian countries. Similarly, Middle East countries are found to be primary energy exporters while the other regions are on average primary energy importers (except for Eurasia in 1990)[40].

	GDP per capita			**Energy intensity per capita**			**Primary energy ex-/importer**		
Region	2010	2000	1990	2010	2000	1990	2010	2000	1990
Africa	2	2	2	1	1	2	Im	Im	Im
Asia & Oceania	2	2	2	2	2	2	Im	Im	Im
Central & South America	3	3	3	3	3	3	Im	Im	Im
Eurasia	2	2	3	3	3	4	Im	Im	Ex
Europe	3	4	4	3	4	4	Im	Im	Im
Middle East	3	3	3	3	3	3	Ex	Ex	Ex
North America	4	4	4	4	4	4	Im	Im	Im

Notes: 1, 2, 3, and 4 refer to the 1st, 2nd, 3rd, and 4th quartile of each indicator's country ranking. Country rankings and quartiles are recalculated for every year. GDP values are translated into 2005 USD (PPP). Energy intensity is calculated as the ratio of national primary energy consumption and population. Countries in which primary energy production exceeds (falls short of) primary energy consumption are classified as primary energy exporters (Ex) (importers (Im)). In this overview table, individual country values have been aggregated on a regional level using arithmetic averages (median for primary energy ex-/importer). For values of individual countries, refer to Appendix 9.

Table 11 – Average indicator cluster values by region
Source: Own illustration based on data from EIA (2015).

[40] Detailed indicator values by country are presented in Appendix 9.

Figure 8 shows the share of countries which have adopted at least one of the eleven support instruments presented in Figure 7. Corresponding to the results from Figure 7, Figure 8 (a) shows a continuous increase in the number of countries which engage in renewable energy promotion. This increase is especially strong from the early 2000s onwards.

However, Figure 8 (b) shows large differences in the implementation rates between regions. In the 1990s, renewable energy support policies were most common in North America[41] and to an even higher extend in Europe, which has traditionally been the leader in renewables support. From the second half of the 2000s onwards, though, Asian and African countries caught up and followed the global trend towards more support for renewable power generation technologies.

Parts (c) and (d) of Figure 8 show that the proliferation of renewable energy support policies is driven by the more developed countries. Those countries with the highest income and energy consumption per capita adopt are first to adopt policy measures. The other countries follow in the order of their respective levels of economic development. However, as for the regional perspective, the increasing proliferation of support policies since the 2000s caused the difference between clusters to decrease and ultimately to disappear.

Finally, the data depicted in Figure 8 (e) indicate that energy importers are earlier to implement renewables support than primary energy exports. As one would expect against the background of today's fossil fuel dependency, the gap increases if the size rather than the sign of the primary energy balance is considered[42]. Large energy importers exhibit much higher levels of renewables support than large energy exporters.

In contrast to Figure 8, which depicted the number of countries with at least one renewable energy support policy in place, Figure 9 reports the overall adoption shares of common renewable energy support policies. Hence, Figure 9 shows which share of the eleven common policy instruments listed in Figure 7 has on average been adopted by countries from a given cluster at a given point in time. Overall, the results based on the average adoption shares (Figure 9) are similar to those based on the adoption of at least one policy measure (Figure 8): Advanced countries are more inclined to support renewables than emerging ones.

---

41 Figures for North America appear low as smaller countries from this region (e.g. Bahamas and Greenland) did not adopt renewables support policies. In contrast, the major North American countries (US, Canada, and Mexico) all have renewable energy support policies in place. Refer to Appendix 4 to Appendix 8 for further details.

42 Unreported analysis. Data is available on request.

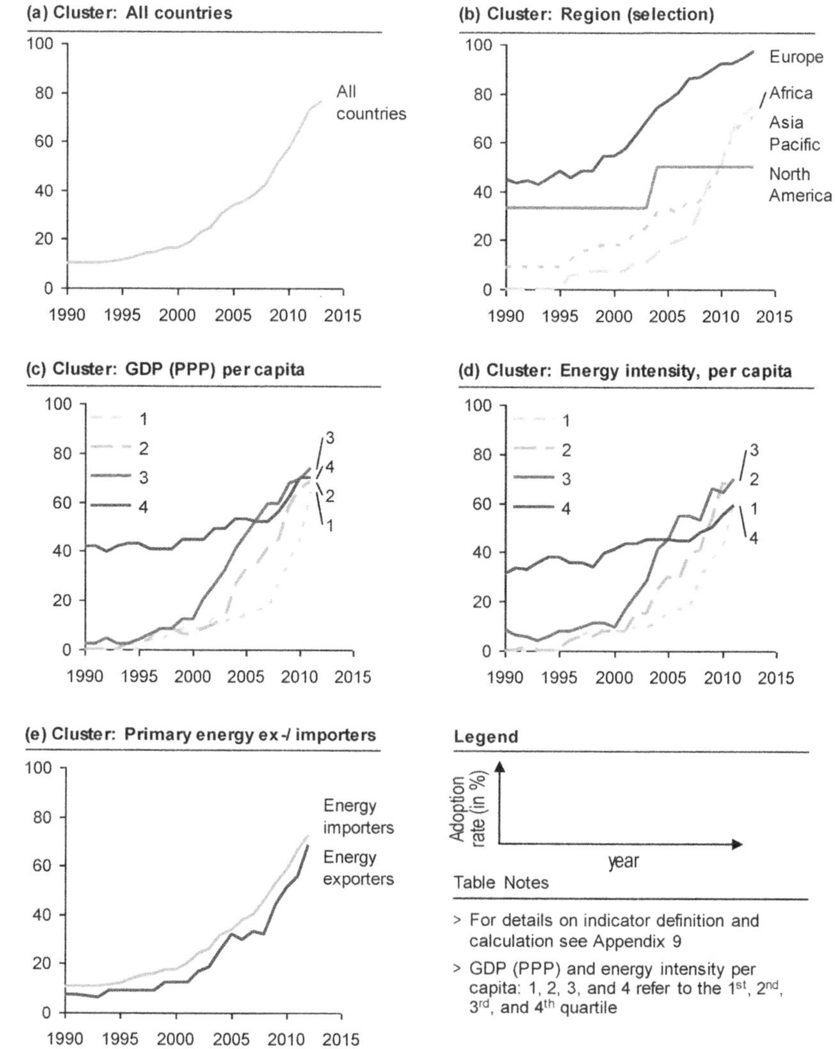

Figure 8 – Share of countries with any RE support policy[43]
Source: Own illustration based on data from EIA (2015), IEA/IRENA (2015), OECD (2015), REN21 (2005, 2006, 2007, 2009, 2010, 2011, 2012, 2013, 2014a, 2014b, 2015).

[43] Figure 8 illustrates changes in the share of countries which have adopted any renewable energy support for different country clusters. For details on the allocation of countries to clusters refer to Appendix 9.

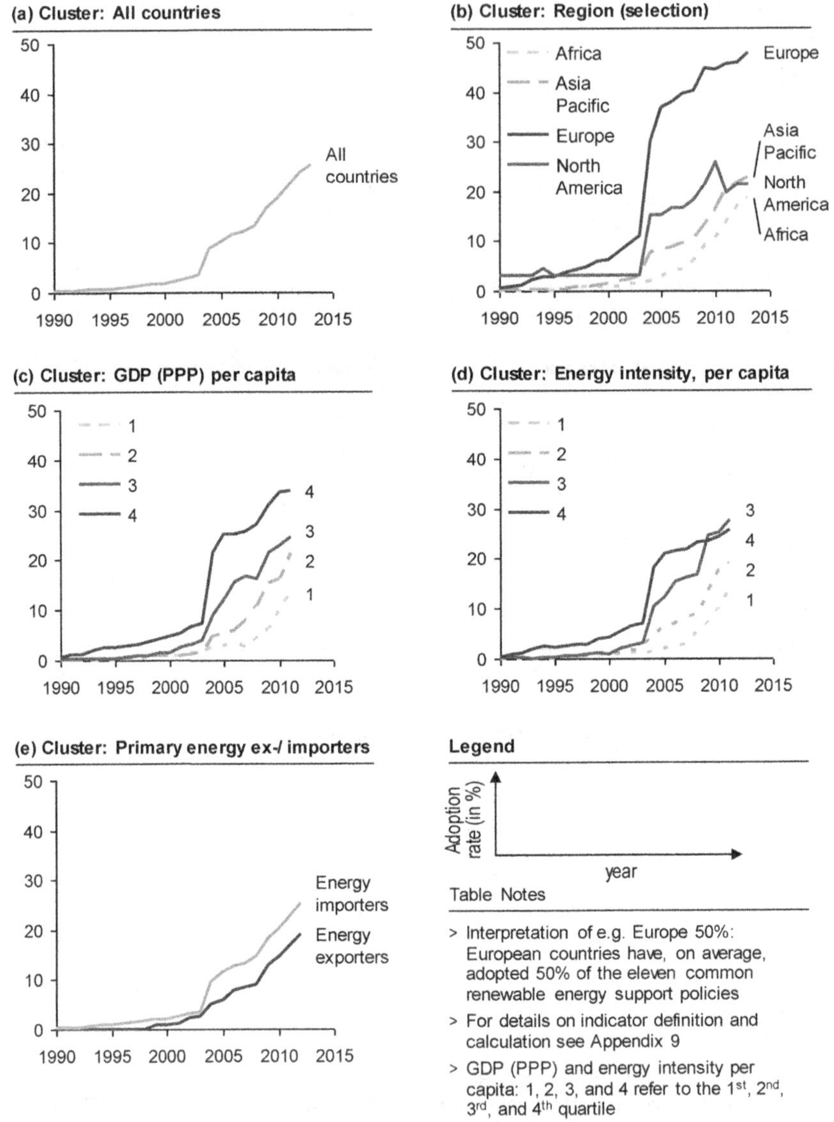

Figure 9 – Adoption rate over all policy instruments (except RD&D)[44]
Source: Own illustration based on data from EIA (2015), IEA/IRENA (2015), OECD (2015), REN21 (2005, 2006, 2007, 2009, 2010, 2011, 2012, 2013, 2014a, 2014b, 2015).

[44] Figure 9 illustrates changes in the overall adoption rates of common policies for different country clusters. For details on the allocation of countries to clusters refer to Appendix 9.

On a detailed level three observations are worth mentioning. First, as shown in Figure 9 (b), European countries adopt higher numbers of different support policies than countries from other regions. Second, the differences between country clusters in Figure 9 (c) and (d) do not converge and remain high throughout the 2010s. Third, based on Figure 9 (a) to (e), portfolios of renewable energy support policies became clearly more differentiated and complex from the early 2000s onwards.

In sum, the results of Figure 8 and Figure 9 are in line with what one would commonly expect. Economically advanced, energy-importing countries from Europe and North America were first to adopt renewables support polices in order to protect the environment, reduce their dependency on foreign energy resources, and possibly promote the development of a domestic equipment industry. Later, countries with lower development levels followed and adopted own support policies. However, their policy portfolios appear to be less comprehensive than those of advanced economies. Hence, the analysis presented in this section suggests that the policy information consolidated in the database is a good representation of the real world situation.

3.3.2 Development of support policies' overall intensity

In the previous section, I have analyzed the policy data and demonstrated that tracking the implementation status of eleven common instrument types is a suitable approach to capture the design of countries' policy portfolios – the first dimension along which renewable energy support schemes are evaluated.

In this section, I will turn to the second evaluation dimension and analyze data on renewable energy shares, the preferred proxy of regulation intensity as defined in Section 3.2.3. Hereby, I distinguish between two alternatives: renewable energies' share in electricity generation and renewable energies' share in electricity generation capacities. The advantage of capacity shares is that they directly measure how much renewable energy equipment has been installed in a given country, certainly a very good measure of market attractiveness for suppliers of such equipment. The disadvantage is that global data for wind and solar installations only exists since 2005. Moreover, this data are only available on an aggregated level also including capacities of tidal and wave power. In contrast, data on renewables' share in power generation is available in great detail from 1990 onwards. The disadvantage of this measure is, however, that it tracks installed capacities only indirectly and is influenced by other factors such as weather conditions or business cycle effects. Hence, if the shares in electricity generation are used, fluctuations in renewables shares might have reasons other than changes in the installed capacity.

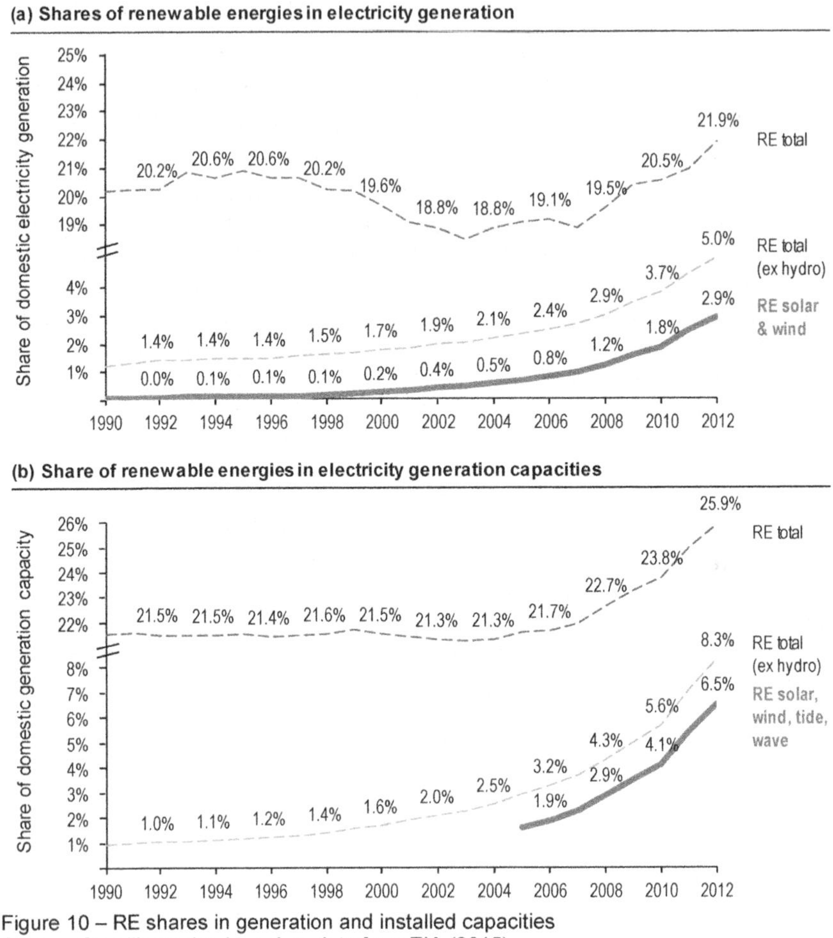

Figure 10 – RE shares in generation and installed capacities
Source: Own illustration based on data from EIA (2015).

Figure 10 illustrates the development of renewable energy shares between 1990 and 2012 in terms of generation and generation capacity for different levels of aggregation. The data on renewables' share in power generation depicted in Figure 10 (a) show that the overall share of all renewable energy technologies has been more or less stable at around 20% over the entire observation period. The technological composition of this block changed considerably, though. In the 1990s the share of non-hydro renewables, such as biomass and geothermal power, was with less than 2% quite low. The contribution of wind and solar was negligible. Since the 2000s, however, the share of non-hydro renewables increased strongly to 5% in 2012. This development was mostly driven by wind and solar power, which exhibited an exponential growth trend. Between 1992 and 2002, the wind and solar share increased tenfold from 0.04% to 0.35%, just to increase about tenfold again over the next decade to reach 2.86% in 2012.

The data on renewables' share in power generation capacity illustrated in Part (b) of Figure 10 show a very similar picture. The main difference is that the boom of wind and solar since the 2000s leads to significant increase in the overall share of renewables in power generation capacities. Moreover, the percentage share of solar and wind capacities is higher than it was when measured in terms of electricity generation. This effect is explained by differences in the average capacity utilization of wind turbine and solar panels compared to conventional technologies such as hydro, nuclear, or fossil power. While most conventional power plants usually operate quite close to their technical capacity limits, wind and solar installations often operate far below their maximum capacity due to unfavorable weather conditions. Hence, a one percent increase in wind and solar capacities usually corresponds to a significantly less than one percent increase in terms of electricity generation.

In order to develop a more profound understanding of the determinants of countries' solar and wind power shares, I follow the approach applied in Section 3.3.1 and explore the differences between clusters of countries grouped by geography, economics performance, energy intensity, and resource abundance.

Figure 11 presents the shares of wind and solar power in total electricity generation for different clusters of countries. In general, the differences in generation shares between country clusters resemble the analysis results of differences in policy proliferation and adoption rates.

Figure 11 (b) shows that European countries clearly exhibit the highest shares of renewables in their electricity mixes. Asian and especially African countries lag considerably behind. The regional differences in terms of generation shares are much bigger than they are in terms of policy adoption rates[45]. Moreover, while 2012 policy adoption rates in Asia Pacific and Africa are similar to those of North American countries, their renewable shares are obviously much lower. This indicates that although Asian and African countries have similar numbers of policy measures in place, the intensity of these measures is relatively low.

---

[45] Regional policy adoption rates are presented in Figure 9 (b) (page 90).

The analyses by GDP and energy intensity clusters, shown in Figure 11 (b) and (c), are in line with the earlier result that advanced countries are more inclined to adopt effective measures to support renewables than developing countries. Renewable energies shares are clearly highest for cluster 4 countries. However, the depicted trends for clusters 1 to 3 are less clear. Strong individual changes between 2005 and 2010 and the fact that countries from GDP cluster 2 have higher renewables shares than those from GDP cluster 3 appear to be counterintuitive. However, there are straightforward explanations. First, the sudden drop in the GDP cluster 1 curve after 2006 and the sudden rise of the energy intensity cluster 3 curve after 2007 are explained by shifts of important countries from one cluster to another. In 2006, India shifts from GDP cluster 1 to GDP cluster 2; in 2007, China shifts from energy intensity cluster 2 to energy intensity cluster 3. Second, the high renewables share reported for GDP cluster 2 countries is mostly driven by the high renewable energy shares of two major countries, namely again China and India.

Finally, the analysis by energy balance clusters shown in Figure 11 (e) is in line with the previous analysis as well. Energy importers have much higher renewables shares than importers. Similar to the regions, the differences are more pronounced if measured in terms of regulation intensity than in terms of regulation design.

Figure 12 shows that using the alternative measure of regulation intensity, renewables' share in generation capacities, does not change the overall results.

Hence, it can be concluded that both renewable energy shares in electricity generation and renewable energy shares in electricity generation capacities, are suitable proxies of countries' reliance on wind and solar as power generation technologies. However, given the considerably better data availability in terms of periods covered and technological disaggregation, renewable energy shares in electricity generation are the preferred option to proxy the overall intensity of countries' portfolios of renewable energy support policies.

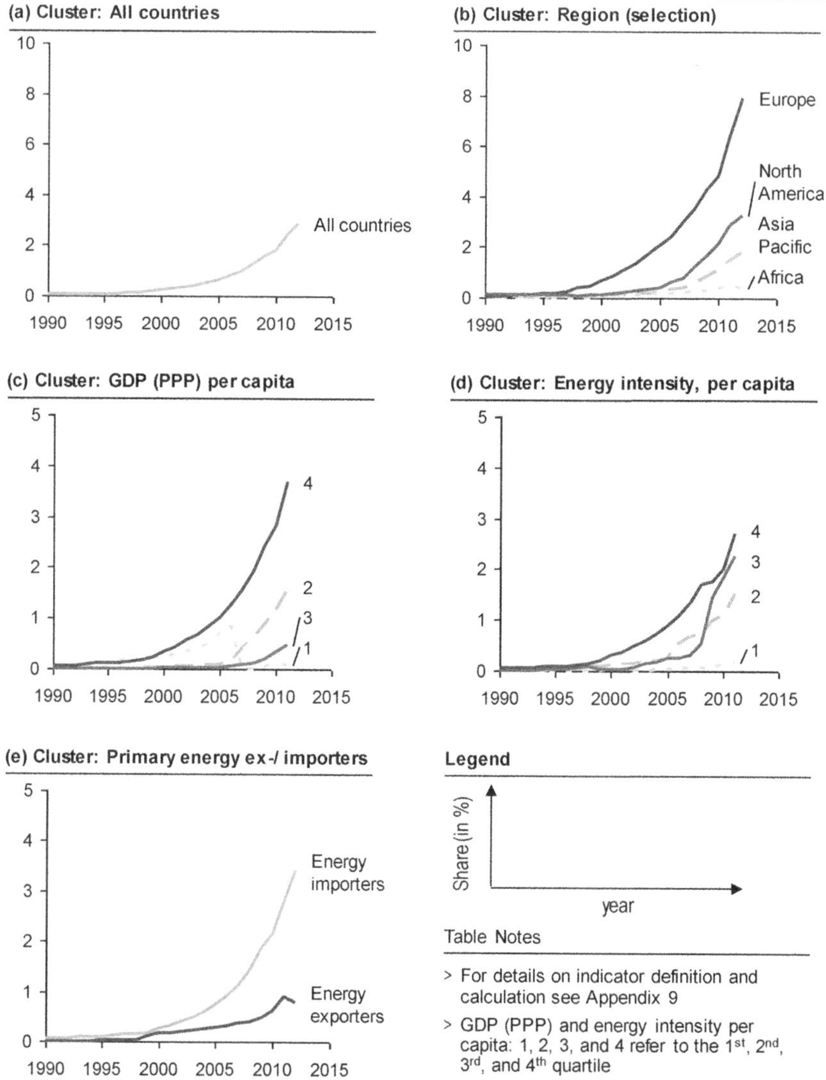

Figure 11 – Share of wind and solar in total electricity generation
Source: Own illustration based on data from EIA (2015), IEA/IRENA (2015), OECD (2015), REN21 (2005, 2006, 2007, 2009, 2010, 2011, 2012, 2013, 2014a, 2014b, 2015).

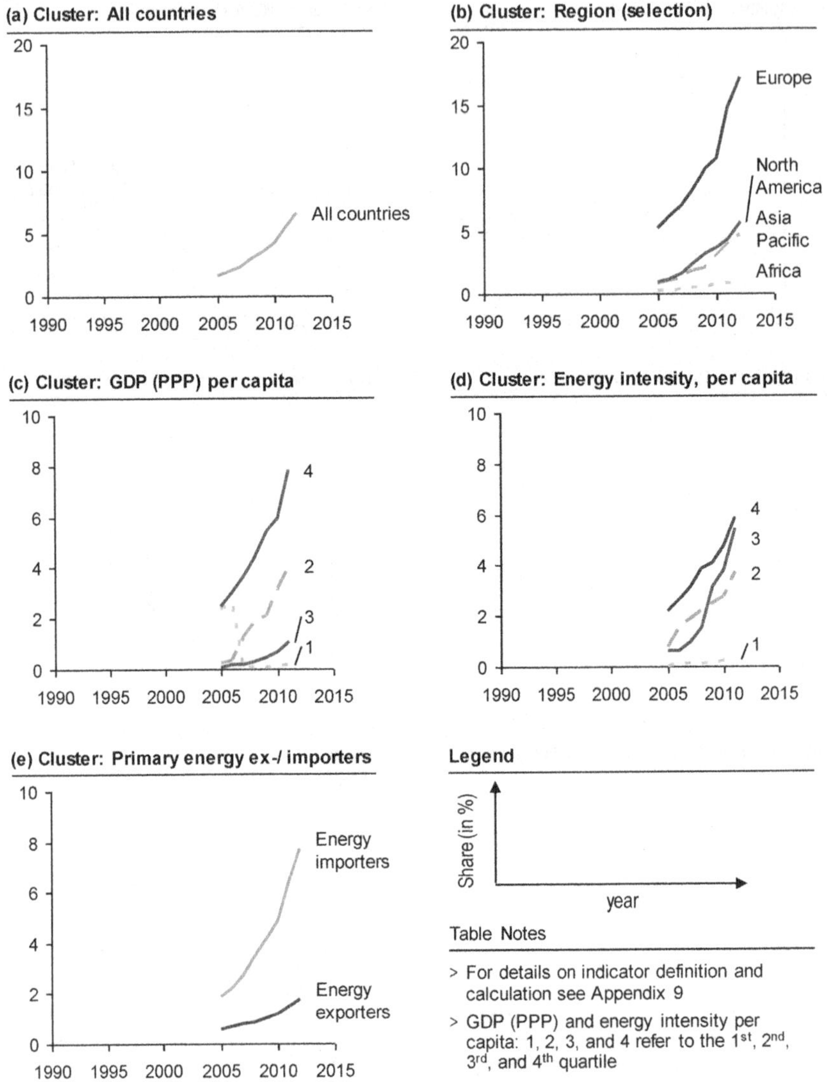

Figure 12 – Share of wind, solar, tide, and wave in total capacity
Source: Own illustration based on data from EIA (2015), IEA/IRENA (2015), OECD (2015), REN21 (2005, 2006, 2007, 2009, 2010, 2011, 2012, 2013, 2014a, 2014b, 2015).

3.3.3 Contribution of individual policies to overall intensity

In the previous sections, the two dimensions of environmental regulation, design and intensity, have been analyzed separately. A comparison of the results yielded two indicative findings. First, regulation design and intensity appear to be closely related. High policy adoption rates seem to coincide with high regulation intensities. Second, the relatedness of these two dimensions appears to vary strongly between country clusters. Country characteristics such as GDP per capita apparently have a considerable impact on the strength of the design-intensity relationship.

This section attempts to advance and substantiate these indicative findings by analyzing both dimensions of renewable energy regulation jointly. The objective is to show that differences in the effect of regulation design on intensity are not just a question of country-specific characteristics. The hypothesis to be tested is that instrument types are not alike and that they differ in their contribution to overall regulation intensity. The existence of such differences would help to resolve the puzzle that support policies sometimes lead to higher regulation intensities and sometimes do not. In other words, if there were systematic, type-specific intensity differences, then country-to-country differences in overall regulation intensity were not only a matter of country-specific characteristics or unobserved differences in detailed policy formulation but also a matter of which types of instrument are in place to support renewable energies.

The estimation of policies' contribution to regulation intensity is based on a set of panel regression models with country-fixed effects (within models). This approach is preferred to pooled estimation and random-effects estimation for the following three reasons. First, the pooled estimation approach is not suitable in this case because it treats all observations as if they were completely unrelated and does not take into account the valuable information that groups of observations belong to the same country. The second argument against the pooled estimation approach is that it does not allow for individual heterogeneity. However, as countries are not alike[46] controlling for individual heterogeneity, i.e. country-specific, time-invariant effects like natural renewable energy potential, will certainly improve estimation precision (Hill, Griffiths, & Lim, 2012). Third, fixed effects estimation is preferable to random effects estimation as the observations represent the entire population and are therefore non-random. The database contains all known renewable

[46] See results of Sections 3.3.1 and 3.3.2 for details.

energy support policies for all countries and territories since 1978, the year when the US adopted their first support instrument (IRENA, 2012)[47].

Equations (3.1) to (3.4) model the effect of the existence of certain renewable energy support policies on countries' regulation intensity.

$$\ln RES\_SW_{it} = \alpha_i + \sum_{c=1}^{C} \beta_{ct} ClusterEx_{cit} + \varepsilon_{it} \quad (3.1)$$

$$\ln REC\_SWTW_{it} = \alpha_i + \sum_{c=1}^{C} \beta_{ct} ClusterEx_{cit} + \varepsilon_{it} \quad (3.2)$$

$$\ln RES\_SW_{it} = \alpha_i + \sum_{p=1}^{P} \beta_{pt} InstruEx_{pit} + \varepsilon_{it} \quad (3.3)$$

$$\ln REC\_SWTW_{it} = \alpha_i + \sum_{p=1}^{P} \beta_{pt} InstruEx_{pit} + \varepsilon_{it} \quad (3.4)$$

Although all models have been designed to explore the (policy) existence-intensity relationship, they differ in terms of dependent variables and level of detailing of explanatory variables. The dependent variable of Equations (3.1) and (3.3) is the preferred measure of regulation intensity, percentage share of solar and wind in total electricity generation (RES_SW). Equations (3.2) and (3.4), in contrast, use the alternative intensity measure, percentage share of solar, wind, tide, and wave power in total power generation capacity (REC_SWTW).

Explanatory variables vary in the level of aggregation. Equations (3.1) and (3.2) analyze the effect of policy existence on regulation intensity on an aggregated cluster level (ClusterEx), while Equations (3.3) and (3.4) are more detailed and estimate the effect on instrument level (InstruEx).

ClusterEx stands for a set of binary variables indicating the existence of each of the six policy clusters: targets (C_TAR_E), RD&D support (C_RDD_E), quotas (C_QUO_E), feed-in tariffs (C_FIT_E), fiscal incentives (C_FIS_E), and carbon trading (C_GHG_E)[48]. Cluster indicators take the value 1 if at least one policy instrument from the cluster exists. Similarly, InstruEx stands for a set of binary variables which indicate the existence of each of the eleven instrument types: renewables energy targets or strategies (TAR_E), research,

47 Observations for RD&D expenditures date back till 1974 but are not available for all countries.

48 For the allocation of individual instruments to policy clusters refer to Table 7 (page 71).

development, and demonstration programs (RDD_E), renewable energy quotas without certificate trading (QUO_E), renewable energy quotas with certificate trading (REC_E), feed-in tariffs (fixed rate or premium) (FIT_E), net metering (NET_E), public competitive bidding (tendering) (TEN_E), tax credits (investment or production) (TXC_E), tax reductions (carbon, energy, sales, VAT, or other taxes) (TXR_E), public spending, capital subsidies, and low cost loans (PUB_E), and greenhouse gas certificate trading systems (GHG_E). The descriptive statistics for the above mentioned variables is presented in Table 12[49]. A list of all variables including a detailed description, units of measurement and data sources is presented in Appendix 10.

Variable	Obs.	Mean	Std. dev.	Min	Max
lnRES_SW	1,426	-1.982	2.661	-11.71	4.604
lnRES_TeH	3,717	.1976	2.160	-8.10	4.604
lnREC_SWTW	793	-.5515	2.478	-10.34	4.604
TAR_E	5,175	.1636	.3700	0	1
RDD_E	5,175	.1111	.3143	0	1
QUO_E	5,175	.0106	.1026	0	1
REC_E	5,175	.0336	.1803	0	1
FIT_E	5,175	.1271	.3332	0	1
NET_E	5,175	.0242	.1535	0	1
TEN_E	5,175	.0354	.1847	0	1
TXC_E	5,175	.0595	.2366	0	1
TXR_E	5,175	.0873	.2824	0	1
PUB_E	5,175	.1246	.3303	0	1
GHG_E	5,175	.0443	.2057	0	1
C_TAR_E	5,175	.1637	.3700	0	1
C_RDD_E	5,175	.1111	.3143	0	1
C_QUO_E	5,175	.0443	.2057	0	1
C_FIT_E	5,175	.1434	.3505	0	1
C_FIS_E	5,175	.1525	.3595	0	1
C_GHG_E	5,175	.0443	.2057	0	1
TAR_D	5,175	.8423	2.482	0	26
RDD_D	5,175	1.324	4.479	0	39
QUO_D	5,175	.0543	.4147	0	6
REC_D	5,175	.1598	.9732	0	11
FIT_D	5,175	.9107	3.014	0	25
NET_D	5,175	.0978	.7676	0	15
TEN_D	5,175	.1179	.7312	0	10
TXC_D	5,175	.3637	2.000	0	35
TXR_D	5,175	.3888	1.602	0	18
PUB_D	5,175	.7190	2.410	0	24
GHG_D	5,175	.1936	1.018	0	8

Table 12 – Descriptive statistics for regulation intensity regressions
Source: Own illustration.

[49] Table 12 (page 99) also contains the descriptive statistics for variables, which will be used in additional regression models discussed in the following course of the thesis.

Variable	Obs.	Mean	Std. dev.	Min	Max
C_TAR_D	5,175	.8423	2.482	0	26
C_RDD_D	5,175	1.324	4.479	0	39
C_QUO_D	5,175	.2141	1.162	0	14
C_FIT_D	5,175	.9731	3.071	0	25
C_FIS_D	5,175	.9266	2.979	0	35
C_GHG_D	5,175	.1936	1.018	0	8
TAR_D2	5,175	6.866	33.08	0	676
RDD_D2	5,175	21.81	100.7	0	1,521
QUO_D2	5,175	.1749	1.740	0	36
REC_D2	5,175	.9726	7.337	0	121
FIT_D2	5,175	9.913	46.39	0	625
NET_D2	5,175	.5986	6.978	0	225
TEN_D2	5,175	.5484	4.711	0	100
TXC_D2	5,175	4.133	47.02	0	1,225
TXR_D2	5,175	2.716	17.25	0	324
PUB_D2	5,175	6.324	31.44	0	576
GHG_D2	5,175	1.074	6.628	0	64
C_TAR_D2	5,175	6.866	33.08	0	1,521
C_RDD_D2	5,175	21.81	100.7	0	676
C_QUO_D2	5,175	1.396	10.03	0	1,521
C_FIT_D2	5,175	10.37	46.76	0	196
C_FIS_D2	5,175	9.733	56.09	0	1,225
C_GHG_D2	5,175	1.074	6.628	0	64

Figure 12 – Share of wind, solar, tide, and wave in total capacity (cont'd)
Source: Own illustration.

Furthermore, comparison of the scatter plots for RES_SW, REC_SWTW and their logarithmic equivalents (see Figure 13 (e) to (h)) show that taking the natural logarithms transforms the exponential trend found in the original data into a more linear one. This is an important property as the OLS estimator, which I intend to use, works best in the presence of a linear relationship between explanatory and dependent variables (Hill et al., 2012). In addition, logarithmic transformation changes the distribution of the dependent variables and therefore also that of the regression errors to a normal one,[50] which is desirable for the computation of interval estimates and significance thresholds (Hill et al., 2012).

50 See Appendix 11 for exemplary pre- and post-transformation histograms and normal quantile plots for the least square residuals of Equation (3.1) and (3.3).

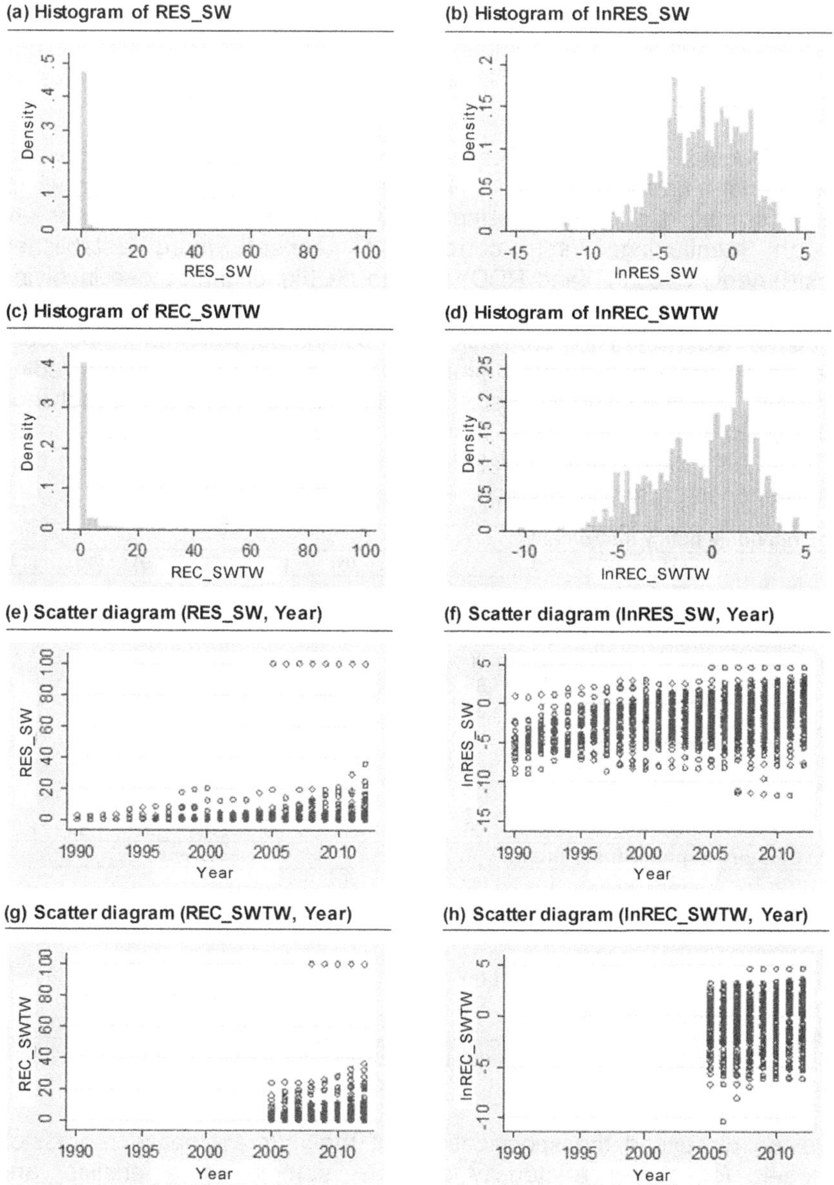

Figure 13 – Histograms and scatter plots by intensity indicator
Source: Own illustration.

The last analytical step, before I enter into the discussion of the regression results, is an examination of pairwise correlations between the explanatory variables include in Equations (3.1) to (3.4). Table 13 shows the correlation matrices.

As expected, correlations between both policy clusters and individual policy instruments are positive. However, there is no combination which only comes close to exact collinearity. A few additional observations are worth mentioning. First, correlations between more established instruments (e.g. FIT and RDD) tend to be higher than those involving more innovative, less wide-spread instruments (e.g. FIT and NET). Second, QUO and REC are basically uncorrelated, what makes perfectly sense as renewable energy quotas with and without certificate trading system are mutually exclusive policies. Last, correlations between clusters of policies are higher than those between individual instruments. This is also logical given clusters' higher level of aggregation and their correspondingly lower variance.

(a) Individual policy instruments

	(1)	(2)	(3)	(4)	(5)	(6)	(7)	(8)	(9)	(10)	(11)
(1) TAR	1.00										
(2) RDD	.34	1.00									
(3) QUO	.14	.05	1.00								
(4) REC	.41	.45	-.02	1.00							
(5) FIT	.52	.47	.14	.35	1.00						
(6) NET	.31	.20	.14	.31	.22	1.00					
(7) TEN	.37	.18	.26	.26	.35	.29	1.00				
(8) TXC	.44	.33	.09	.40	.42	.32	.43	1.00			
(9) TXR	.51	.28	.20	.36	.45	.25	.40	.49	1.00		
(10) PUB	.63	.41	.19	.47	.53	.30	.41	.50	.58	1.00	
(11) GHG	.47	.36	.06	.56	.45	.19	.30	.42	.43	.51	1.00

(b) Clusters of policy instruments

	(1)	(2)	(3)	(4)	(5)	(6)
(1) C_TAR	1.00					
(2) C_RDD	.34	1.00				
(3) C_QUO	.43	.42	1.00			
(4) C_FIT	.58	.58	.42	1.00		
(5) C_FIS	.66	.66	.49	.63	1.00	
(6) C_GHG	.47	.47	.52	.47	.48	1.00

Table 13 – Correlation matrices for regulation intensity regressions
Source: Own illustration.

Having discussed the specifications of the four alternative regression models for existence-intensity analysis, sample characteristics, and estimation approach, the remainder of this section is reserved for the discussion of regression results. To avoid repetition, I will in most cases only refer to those model specifications which use solar and wind powers' share in total electricity generation (lnRES_SW), the preferred intensity measure, as dependent variable. As discussed earlier the key advantage of this variable is that is available for much longer periods of time than the alternative variable based on capacity shares. Whenever changing the dependent variables leads to considerable differences in regression results, these differences are highlighted and thoroughly discussed.

The estimation results for Equations (3.1) to (3.4) are presented in Table 14. As mentioned above, these estimates have been obtain using a fixed effects ordinary least squares approach, which allows for individual heterogeneity on country level. The results for regression model (3.1) show that five out of six policy clusters' contribution to overall regulation intensity is significantly positive. Only the otherwise positive coefficient of the RD&D cluster fails to fulfill the minimum requirements of statistical significance. Coefficient values of the five significant policy clusters are all in the range between 0.7 and 1.2[51]. Hence, the results indicate that implementing any of these policy clusters increases the share of wind and solar in the electricity mix by roughly one percent. The values of F-test, 56.12, and R^2, 0.52, indicate that the model has good explanatory power.

As the point estimates reported for Equation (3.2) show, changing the dependent variable to renewables capacities (lnREC_SWTW) does not change results much. However, two differences are worth mentioning. Firstly, using the alternative intensity measure turns the coefficient of C_RDD_E significant, while all other coefficients retain statistical significance as well. Secondly, Equation (3.2) has with 13.06 and 0.18 considerably lower values for F-test and R^2. This is probably due to the much shorter observation period of 8 years, versus 23 years for Equation (3.1), and the reduced number of just 793 observations, versus 1,426 observations for Equation (3.1). Overall, the results of Equations (3.1) and (3.2) are consistent.

The two regressions using individual policy instruments instead of policy clusters yield similar results. Regression model (3.3) produces significantly positive coefficient values for renewable energy targets (TAR_E), quotas without trading systems (QUO_E), feed-in tariffs (FIT_E), tax reductions (TXR_E), public spending and related measures (PUB_E), and greenhouse gas trading systems (GHG_E). In addition, four of the remaining five coefficients have positive values as well, however, not at statistically significant levels. The coefficient values are generally smaller compared to the regressions on cluster level, what is

51 Coefficient values are rounded to one decimal place.

logical given that the support effect spreads out over a greater number of policy measures.

Dep. var.	lnRES_SW	lnREC_SWTW	lnRES_SW	lnREC_SWTW
Variable	(3.1)	(3.2)	(3.3)	(3.4)
C_TAR_E	.8122 ***	.3808 *		
C_RDD_E	.3557	.6769 **		
C_QUO_E	.7449 **	.7958 ***		
C_FIT_E	1.087 ***	.3956 *		
C_FIS_E	.6903 ***	.4164 *		
C_GHG_E	1.203 ***	1.948 ***		
TAR_E			.7941 ***	.3790 **
RDD_E			.3740	.2971
QUO_E			.9660 ***	.4002
REC_E			.4379	.7082 **
FIT_E			.8435 ***	.0272
NET_E			.2387	-.2770
TEN_E			.3312	1.116 ***
TXC_E			-.0331	-.2867
TXR_E			.4739 *	.6294 ***
PUB_E			.8195 ***	.2442
GHG_E			1.078 ***	1.942 ***
CONST	-3.528 ***	-2.215 ***	-3.500 ***	-2.063 ***
F	56.12 ***	13.06 ***	34.98 ***	9.58 ***
R^2	0.52	0.18	0.53	0.29
Obs.	1,426	793	1,426	793
Groups	109	124	109	124

Notes: Results are estimated using fixed effects (within) regression with observation grouped by country. *, **, and *** indicate statistical significance at 10%, 5%, and 1% level respectively. Statistical significance is based on cluster-robust standard errors.

Table 14 – Results of policy existence on reg. intensity regression
Source: Own illustration.

A closer look at the results of the alternative regression (3.4) using capacity data reveals that statistical significance shifts between policy instruments. While tendering (TEN_E) and quotas with certificate trading system (REC_E) are now significant at five and one percent levels, feed-in tariffs (FIT_E) and quotas without certificate trading (QUO_E) lose their statistical significance. If one recalls that the average observation used for Equation (3.4) is much more recent than those used for Equation (3.3), these differences are interesting as they tell something about the policy preference in recent years. Tendering (TEN_E) and certificate trading (REC_E) can be viewed as advanced versions of classical feed-in tariffs (FIT_E) and quotas systems without trading option (QUO_E)[52]. They increase flexibility and allow governments to achieve their policy targets in the energy sector at lower economic cost.

[52] See discussion in Section 3.1.2 for further details.

Hence, this shift of significance within policy clusters[53] shows that governments recently increased the relative intensity of more flexible and therefore more efficient support instruments. These results can be replicated by restricting the sample of Equation (3.3) to contain just observations from 2005 onwards.

Overall, the results for regression models (3.1) to (3.4) provide evidence for the hypothesized positive relationship between the existence of support policies and overall regulation intensity. However, there is good reason to believe that the relationship between the design of policy schemes and overall regulation intensity is not only determined by the current composition of countries' policy portfolios but also by their previous compositions. Hence, I hypothesize that the length of policy existence, i.e. policy duration, explains overall policy intensity even better than pure duration alone.

Four additional regression models have been formulated to test this hypothesis and estimate the effect that policy duration has on overall regulation intensity. Corresponding to the set-up used to explore the existence-intensity relationship, the models on the duration-intensity relationship combine different dependent variables and detailing levels. Equations (3.5) and (3.6) regress renewable energy generation and capacity shares on policy clusters while Equations (3.7) and (3.8) use individual policy instruments as explanatory variables.

In contrast to Equations (3.1) to (3.4), Equations (3.5) to (3.8) use count instead of binary variables to estimate the effect of individual instruments or policy clusters. The variables with the suffix _D, summarized by InstruDur and ClusterDur, are set to one in the first year a country has adopted a certain policy or, in the case of cluster variables, at least one policy from the respective cluster. The value increases by one each year the policy or policy cluster remains active.

In order to account for the expected decreasing marginal returns of policy measures over time, a squared equivalent of each cluster or instrument variable is added to the equations. In Equations (3.5) to (3.8) these squared variables are summarized as $ClusterDur^2$ and $InstruDur^2$. In the regression model the squared terms of clusters and instruments are indicated by the suffix _D2. As in the previous models, α is a country-fixed constant term, the β's are the coefficients of the explanatory variables, and ε the cluster-robust error term. The index i

53 Classical feed-in tariffs (FIT_E) and tendering (TEN_E) both belong to the feed-in tariff cluster (C_FIT_E) while renewable energy quotas with (REC_E) and without (QUO_E) certificate trading system both belong to the quotas cluster (C_QUO_E).

stands for the country, t indicates time, and c and p as well as d and l stand for the count of different policy instrument and cluster variables included in the regression model.

$$\ln RES\_SW_{it} = \alpha_i + \sum_{c=1}^{C} \beta_{ct} ClusterDur_{cit} + \sum_{d=1}^{D} \beta_{dt} ClusterDur^2{}_{dit} + \varepsilon_{it} \quad (3.5)$$

$$\ln REC\_SWTW_{it} = \alpha_i + \sum_{c=1}^{C} \beta_{ct} ClusterDur_{cit} + \sum_{d=1}^{D} \beta_{dt} ClusterDur^2{}_{dit} + \varepsilon_{it} \quad (3.6)$$

$$\ln RES\_SW_{it} = \alpha_i + \sum_{p=1}^{P} \beta_{pt} InstruDur_{pit} + \sum_{l=1}^{L} \beta_{lt} InstruDur^2{}_{lit} + \varepsilon_{it} \quad (3.7)$$

$$\ln REC\_SWTW_{it} = \alpha_i + \sum_{p=1}^{P} \beta_{pt} InstruDur_{pit} + \sum_{l=1}^{L} \beta_{lt} InstruDur^2{}_{lit} + \varepsilon_{it} \quad (3.8)$$

Descriptive statistics for all variables included in the duration-intensity models are presented in Table 12. Appendix 10 contains a list of all variables including detailed description, units of measurement, and data sources. The correlation matrices for the duration-based cluster and instrument variables show the same pattern as the equivalent matrices for the existence-based variables. Most pairs of explanatory variables have a considerable positive correlation but there are no situations in which exact collinearity becomes an issue[54].

The results for Equations (3.5) to (3.8) are presented in Table 15. Again, all results have been obtained using fixed effects OLS regression.

First of all, the F- and R^2-values for all four specifications are much higher than their equivalents for the existence-based models. This is especially the case for Equations (3.6) and (3.8) which use capacity shares as independent variable. This result indicates that, overall, policy duration models outperform the previously discussed policy existence models in terms of goodness of fit. Thanks to its richer information content, policy duration is a better predictor of regulation intensity than policy existence alone.

54 Refer to Appendix 12 for a graphical representation of the correlation matrices for variables used in duration-intensity regression.

Dep. var.	lnRES_SW	lnREC_SWTW	lnRES_SW	lnREC_SWTW
Variable	(3.5)	(3.6)	(3.7)	(3.8)
C_TAR_D	.2629 ***	.0856		
C_RDD_D	.2162 ***	-.1704		
C_QUO_D	.0036	.0631		
C_FIT_D	.2604 ***	.2384 *		
C_FIS_D	.0853	.2109 *		
C_GHG_D	-.0959	.1659		
TAR_D			.2444 ***	.1882 **
RDD_D			.2897 ***	-.0786
QUO_D			.6185 **	.4705
REC_D			-.2495 **	.0960
FIT_D			.1993 ***	.1709 *
NET_D			.1142	-.0582
TEN_D			.0661	.1267
TXC_D			.0260	-.0872
TXR_D			.1613 **	.2125 **
PUB_D			.1163	.1541
GHG_D			.0077	.0755
C_TAR_D2	-.0063 **	-.0003		
C_RDD_D2	-.0024	-.0009		
C_QUO_D2	-.0060	-.0043		
C_FIT_D2	-.0138 ***	-.0040		
C_FIS_D2	-.0001	-.0009		
C_GHG_D2	.0161	-.0145		
TAR_D2			-.0059 **	-.0021
RDD_D2			-.0034 **	-.0018
QUO_D2			-.0589	-.0706
REC_D2			.0022	-.0093
FIT_D2			-.0142 ***	-.0058 *
NET_D2			-.0106	.0044
TEN_D2			-.0114	-.0236
TXC_D2			.0011	.0051
TXR_D2			-.0191 ***	-.0105 **
PUB_D2			-.0017	-.0019
GHG_D2			.0200	-.0002
CONST	-3.885 ***	-1.800 ***	-3.981 ***	-1.881 ***
F	34.58 ***	15.96 ***	93.87 ***	8.86 ***
R^2	0.64	0.48	0.68	0.50
Obs.	1,426	793	1,426	793
Groups	109	124	109	124

Notes: Results are estimated using fixed effects (within) regression with observation grouped by country. *, **, and *** indicate statistical significance at 10%, 5%, and 1% level respectively. Statistical significance is based on cluster-robust standard errors.

Table 15 – Results of policy duration on reg. intensity regression
Source: Own illustration.

In terms of coefficient values and significance levels the results of Equations (3.5) to (3.8) are similar to those of Equations (3.1) to (3.4). However, there are some noteworthy differences in the details. The results of model (3.5) show that the coefficients of quotas (C_QUO), fiscal incentives (C_FIS), and GHG trading systems (C_GHG) are no longer statistically significant at cluster level. At the same time, the RD&D cluster (C_RDD) is now highly significant at the one percent level. A comparison of results to those of Figure 7 reveals that clusters with statistically significant coefficients in model (3.5) also tend to have a long history of implementation. In contrast, those clusters without statistical significance tend to be more recent developments. These results indicate that it takes some time until policy measures unfold their full effects and hence support the hypothesis that it makes sense to control for duration than just for policy existence.

However, differences in average policy duration do not explain why the quotas cluster (C_QUO) lost its statistical significance and, based on the coefficient size, also importance in general. The results of the instrument-based regression model (3.7) resolve this puzzle.

Corresponding to the results of model (3.5), the results of model (3.7) show an increased significance for RD&D support (RDD), and lower or no significance for fiscal incentive measures (TXC, TXR, PUB), and greenhouse gas trading systems (GHG). More interesting, however, are the opposite signs on renewable energy quotas with (REC) and without trading systems (QUO). While the effect of classical quota systems (QUO) is positive, as it was in the duration-intensity models, the effect of the more advanced quota systems with certificate trading (REC) is now negative at a statistically significant level.

On the one hand, this result explains why the intensity effect of the quotas clusters (C_QUO), which consists of the two instruments with opposing signs (QUO and REC), is no longer significantly different from zero. On the other hand, this result raises another question: How can a policy instrument designed to promote renewable energies have a negative effect on the same?

Further analysis shows that the negative effect found for quota systems with certificate trading (REC) is an artefact of the definition of the dependent variables used throughout Equations (3.1) to (3.8): lnRES_SW and lnREC_SWTW. These variables only cover the shares of *selected* renewable energy technologies in electricity generation and generation capacities, namely wind and solar. The seemingly negative impact of quotas with trading system (REC) vanishes if the share of *all* non-hydro renewable energy technologies in electricity generation (lnRES_TeH) or generation capacity (lnREC_TeH) is used as dependent variable[55]. An effect which makes perfectly sense if one considers how certificate trading systems for renewables work. While it certainly

[55] The regression results are reported in Appendix 13 and Appendix 14.

increases regulation intensity and therefore demand for renewables in general, it also leads to a shift in the structure of this demand. The flexibility of the trading systems (REC) allows utilities to substitute rather expensive technologies such as solar PV by more cost-competitive technologies such as biomass and geothermal. Many classical quotas systems (QUO) are less flexible and often even prescribe fixed installation targets by type of technology.

All in all, the results of the duration-intensity regression support the hypothesis that policy durations on cluster and policy level are well suited to explain the overall intensities of countries' portfolios of renewable energy support policies.

In order to test the robustness of the results presented for Equations (3.1) to (3.8), I have estimate two alternative specifications for each regression model. In the first robustness test, the variable(s) for research, development, and demonstration programs[56] is left out. The second robustness test does not control for the effect from the existence greenhouse gas trading systems[57].

The rationale for the first robustness test is the limited availability of data on the proliferation of research, development, and demonstration programs. While reliable data are available for the member states of the OECD and some other highly developed countries, information on less developed countries is scarce. Hence, the respective policy design indicators have been removed on test purpose to rule out that a potential selection bias in this variable affected the coefficients of correlated policy design indicators.

The rationale for the second robustness test is uncertainty in the appropriateness of the variable on the existence greenhouse gas trading systems. Although such trading systems are theoretically important indirect support mechanisms for renewable energies, as discussed in Section 3.1.3, the actual configuration of some existing greenhouse gas trading systems puts this relationship into question. In the early stages of the EU ETS, for instance, emission permits were freely allocated to power plant operators and hence presumably did not have a strongly negative effect on the attractive of the substitutes of wind and solar power (Directive 2009/29/EC).

---

56 Depending on the regression model either C_RDD_E, RDD_E, C_RDD_D and C_RDD_D2, or RDD_D and RDD_D2.

57 Depending on the regression model either C_GHG_E, GHG_E, C_GHG_D and C_GHG_D2, or GHG_D and GHG_D2.

The results of the robustness[58] tests are similar to those of Equations (3.1) to (3.8) and hence indicate that neither the inclusion of RD&D programs nor the inclusion of greenhouse gas trading has an adverse effect on the estimation results of the remaining coefficients. Therefore, I prefer to stay with the original specification and keep RD&D programs and greenhouse gas trading in scope so that the full range of renewable energy support policies remains covered.

In summary the results of the econometric analyses presented in this section, allow to draw the following five conclusions. First, the effects of individual policy support policies and clusters of policies add up. More policy instruments mean more support for solar and wind and therefore increased regulation intensity. Second, the identified clusters and instrument types represent the policy landscape well, which is reflected by the generally high scores of the goodness-of-fit measures. Third, policy instruments differ in their impact on regulation intensity. Feed-in tariffs and quotas, for instance, are found to have a much stronger individual impact on regulation intensity than other measures such as net metering or tax credits. Fourth, measures based on policy duration are preferable to measures based on policy existence due to their higher information content. Fifth and final, the results are in line with the predictions of the Porter Hypothesis. Policy intensity is found to increase in policy duration, which stands for the importance of predictability stressed by Porter & van der Linde (1995). Similarly, there is evidence that build-in flexibility, another key feature of well-crafted environmental regulation, shifts demand to the most cost-efficient technologies.

Besides its above-listed strengths, the selected approach to capture differences in environmental regulation between countries and over time has also its limitations, especially with respect to the design dimension. Due to the lack of more detailed data on the specific provisions of past and present policy instruments, the proposed policy indicators are subject to two types of unobserved heterogeneity.

On the one hand, two policy measures from the same category are not necessarily identical. The detailed provisions of like instruments might vary strongly between countries and over time. In the case of renewable energy quotas (REC), for instance, country A might enact very strict quotas and require a renewables share of 10% while country B is more moderate and requires only a share of 1%. On the other hand, some policy indicators such as public spending, capital subsidies, and low cost-loans (PUB) are aggregated bundles of minor policy measures for

[58] The results of robustness tests are presented in Appendix 15 to Appendix 18.

which no individual data exist. Hence, the PUB indicator does not differentiate between the existence of one or multiple of these measures.

Irrespective of these limitations, it still seems reasonable to use the previously defined categories to distinguish between types of policies. Despite the undisputed heterogeneity among policy categories, design differences between categories are certainly more fundamental than design differences within categories. Hence, keeping the design dimension will yield additional insights which would be foregone otherwise. However, the results certainly require careful interpretation.

Overall, the measures of regulation intensity and regulation design perform as expected and its limitations seem manageable. Therefore, the intensity measure, renewables energies' share in electricity generation and the various design indicators are ready for application in the empirical tests of the narrowly strong Porter Hypothesis presented in Chapters 4 and 5.

4 Environmental regulation and renewable energy innovation

From the discussion in the introduction (Chapter 0) and the subsequent literature review (Chapter 2) follows that empirical research on the narrowly strong Porter Hypothesis is best conducted in two steps[59]. The first step should address the *weak* aspect of the narrowly strong Porter Hypothesis and analyze the innovation inducement effect of environmental regulation. The second step should address the *strong* aspect and analyze the effect of regulation-induced eco-innovations on countries' export competitiveness in environmental goods and services[60].

The idea to disaggregate the narrowly strong Porter Hypothesis into two steps and to analyze them separately is also applied in the empirical part of this doctoral thesis. Consequently, the analysis of the hypothesis' weak part is carried out in this chapter while the analysis of the strong part is presented in Chapter 5.

The main objective of this chapter is to generate new insights on the relationship between different types and intensities of environmental regulation, as developed in Sections 3.1 and 3.2, and innovation in renewable energy technologies.

This analysis is carried out at different levels of aggregation. Initially, the inducement effect of environmental regulation is analyzed at an aggregated level covering all renewable energy technologies. Thereafter, innovation effects are broken down by technology and analyzed separately. The analysis of differences in the technology-specific inducement effect between policy measures is important for the analysis of the *strong* part of narrowly strong Porter Hypothesis. If the results of the separate analysis suggest that the innovation inducement effect of specific regulatory measures differs by technology, then the competitiveness enhancement effect of these measures can be expected to differ to a similar extend. To the contrary, increases in

---

59 Idea to decompose the Porter Hypothesis is based on Ambec & Barla (2006), Figure 1.

60 The differentiation between a weak and a strong part of the narrowly strong Porter Hypothesis refers to the terminology introduced by Jaffe & Palmer (1997) which was discussed in Section 2.1. Because the weak Porter Hypothesis, as defined by Jaffe & Palmer (1997), refers to regulation-induced product and/or process innovations and the strong Porter Hypothesis to the potential increase in export competitiveness (win-win situation) developed based on these innovations, I will use the terms weak and strong also to refer to the innovation inducement and competitiveness enhancement components of the narrowly strong Porter Hypothesis.

countries' export competitiveness without prior innovation inducement could not be explained using the line of argumentation brought forward by Porter (1991) and Porter & van der Linde (1995) and would therefore be due to other reasons than environmental regulation.

The subsequent part of this chapter is structured as follows. Section 4.1 provides a review of the empirical literature on the determinants of innovation in environmentally-friendly technologies with a special emphasis on renewable energy equipment. Section 4.2 introduces the concepts of patents and patent analysis as key tools in technological change and especially innovation research. Section 4.3 develops the research model and discusses the respective empirical data alongside their corresponding data sources. Section 4.4 presents the results and the discussion of the same. Section 4.5 concludes.

4.1 Empirical research on green-tech innovation

In this section, I review the empirical literature[61] on the impact of environmental regulation on technological change in the field of environmentally-friendly technologies. The objective of this additional literature review section is to provide, on the one hand, a general overview on the seminal contributions in this research area and, on the other hand, a detailed discussion of studies on determinants of innovation in renewable energy technologies. This discussion clearly concentrates on the role of environmental regulation in the context of induced innovation which is most relevant for this research project. The discussion of other determinants of innovation activity, which are certainly needed as model controls, follows in Section 4.3, where I develop the generalized research model.

Following the steps of the Schumpeterian technological change process, research in this field is commonly subdivided into two broad streams: research on invention and innovation, and research on technology diffusion (Jaffe et al., 2003). This subdivision is also used for technological change research in environmental economics (Popp, Newell, & Jaffe, 2010). As technology diffusion is not in the scope of this doctoral thesis, I will concentrate exclusively on empirical research on the determinants of innovation[62] in environmentally-friendly technologies.

---

[61] For an overview on the theoretical literature, refer to the reviews of Jaffe et al. (2002, 2003). Another review of the empirical literature is provided by Vollebergh (2007).

[62] In the following, I will not distinguish between invention and innovation. Hence, whenever the term innovation is used, I refer to the same extend to invention and innovation as the early steps in the Schumpeterian technological change process. For a discussion on the subtle difference in the definitions of these two steps, refer to Section 2.3.1.

Hereby, I will lay a special emphasis on the determinants of renewable energy innovations.

Due to the lack of suitable empirical data on innovation, early research on technological change in the field of environmental economics is almost exclusively of theoretical nature. This changed considerably in the mid-1990s when detailed and reliable data on public and private R&D expenditures as well as searchable, digital patent databases became widely available (Popp et al., 2010). As I will show in the following discussion, especially the development of accessible patent databases represents a real step change for research on renewable energy innovation and certainly also for innovation research in general.

The earliest study using patent information to explore the innovation inducement effect of environmental regulation is Lanjouw & Mody (1996). They use data on pollution abatement and control expenditures to explain differences in the number of environmentally-friendly patents between countries and over time. Their sample consists of data from the United States, Germany, Japan, and 14 countries with low to medium levels of development. They find a significant, positive correlation between the number of patent applications on environmentally-friendly technologies and lagged pollution abatement and control expenditures.

Jaffe & Palmer (1997) study the impact of industry-specific pollution abatement and control expenditures in the United States on industries' inventive activity, proxied by R&D expenses, and their inventive output, proxied by patent applications. In contrast to Lanjouw & Mody (1996), they do not find a positive link between increases in regulation and upswings in patenting activity. However, they do find a small, positive relationship between increasing pollution abatement and control expenditures and R&D expenses with a time lag of one to two years. A similar US study by Brunnermeier & Cohen (2003) finds a statistically significant positive relationship between investments in pollution-control and the number of patent applications in environmental patents. In absolute terms this relationship is very small though and therefore not relevant from an economic perspective.

According to Popp et al. (2010), the studies of Jaffe & Palmer (1997) and Brunnermeier & Cohen (2003) fail to find a statically and economically meaningful relationship between investments in environmental protection and patent applications in this field because they measure patent applications too roughly. While Jaffe & Palmer (1997) use total patents as innovation indicator and therefore do not distinguish between types of innovation at all, Brunnermeier & Cohen (2003) use environmental patent data aggregated by industry. In contrast, studies like Lanjouw & Mody (1996) and Vries & Withagen (2005), which break down patent applications by technology[63], find a much stronger relationship between environmental regulation and eco-innovations.

Following the discussion of early seminal contributions to the literature on regulation-induced innovation in environmental technologies, I will now turn back to the focal area of this research project and review the few existing studies which explore regulation's impact on innovation in renewable energy technologies. This specific research area has long been ignored by scientists who were more interested in other fields of environmental innovation such as exhaust gas treatment (e.g. Popp, 2002). However, interest in the determinants of renewable energy innovation grew considerably from 2010 onwards. One reason is certainly the huge progress that renewables made over the last decade in terms of cost competitiveness and share in electricity generation. Based on literature research, I have identified a small set of six studies which are directly concerned with the impact of environmental regulation on innovation in renewable energy technologies. An overview of these studies is presented in Table 16.

The earliest study dedicated to regulation-induced renewable energy innovation is Johnstone, et al. (2008). The authors explore how effective commonly used renewable energy support policies are in inducing innovation in specific classes of renewable energy technologies. Johnstone et al. (2008) distinguish seven types and three clusters of regulatory instruments to control for differences in countries' policy regimes. Innovation is measured by technology-wise patent counts for six types of renewable energies[64]. A negative binomial model with country-fixed effects is used to estimate the technology-specific impact

63 Based on the discussion on patents and the patent analysis, I will show that the allocation of patents to industries instead of technologies leads to spurious results. This is due to the fact that the cost of regulation and the innovation induced by this regulation may occur in different industries. For example, regulation requires utilities to install exhaust gas scrubbers in coal-fired power plants, hence utilities report increased pollution abatement and control expenditures. The scrubber technology, however, is developed elsewhere, namely in the energy equipment industry. Consequently, pollution-control expenditures and patenting activities are associated with different industries. The research approach of Brunnermeier & Cohen (2003) would not be able to establish a connection between these two effects. For a more detailed discussion on this topic refer to Section 4.2.

64 The policy indicators are public sector R&D expenditures, investment incentives (e.g. low-cost loans), tax incentives, feed-in tariffs, voluntary programs, renewable energy quotas, and tradable renewable energy certificates. The renewable energy technologies covered in the study are wind, solar, geothermal, ocean, biomass, and waste-to-energy.

of regulation on innovation for their sample of 25 OECD countries between 1978 and 2003. The results of Johnstone et al. (2008) suggest that, while environmental regulation generally has a positive effect on innovation in renewable energy technologies, the effectiveness of specific regulatory instruments might vary strongly between technologies.

A study by Böhringer, Cuntz, Harhoff, & Otoo (2014) on the effectiveness of feed-in tariffs in fostering innovation arrives at a similar conclusion. The authors find for their sample of German innovation data between 1990 and 2009 that feed-in tariffs had no or only small positive impacts on renewable energy innovation. In contrast, they do find significant innovation inducement effects for public R&D expenditures.

Another driver of environmental regulation, besides policy, which attracts the interest of researchers are spillovers. Braun, Schmidt-Ehmcke, & Zloczysti (2010) explore the role of knowledge spillovers on renewable energy innovation in 21 OECD countries between 1978 and 2004. Using a zero-inflated Poisson model, they find that national, intra-industry spillovers foster innovation in renewable energy technologies. International or inter-industry spillovers, in contrast, are not found to have a significant impact on renewable energy innovation.

However, knowledge spillovers are not the only kind of spillover effect found in renewable energy innovation. Peters, Schneider, Griesshaber, & Hoffmann (2012) find in their study on solar energy innovations in 15 OECD countries between 1978 and 2005 that countries' demand-side policies, proxied by renewable energy capacities, likewise induce innovation domestically and abroad. In other words, the demand pull from country A's regulatory instruments spills over to country B and induces innovation activity in country B's renewable energy equipment industry. In contrast, the innovation inducement effect of supply-side policies, such as R&D programs, is purely domestic and does not spill over to other countries. Walz, Schleich, & Ragwitz (2011) find equivalent results for wind power innovations.

Finally, another recent study by Nesta et al. (2014), which was already discussed in the literature review on the weak Porter Hypothesis, finds that electricity market deregulation also has a positive effect on renewable energy innovation. However, as according to Nesta et al. (2014) only environmental regulation induces what they call high-quality innovation, i.e. real technological advancement, the innovation effects from electricity market deregulation are not relevant for the discussion in this chapter.

Study	Research focus	Sample	Research approach	Results (selection)
Johnstone, Haščič, & Popp (2008)	Differences in renewable energy support policies' impact on technology-specific innovation	> Wind, solar, geothermal, ocean, biomass, and waste > 25 OECD countries > 1978-2003	Reg: > Six policy dummies + R&D > Three cluster dummies > Composite policy variable Inno: > Patent counts Est: > Negative binomial model with country-fixed effects	> Environmental regulation generally has a positive impact on innovation in renewable energy technologies > Effectiveness of policy measures varies between different renewable energy technologies
Braun, Schmidt-Ehmcke, & Zloczysti (2010)	Role of knowledge spillovers in renewables innovation	> Wind and solar > 21 OECD countries > 1978-2004	Reg: > Lagged R&D investments > Three policy dummies Inno: > Patent counts Est: > Zero-inflated Poisson	> National, mainly intra-industry, spillovers foster innovation in solar energy technologies > International spillovers are rare
Walz, Schleich, & Ragwitz (2011)	Impact of specific renewable energy support policies on wind power innovations	> Wind > 12 OECD countries > 1991-2007	Reg: > Three policy dummies > Renewable energy shares Inno: > Patent counts Est: > Negative binomial model with country-fixed effects	> (Lagged) R&D expenditures, domestic and foreign demand-side policies, and a strong national innovation system have a positive impact on wind energy innovation
Peters, Schneider, Griesshaber, & Hoffmann (2012)	Impact of the locus of renewable energy support policies on renewable energy innovation	> Solar > 15 OECD countries > 1978-2005	Reg: > Domestic, regional, global R&D funding/solar capacity Inno: > Patent counts Est: > Negative binomial model with country-fixed effects	> Technology-push policies have a purely domestic impact on innovation > Domestic and foreign demand-pull policies cause (domestic) innovation > Innovation effect of demand policies is similar at home and abroad
Böhringer, Cuntz, Harhoff, & Otoo (2014)	Impact of feed-in tariffs on renewable energy innovation	> Solar, wind, geothermal, biomass, and hydro > Germany > 1990-2009	Reg: > Feed-in tariff rate > R&D expenditures Inno: > Patent counts Est: > Negative binomial model with time-fixed effects	> Innovation effects of feed-in tariffs are insignificant > Innovation is rather driven by public R&D expenditures, electricity prices, and growth in electricity consumption
Nesta, Vona, & Nicolli (2014)	Role of electricity market deregulation on renewable energy innovation	> Wind, solar, hydro, geothermal, ocean, biomass, and waste > 27 OECD countries > 1976-2007	Reg: > Index based on eight RE support policies Inno: > Patent counts Est: > Pre-sample mean Poisson model	> Renewable energy policies are more effective in deregulated markets > High quality patents are associated with env. reg. and low quality patents with electricity market deregulation

Table 16 – Studies on the regulation-innovation relationship
Source: Own illustration.

In summary, the existing literature on regulation-induced innovation in renewable energy technologies offers four valuable insights for future empirical inquiries in this research area. First, differentiation between alternative types of renewable energy technologies is essential as the strength of the regulation-innovation relationship varies for different policy-technology combinations. Second, the presence of knowledge spillovers suggests that the size of countries' knowledge stocks matters as innovation driver. Third, the possibility of demand-policy spillovers suggests that models should control for both domestic and international demand. Fourth, patent counts and the corresponding estimation techniques are unanimously applied in all six studies and appear to be the strongly preferred research approach.

4.2 Introduction to patent analysis

The review of the empirical literature on regulation-induced innovation in the renewable energy industry revealed that patent analysis is scholars' clearly preferred approach to measure innovation in this research area. I will follow their example and also use countries' patenting activity to measure innovativeness. Therefore, this section provides, first, some basic information on patenting systems and patents themselves and, second, an evaluation of the benefits and drawbacks of patent analysis as method of economic research.

4.2.1 Fundamentals of patents and the patenting system[65]

Patents are legal titles which grant their owners the exclusive right to commercially exploit the technical or procedural innovation described in the patent document for a certain period of time. This temporal protection against imitation by competitors, however, comes at the cost of disclosure. Latest at the time of publication, all patents including their full technical documentation become available to the general public. After patent expiration, the innovation described in the document loses its legal protection and may be applied by any firm or individual free of charge.

If an inventor decides that the benefits of legal protection outweigh the drawbacks of disclosure and the costs of the patenting process, she may apply for patent registration with her national patenting authority. These national authorities include the United States Patent and Trademark Office (USPTO), the European Patent Office (EPO), and the Japan Patent Office (JPO) to mention only the most important ones. Once the applicant has transmitted her patent application, the technical experts at

[65] This section builds on Nagaoka, Motohashi, & Goto (2010) if not indicated otherwise.

the national patent authority review the proposal and assess whether the applicant is eligible for a patent grant. Very roughly, a patent is granted if it describes a true innovation which has not been filed for patent application before. There are subtle differences in the patenting process between countries, which I will not describe in detail, as they are not relevant for the subsequent analysis and would hence carry the discussion too far.

As patent authorities can, for obvious reasons, only grant legal protection within the borders of their respective jurisdictions, applicants who seek international protection have to file separate applications with each national patent office. In order to ease the registration of international patents, the Patent Cooperation Treaty (PCT), which has been ratified by 148 of the 193 UN countries, streamlines the process of filing applications with multiple authorities. The first simplification measure is the so called international patent application, which allows applicants to simultaneously file patent applications with all member authorities of the PCT via their national patent offices. The second simplification measure is the priority date – the date at which a patent application for a specific innovation has been first transmitted to any member authority of the PCT. Within one year from this priority date, all additional patent applications of the same applicant with any other national patent authority under the PCT enjoy priority over competing patent applications (by other applicants) on the same innovation. Hence, the priority date gives inventors another twelve months of quasi-protection, which they can use to assess the value of their innovation before incurring the considerable cost of a multinational patenting process.

Once a patent is granted, or sometimes even at application, all information contained in the patent document becomes available in public patent databases. Examples are the patent databases of the National Bureau of Economic Research (NBER) for US patents, the OECD database for patents of its member states, the database of the Japanese Institute of Intellectual Property (IIP), and, most importantly, the PATSTAT database of the European Patent Office (EPO), which is the only patent database with a truly global coverage[66].

The information available in the different patent databases usually includes patent or application number, title, abstract, technical drawings and descriptions, inventor(s) and applicant(s) name(s), technology class,

---

66 As of 2010, the PATSTAT database consolidates data on patent applications filed with 172 national patent authorities. All other major patent databases listed above only contain domestic data based on patent applications with the respective national patent office (Nagaoka et al., 2010).

citations of other patents[67], affiliation with patent families, etc. Out of this list, two types of information are especially valuable for the analysis carried out in this chapter and therefore deserve additional explanation.

The first piece of information which is of special interest is the technology class which assigns patents to a specific category from a standardized patent classification system based on their technological content. The most prominent system is the International Patent Classification (IPC) which is administered by the United Nations' World Intellectual Property Organization (WIPO). The IPC code F03D3/06, for instance, identifies patents on rotors of wind motors with rotation axis substantially perpendicular to the air flow entering the rotor (WIPO, 2015). Given their high level of detail the IPC and comparable classification systems allow interested parties to easily and reliably identify all existing patents in a given field of technology.

The second interesting piece of information is the so called patent family. Patent families consist of all patents on the same innovation registered in different countries[68]. Hence, patent families occur if an applicant decides to protect an innovation internationally and therefore applies for registration with multiple national patent offices. A special case of patent families are triadic patents. A patent is called triadic if it has been filed for application with the patent offices of the US, Europe, and Japan[69] (Dernis, Guellec, & Van Pottelsberghe, 2001).

4.2.2 Patent analysis as method of economic research

Following the discussion on the fundamentals of patents and the corresponding patenting system, this section introduces the virtues of patents, or more specifically counts of patents, as measure of innovation in economic research.

Patent counts are fundamentally different from R&D expenditures, another common innovation indicator in economics, in terms of measurement approach. While R&D expenditures capture the effort which public or private research organizations invest into the innovation

---

67 If an innovation builds on knowledge protected under other patents, the applicant is legally required to point out this fact by citing these patents. Hence, the citation of other patents reduces the scope of the legal protection granted for the newly patented innovation to the technical advancements which go beyond the underlying, already existing patents.

68 Technically speaking all patents from a given family are identical in terms of title, technical content, inventor/applicant, and priority date.

69 An alternative definition of triadic patents is: US, Europe, and Japan or China.

process, patent counts measure the output[70] of this process (Popp, 2005; Nagaoka, Motohashi, & Goto, 2010). This feature makes patent counts the instrument of choice for research on the narrowly strong Porter Hypothesis. Their output-orientation is especially relevant for the second, the strong part of the hypothesis which links induced innovation to export competitiveness. If export success actually depends on innovation, then logic suggests that this success is more directly related to a country's innovative output than to the financial effort which was required to generate this output.

Output-orientation, however, is certainly not the only reason why patent counts have such a great appeal with economic researchers. As already mentioned in the review of the literature on renewable energy innovation and in the introductory section on patents, the development of publically accessible patent databases worked like an initial spark for research in this field. With this step, data on inventive output became as available as GDP figures, inflation rates, and other macroeconomic indicators. In addition, the data are also very information rich and structured in a standardized format. Hence, patent data are ready for use for myriads of research questions (Nagaoka et al., 2010).

Another key feature of patent data besides availability, richness, and standardization is their comprehensiveness. According to Dernis et al. (2001), all major technological innovations since the development of the steam engine have been patented. Therefore, it is reasonable to assume that the 70,000,000 plus patents currently included in PATSTAT, the global patent database of the EPO, are a good representation of the present state of technological development[71].

The last feature of patent data which is essential for this research project is its technology-orientation. As mentioned in the previous section, patent data are usually categorized based on the IPC or other patent classification systems. This aspect is very important as it enables researchers to capture the innovative output within a certain field of technology. Technology-wise allocation is not possible based on R&D expenditure data, which are at most available on industry level. Even at the highest level of detail, an unambiguous mapping between

70 Due to its very high correlation with R&D expenditures, patent counts can likewise be used as measure of innovative input. Moreover, as patent applications are usually filed shortly after or during the innovation process, the time lag between R&D expenditures and patent applications is considered negligible (Griliches, 1990; Popp, 2005).

71 In order to be really precise here, one would have to take into account the time lag between the actual knowledge generation and the transmission of the patent application to the patent authority.

technologies and industries is not possible. There will always be industries which are associated with multiple technologies or vice versa. For research on innovation in wind and solar power, it would, for instance, not be sufficient to know the R&D expenditures of the renewable energy equipment industry as a whole. The noise from more established technologies such as hydro power, biomass, geothermal, or waste-to-energy would just be too strong. Hence, only patent data structured by technology class ensure precise measurement of innovation in narrow technological fields such as specific renewable energy technologies (Johnstone et al., 2008).

However, besides the indisputable advantages of patent analysis, this method has also a number of considerable drawbacks. One of the most critical issues is the highly skewed distribution of patent values. According to a study by Scherer & Harhoff (2000) the top 10% account for 48% to 93% of the total commercial value of all patents. Given its magnitude, it is not an option to ignore this effect. As assessing the commercial value of patents manually is certainly not a workable solution either, the most common remedy is to count patent families instead of single patents (Harhoff, Scherer, & Vopel, 2003). These authors argue that the cost associated with the application of patents in multiple countries ensures that single-country patents with little or no commercial value are not counted. Moreover, the size of the patent family in terms of countries covered serves as a reliable indicator of patent value.

Another problem of patent data is that the propensity to patent varies considerably across countries and industries (Cohen, Goto, Nagata, Nelson, & Walsh, 2002). A similar effect is observed for changes in patent laws over time (Dernis et al., 2001). These changes in the propensity to patent make it more difficult to establish a causal link between regulation and innovation activity. Popp (2005) proposes a solution for this issue and suggests controlling for temporal and/or national differences in the propensity to patent. His preferred control variable for this purpose is changes in total annual patent applications by jurisdiction.

A similar issue is the so called home bias which describes the effect that patent applicants are more inclined to apply for registration with the patent authorities in their respective home countries than with international offices. There are two common remedies which overcome the home bias. First, the usage of international patent databases like PATSTAT ensures that all patents, irrespective of the authority of registration, are included in the sample. Hence, while the home bias is an issue for single country studies, it is uncritical for international studies like the one conducted here. Second, using triadic patent families instead of simple patent counts is another option to reduce the home bias (Dernis et al., 2001). As mentioned above, triadic patents have been filed for application in the US, Europe, and Japan. In 1995, 96.34% of the triadic patents were filed by applicants from one of these countries. Therefore, using triadic patents or patent families in general renders the home bias negligible (Dernis et al., 2001).

The final drawback of patent counts is the phenomenon of strategic non-patenting. Firms may decide not to protect their innovations if the implicit costs of application, i.e. publicity, outweigh the benefit of legal protection. This effect is especially prevalent in industries which are characterized by short product lead times and lifecycles, or by unevenly distributed market power (Arundel, 2001; Cohen, Nelson, & Walsh, 2000). However, if strategic non-patenting exists, it is mostly a phenomenon associated with specific industries. Hence, although it is unlikely that strategic non-patenting is an issue in long-lifecycle products like energy equipment, its presence would affect all firms and therefore would have no severe implications for an analysis of changes in innovation output.

Overall, after controlling for the drawbacks, the benefits of patent analysis shine even brighter. The technology-orientation of patent data allows researchers to conduct targeted studies on innovation activity, even in specialized fields. Thanks to the wide availability, consistent structure, and richness of this source of information, patent counts have a long history of application in economic research. They likewise measure current innovation activity at specific points in time, changes in the research focus, the stock of knowledge accumulated over time, or the flow and diffusion of knowledge between countries or industries.

4.3 Research model

This section introduces the formal econometric model which I use to explore the weak, or first, part of the narrowly strong Porter Hypothesis. The specification of this model takes carefully into account the empirical lessons learned from existing research on the relationship between environmental regulation and innovation in renewable energy technologies and the methodological lessons learned from scientific applications of patent analysis in general.

The discussion of the research model is subdivided into two parts. The first part, presented in Section 4.3.1, introduces the patent data used in the subsequent estimation process and discusses the results of first descriptive analyses of the same. The second part, presented in Section 4.3.2, describes the building blocks of the econometric regression model element by element and presents the preferred model specification which is used for the following more detailed analyses.

4.3.1 Patent data

The patent information used throughout this research project has been extracted from the spring 2015 version of the PATSTAT database (EPO, 2015) provided by the European Patent Office. PATSTAT is currently the most comprehensive open access patent database (Nagaoka et al., 2010). The spring 2015 version contains over 70 million patent applications from more than 100 countries (EPO, 2015). PATSTAT's broad geographic coverage ensures that home bias (Dernis et al., 2001) is not an issue for the analyses of this and subsequent chapters. Generally, PATSTAT provides reliable data on technology classes, applicant country, priority date, and family affiliation and therefore fully meets the critical information requirements for meaningful patent analysis as describes in Section 4.2.2.

The initial two steps in literally every patent analysis project are first to define the scope of analysis and second to identify all patents according to this definition. While defining the scope is mostly quite easy, for this thesis it has been defined as technologies to generate electricity from wind and solar radiation, selecting the corresponding patents is less straight forward. Table 17 provides an overview of the identification approaches used in previous studies on renewables innovation.

All previous studies use the IPC system to identify patent applications on wind and solar innovations. Hereby, most studies follow Johnstone et al. (2008), the earliest publication in this field, and rely on the same or similar sets of IPC classes to identify relevant patents for their research.

However, even though the IPC system has been applied without exception in all previous studies on renewable energy innovation, the technology classes of the IPC system are not very well suited for research on renewables or more generally climate change mitigation technologies (CCMT). Using IPC classes to identify patent applications of CCMT leads to considerable type I and II errors, i.e. the selection of irrelevant patents or the failure to select relevant patents (Veefkind, Hurtado-Albir, Angelucci, Karachalios, & Thumm, 2012).

Hence, a consortium of experts from the EPO, the United Nations Environment Programme (UNEP), and the International Center for Trade and Sustainable Development (ICTSD) developed an alternative classification system. The so called Y02E system has been set up between 2009 and 2011 to identify patent applications on "technologies which control, reduce, or prevent greenhouse gas emissions of anthropogenic origin, as set forth by the Kyoto Protocol" (Veefkind et al., 2012, p. 107). Hereby, it is important to note that the Y02E has been developed as tagging system which exists in addition to the IPC. One benefit of this approach is that it can be applied to new as well as existing patents and patent applications. Therefore, the Y02E is equally suitable to identify CCMT patent applications filed before and after its introduction in 2011, which is an important prerequisite for its applications in this research project.

Overall, the newly developed Y02E system is clearly superior to the traditional IPC system in the identification of renewable energy and CCMT innovations in general. Thanks to its novel coding structure which has been tailored to the needs of green-tech research and the reliable patent identification process lead by EPO experts, the Y02E reduces type I/II errors to a minimum (Veefkind et al., 2012; EPO, 2013; IRENA, 2013b). Hence, the Y02E system is now the preferred approach to identify patent applications on wind and solar power technologies.

Table 17 compares the number of renewable energy patents identified using Y02E codes, Y02E 10/7 for wind and Y02E 10/5 for solar energy technologies, to the number of patents identified using the IPC classes applied in previous studies. In terms of wind energy technologies the IPC system works quite well. There is a distinct category, F03D (wind motors), which makes it easy to identify relevant patents. This implies that the risk of type I/II errors as well as the difference in the number of patents identified using IPC and Y02E are quite small.

For solar energy technologies, however, the situation is completely different. The list of potentially relevant IPC classes is long and highly fragmented. Many of the IPC codes listed in Table 17 are ambiguous and apply similarly to solar cells as well as other types of semiconductors. Hence, there is a high risk of false or incomplete identification of solar energy patents. This high degree of uncertainty in patent selection is also reflected in the variation of results based on alternative sets of IPC codes. While the approach of Peters et al. (2012) yields just 104,000 solar energy patents between 1980 and 2011, the approach of Böhringer et al. (2014) suggests that the number of patents applied in this period was in excess of 3,000,000. Even if one classifies the very broad selection approach of Böhringer et al. (2014) as outlier, there is clearly no consensus on the question which IPC classes to cover. A good example is the IPC code H01L 31. Although all studies agree that this code is relevant, the inclusion of different sub-codes leads to results which differ by almost one magnitude (32,000 to 303,000).

Technology class	Description	Patent applications on selected technologies from 1980 to 2011				
		Johnstone et al. ('08)	Braun et al. ('10)	Peters et al. ('12)	Böhringer et al. ('14)	Nesta et al. ('14)
(a) Wind energy technologies						
F03D	Wind motors	104	104		104	104
B60L 8/00	Electric propulsion (...) force of nature	2			2	2
B63H 13/00	Effecting propulsion by wind motors (...)	*			*	*
Total IPC		106	104		106	106
Y02E 10/7	Energy generation through (...) Wind	95	95		95	95
Delta (IPC ./. Y02E)		+11	+9		+11	+11
(b) Solar energy technologies						
B60L 8/00	Electric propulsion (...) force of nature	2				2
C30B 15	Single-crystal growth (...)				27	
C30B 28	Production of (...) polycrystalline (...)				3	
C30B 29	Single crystals or homogeneous polycrystalline (...)				58	
C23C 14	Coating by vacuum evaporation, by sputtering or by ion implantation (...)				214	
C23C 16	Chemical coating by (...)				223	
E04D 13	Roof covering (...)collecting devices				66	
E04D 13/18	Roof covering (...) energy collecting devices, e.g. including solar panels	9	9			9
F03G 6/00-F03G 6/08	(...) producing mechanical power from solar energy	4	4			4
F24J 2/00-54	Use of solar heat (...)	95	95			95
F25B 27/00	Machine plant or systems using (...) sun	7				7
F26B 3/28	Drying (...) by radiation - e.g. sun	24				24
H01G 9/028	Organic semiconducting electrolytes				2	
H01L 21	Processes or apparatus adapted for the manufacture (...) of semiconductor (...)				2,331	
H01L 27/142	Devices (...) sensitive to infra-red radiation, light-specially adapted		3	3		
H01L 31	Semiconductor devices sensitive to (...)				303	
H01L 31/042	Semiconductor devices sensitive to infra-red radiation (...) e.g. solar cells	32				32
H01L 31/042-	Semiconductor devices sensitive to (...)			102		
H01L 31/04-	Semiconductor devices sensitive to (...)		118			
H01L 51	Solid state devices using organic (...)				190	
H02N 6/00	Generators in which light radiation is directly converted into electrical energy	*	*		*	*
Total IPC		172	228	104	3,414	172
Y02E 10/5	Energy generation through (...) PV	145	145	145	145	145
Delta (IPC ./. Y02E)		+27	+83	-41	+3,269	+27

Notes: Aggregated counts of patent applications based on the spring 2015 version of PATSTAT (EPO, 2015). Figures in thousands. Asterisks (*) indicate values < 1,000. Walz et al. (2011) is not included due to missing information on the technology classes covered.

Table 17 – Patent identification approaches of related publications
Source: Own illustration based on data from EPO (2015).

In sum, the results presented in Table 17 confirm the notion that the Y02E is the more reliable and for that reason preferable approach to identify renewable energy innovations. Therefore, I will use patent applications allocated to Y02E 10/7 and its subclasses as proxy for wind energy innovation and patent applications allocated to Y02E 10/5 and its subclasses as proxy for solar energy innovation.

Following the discussion on the right patent identification strategy, I will now present some preliminary analyses of the data extracted from PATSTAT based on this identification approach and used throughout the remainder of the thesis.

Figure 14 shows the trend of total and renewable energy patent applications between 1990 and 2011. While the number of total annual patent applications exhibits a smooth growth trajectory over the entire observation period only interrupted by the recessions in the early 1990s, 2000s, and the great recession of 2008/09, the number of annual patent applications in renewable energy technologies shows an exponential growth trend. Especially after 2005/06, the speed of technological development in solar and wind increased considerably.

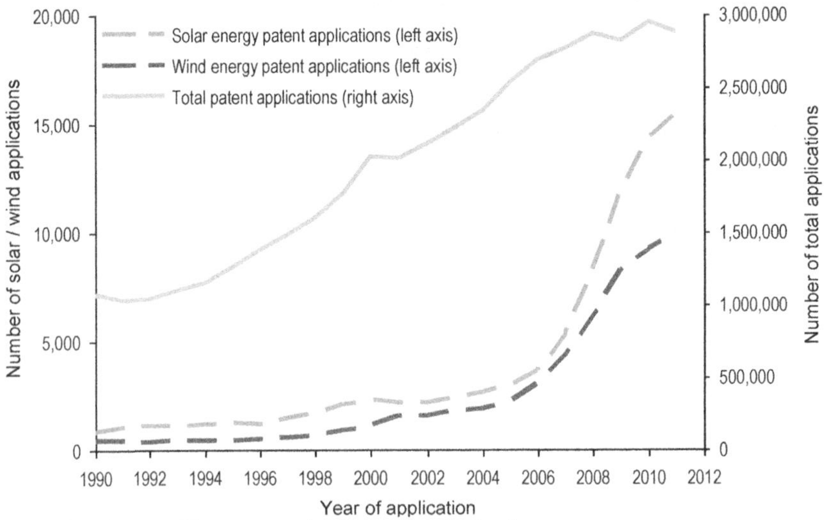

Figure 14 – Renewable energy patenting vs. total patenting
Source: Own illustration based on data from EPO (2015).

Against the background of the strong increase in adoption rates of renewable energy support policies in the same period[72], this finding

---

[72] For details on the dissemination of RE support policies, refer to Section 3.3.1.

already provides first indicative support for the hypothesis that environmental regulation has a positive impact on innovation in renewable energy technologies. From a technology perspective, Figure 14 confirms the data presented in Table 17 and reports generally higher numbers of patent applications for solar than for wind energy technologies. However, one should be careful to draw inferences from the number of patent applications on the innovativeness of areas of technology because the propensity to patent or the complexity of patenting issues might differ largely.

In addition to the development over time, I have also analyzed country-to-country differences in renewable energy patenting. The results of this similarly insightful analysis are presented in Table 18. First of all, the data show a strong concentration of innovation activity. The top five countries in terms of wind and solar energy innovation, the United States, Germany, South Korea, Japan, and China, account for two thirds of total patent applications between 1980 and 2011. The patent applications of the top 20 countries even make up 90 percent of the (allocable) innovative output in this area. However, given the top five countries' economic power and the strength of their innovation systems, these countries are likely to produce higher numbers of patent applications in any field of technology.

Hence, controlling for countries' overall innovative output, defined as total patent applications, yields a quite different picture and constitutes the second main insight from this analysis. Although the United States and Germany are the leaders in solar and wind energy technology in absolute terms, other countries are, relative to their innovative output, much more productive innovators in these fields. While just 1.0 in 1,000 US patents is related to solar power, the corresponding ratio is 4.9 in 1,000 for Taiwan and 3.0 in 1,000 for South Korea. This effect is even more pronounced for wind energy where Denmark and the United Arab Emirates lead with 12.2 and 9.2 wind energy patents per 1,000 patent applications. Germany, the innovation leader in absolute terms, only generates 1.7 wind energy patents per 1,000 patent applications. In short, relative patent outputs are more suitable than absolute figures, which give preference to large countries, to identify economies which are forerunners in renewable energy innovation.

A comparison of renewable energy patents per 1,000 patents between the United States and Germany supports this finding. While the US generates a mere 1.6 wind and solar patents in 1,000, relative innovativeness in Germany, which generates 3.1 renewable energy patents per 1,000 patent applications, is clearly higher. It will be interesting to explore the role which environmental regulation plays as a determinant of these considerable country-to-country differences in renewable energy patenting.

	Number of renewable energy patents			Number of renewable energy patents per 1,000 patents		
Country	Solar	Wind	Total	Solar	Wind	Total
United States	10,743	5,410	16,153 (19.6%)	1.0	0.5	1.6
Germany	5,807	6,871	12,678 (15.4%)	1.4	1.7	3.1
South Korea	7,121	3,431	10,552 (12.8%)	3.0	1.4	4.4
Japan	8,381	1,449	9,830 (11.9%)	1.6	0.3	1.9
China	2,216	4,201	6,417 (7.8%)	2.0	3.7	5.7
Taiwan	2,955	1,012	3,967 (4.8%)	4.9	1.7	6.6
Denmark	60	2,381	2,441 (3.0%)	0.3	12.2	12.5
France	1,138	1,005	2,143 (2.6%)	0.7	0.6	1.3
United Kingdom	817	1,271	2,088 (2.5%)	0.7	1.1	1.9
Spain	365	1,094	1,459 (1.8%)	1.7	5.2	6.9
Netherlands	467	535	1,002 (1.2%)	0.7	0.8	1.6
Russia	186	814	1,000 (1.2%)	0.5	2.3	2.9
Canada	404	583	987 (1.2%)	0.7	1.0	1.8
Chile	607	256	863 (1.0%)	0.9	0.4	1.3
Italy	429	316	745 (0.9%)	0.7	0.5	1.2
United Arab Emirates	49	528	577 (0.7%)	0.9	9.2	10.1
Austria	258	252	510 (0.6%)	1.1	1.1	2.3
Sweden	120	383	503 (0.6%)	0.2	0.7	0.9
Belgium	259	206	465 (0.6%)	1.2	1.0	2.2
Poland	29	419	448 (0.5%)	0.2	3.4	3.6
other	2,732	4,734	7,466 (9.1%)			
unknown	49,576	22,802	72,378			
Total	94,719	59,953	154,672	**1.4**	**1.0**	**2.4**

Notes: This table gives the total number of all patent applications by domestic applicants between 1980 and 2011. If a patent application is filed by applicants from multiple countries, the application is equally considered for the patent counts of all applicant countries. The total number of patents is lower compared to the figure presented in Table 17 because the database underlying this table is restricted to patent applications for which applicant information is available.

Table 18 – Patent applications on RE technologies by country
Source: Own illustration based on data from EPO (2015).

Moreover, it is worth noting that the results of Table 18 also fit well into the previous discussion on countries' revealed comparative advantage in renewable energy equipment. The respective indicator values from Part (c) of Table 2[73] show that Denmark, China, Spain, and Germany are the most competitive countries in wind power solutions, while Malaysia, China, and Japan lead in solar power equipment. A quick view on Table 18 reveals that these countries are also particularly strong innovators in the field of renewable energy technologies. Taken together, the data on

[73] Table 2 is presented in Section 1.3 on page 14.

countries' patenting activity and revealed comparative advantage in renewable energy equipment point towards the existence of a positive relationship between innovation and export success, i.e. the strong part of the narrowly strong Porter Hypothesis. As this chapter is concerned with the weak part of the narrowly strong Porter Hypothesis, I will leave a more detailed discussion on competitiveness effects aside till Chapter 5.

A last aspect of patent data which needs to be discussed before I start with the development of the regression model is the idea of knowledge stocks. On an abstract level, knowledge generation is a collaborative effort. New technologies are rarely developed entirely from scratch. In most cases, innovators build on existing knowledge and advance it gradually. Consequently, innovators find it the easier to invent new technologies the bigger the stock of existing knowledge is (Popp, 2002). The exponential growth in solar and wind energy patenting shown in Figure 14 supports this notion. These data show that the number of newly applied patents per year is clearly trending. The number of annual patent applications increases in the cumulative number of innovations, i.e. the size of the knowledge stock. For this reason, knowledge stocks are often applied in empirical research as a tool to control for the self-enhancing feature of innovation.

The standard approach to calculate knowledge stocks in environmental economics was initially developed by Popp (2002, 2005) and advanced further by Popp, Haščič, & Medhi (2011). They calculate knowledge stocks (knowledge stock) as sums[74] of annual counts of patent applications (pat. appl.) which are adjusted by the rate of decay (β_1), i.e. the speed at which new innovations become obsolete, and the rate of diffusion (β_2), i.e. the speed at which knowledge spreads and becomes available to other inventors. Building on this basic idea, Popp et al. (2011) propose four alternative formulations: Equations (4.1) to (4.4).

The difference between these four knowledge stock formulations is their approach to count patent applications. As discussed in Section 4.2.2, patents are subject to a skewed value distribution characterized by many low and few high value patents. In order to exclude low value patents, some researchers (e.g. Harhoff et al., 2003) proposed to use counts of patent families instead of simple patent counts. Popp et al. (2011) build on this idea and propose to calculate patent stocks based on simple counts (SC) (4.1) as well as family counts (FC) (4.2). Further, they propose to weigh patent counts by family size (SCw, FCw), i.e. the number of countries in which an invention has been applied for patent

[74] From the starting period (s) to the current or final period (t).

registration, in order to even better account for the long tail nature of the distribution of patent values, Equations (4.3) and (4.4)[75]. While, Popp et al. (2011) use all four count strategies, they prefer size-weighted family counts, Equation (4.4), because it fits their data best.

$$knowledge\ stock\ (SC)_t = \sum_{s=0}^{t} e^{-\beta_1(s)}\left(1 - e^{-\beta_2(s+1)}\right) pat.appl.(SC)_{t-s} \tag{4.1}$$

$$knowledge\ stock\ (FC)_t = \sum_{s=0}^{t} e^{-\beta_1(s)}\left(1 - e^{-\beta_2(s+1)}\right) pat.appl.(FC)_{t-s} \tag{4.2}$$

$$knowledge\ stock\ (SCw)_t = \sum_{s=0}^{t} e^{-\beta_1(s)}\left(1 - e^{-\beta_2(s+1)}\right) pat.appl.(SCw)_{t-s} \tag{4.3}$$

$$knowledge\ stock\ (FCw)_t = \sum_{s=0}^{t} e^{-\beta_1(s)}\left(1 - e^{-\beta_2(s+1)}\right) pat.appl.(FCw)_{t-s} \tag{4.4}$$

Figure 15 illustrates the size of the global knowledge stocks for solar and wind power technologies calculated using Equations (4.1) to (4.4). The results show a strong increase in the size of the knowledge stocks for both technologies. Such strong increases are typically associated with booming fields of technology in which the number of new ideas grows far above the rate of decay (Popp, 2005).

Moreover, Figure 15 shows an increasing gap between the unweighted and weighted knowledge stocks which indicates that, on average, innovations become more and more valuable. The tendency to file for patent application in multiple countries also reflects the increase in the number of markets with considerable renewable energy shares. Especially in the case of solar energy, the geographic spread of global demand increased considerably over the last decade[76]. From a technological perspective, the data suggest that the internationalization process of technology and therefore patenting started first in wind and later on also in solar energy technologies. One reason for this effect might be the consistently lower levelized cost of electricity of wind, which makes it more independent from national demand side policies.

75 Simple count (SC): Every patent is counted (weight = 1). Family count (FC): Only patents with a family size >1 are counted (weight = 1). Simple count, size weighted (SCw): Every patent is counted (weight = family size of the patent). Family count, size weighted (FCw): Only patents with a family size > 1 are counted (weight = family size of the patent). Hence, the patent scope of FC/FCw, which leaves aside single country patents, is a subset of the one of SC/SCw.

76 For further details on the geographic split of renewables demand, refer to Section 1.1.

(a) Global knowledge stock for solar power technologies

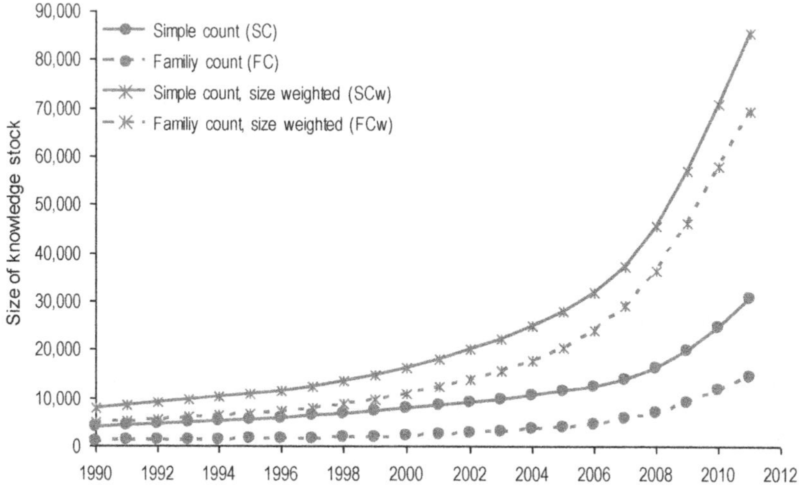

(b) Global knowledge stock for wind power technologies

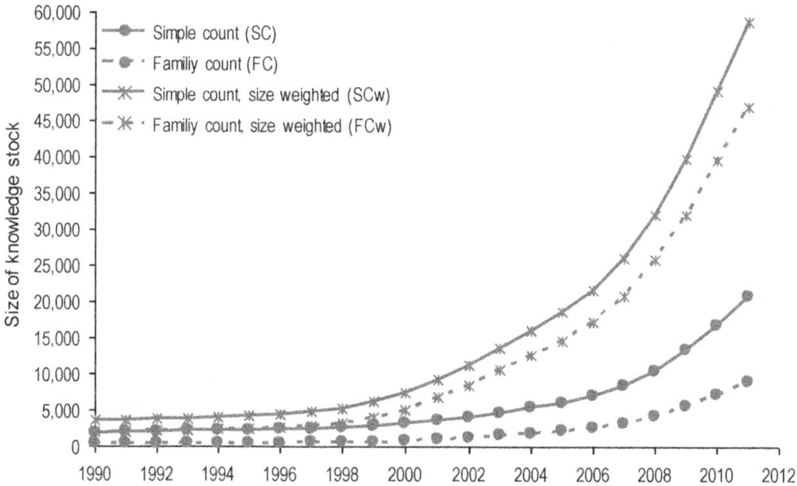

Figure 15 – Global knowledge stocks on solar and wind technologies
Source: Own illustration based on data from EPO (2015).

In summary, the discussions and analyses presented above yield three main results which are important for the econometric analysis of the innovation inducement effect of environmental regulation in wind and solar power technologies. First, the newly developed Y02E classification systems for patents on climate change mitigation technologies considerably improves the accuracy by which patents on wind and solar power technologies can be identified. Consequently, identification of relevant patents based on Y02E, which is applied here, improves the accuracy of results compared to previous studies using the conventional IPC system, esp. in terms of solar energy technologies. Second, the preliminary analysis of the patent data shows a strong increase in solar and wind energy patenting particularly over the last decade. This boom in patenting coincides with the adoption of more and more intense renewable energy support policies in many countries and with the growth of the existing knowledge stocks in these fields of technology. Third, while large economies with strong innovation systems also lead the technological development in renewable energies, small countries, like Denmark, Taiwan, and South Korea, are also remarkably successful in this field. Similarly, some countries seem to focus on specific renewable energy technologies. It will be interesting to explore to what extend these temporal and cross-country differences can be explained by regulation.

4.3.2 Model specification

The objective of Section 4.3 is to define an econometric model to empirically analyze the relationship between environmental regulation and innovation in wind and solar power technologies. While the previous section introduced the patent data used as dependent variable in this analysis, this section evaluates potential explanatory variables and presents the regression model in its generalized form.

In order to arrive at a well-specified regression model, I will first identify and discuss the main drivers of innovation in wind and solar energy technologies other than environmental regulation. Afterwards, I will add the indicators of regulation intensity and regulation design, developed throughout Chapter 3, to control for the innovation inducement effect of common renewable energy support policies.

Based on a review of the empirical literature, three non-regulatory forces appear to determine how many renewable energy innovations a given country generates and hence should be considered as explanatory variables. The first innovation determinant is the level of technological advancement in renewable energy equipment, i.e. the starting point for further technological development. The second innovation driver is the existence of attractive market opportunities for manufacturers of renewable energy equipment, which proxies the incentive to innovate. The third factor is an additional control for changes or differences in the country-specific propensity to patent (Johnstone et al., 2008; Braun et al., 2010; Walz et al., 2011; Peters et al., 2012; Böhringer et al. 2014; Nesta et al., 2014).

The first non-regulatory explanatory variable which should be included in the model is an appropriate indicator of the current level of technical development in renewable energy equipment. From the discussion in Section 4.3.1 and Popp (2005) follows that access to existing knowledge facilitates innovativeness and the creation of new, farther-reaching knowledge. Hence, it is expected that the innovation output in solar and wind power technologies increases with the level of technical development in this very field.

Many studies on renewable energy innovation use trend variables or time-fixed effects to model technological advancement in renewables technology (e.g. Braun et al., 2010; Peters et al., 2012; Böhringer et al., 2014; Nesta et al., 2014). Yet, Popp (2005) states in his summary of lessons learned from patent analysis that neither time dummies nor trend variables are suitable instruments for this purpose. He argues further that only knowledge stocks are reliable measures of the development level in a given field of technology at a given point in time. Therefore, I will follow Popp (2005) and use knowledge stocks as indicators of the current state of technical development.

The second non-regulatory innovation driver which should be part of the model is an indicator which captures the wind and solar industry's incentive to innovate based on the existence of general market opportunities for manufacturers of energy equipment. Hereby it is important to note that those general market opportunities should not be directly related to demand-creating renewable energy support policies such as feed-in tariffs. The whole point of including non-regulatory innovation determinants is to capture inducement effects from other sources than environmental regulation.

Multiple related studies propose to proxy market opportunity by year-on-year growth in domestic electricity consumption (e.g. Johnstone et al., 2008; Böhringer et al., 2014; Nesta et al., 2014). In contrast, a study by Peters et al. (2012) suggests that energy equipment is a global product category which therefore should not only depend on local but also on international demand. Their empirical results provide support for this notion. Moreover, they suggest that capacity additions are a better proxy of the demand for energy equipment than changes in electricity consumption, as the latter also depends on, for instance, business cycle effects. This view is consistent with my line of argumentation in Section

3.2.3, where I also concluded that capacity changes are the preferable demand proxy.

Therefore, I follow the example of Peters et al. (2012) and use year-on-year changes in global installed electricity generation capacities as indicator of business opportunity[77]. As it seems reasonable to assume that overall demand for power plants is more driven by general factors such as economic progress, population growth, and plant age, this indicator fulfills the requirement of being unaffected by renewable energy support policies.

The third non-regulatory determinant of renewable energy innovation proposed in the literature is countries' general propensity to patent. As discussed previously, the likelihood of filing patent applications for newly developed innovations varies between countries, industries, as well as over time (Dernis et al., 2001; Cohen et al., 2002). Considering this point, I implement a proposal of Popp (2005) and use the total number of domestic patent applications to control for temporal changes or country-specific differences in the propensity to patent.

For the sake of completeness, it needs to be stated that related studies used additional non-regulation-based determinants of renewable energy innovation which I have not included in my regression model. Nesta et al. (2014), for instance, also included the degree of product market (de)regulation in their model. This variable is not applied here as it was found to only affect low value innovations, which are not what I intend to investigate. Moreover, Johnstone et al. (2008), Böhringer et al. (2014), and Nesta et al. (2014) all include changes in electricity prices as additional driver of renewables demand and therefore incentive to innovate in this field of technology. However, the significance of their results is mixed. Moreover, it is not clear whether the price increases are neutral or (partially) caused by renewable energy support policies. Similarly, Peters et al. (2012) proxy changes in energy prices and therefore the attractiveness of the market environment for renewables by the crude oil price. The drawback of this measure is that crude oil prices are more or less equal across countries. They are therefore not very suitable to explain country-to-country differences in innovation, which is what I attempt to explain in this research project. Finally, Walz et al. (2011) use the share of green party votes in general elections to

[77] While Peters et al. (2012) actually use data on capacity additions, I have to use changes in installed capacity due to the unavailability of data on capacity additions. The drawback of installed capacity is that it only measures the net demand for new power plants (net of replacements) and therefore underestimates the business opportunities for equipment manufacturers.

measure public support for environmental protection and thus investment in renewable energies. However, they fail to show a statically significant effect. In sum, all additional model controls discussed in this paragraph are either statistically insignificant or at least disputed, or lie outside my research focus.

Finally, Equation (4.5) states the generalized econometric regression model which I use to estimate the impact of environmental regulation on countries' innovative output in solar and wind power technologies.

$$\begin{aligned} \textit{solar and wind energy patents} \\ &= \textit{domestic stock of solar and wind patents} \\ &+ \textit{total domestic patents} \\ &+ \textit{changes in global generation capacity} \\ &+ \textit{regulation intensity} + \textit{regulation design} + \varepsilon \end{aligned} \tag{4.5}$$

Besides the three non-regulatory innovation drivers introduced throughout this section, the domestic knowledge stock, total domestic patents, and changes in global installed capacity, Equation (4.5) also includes two sets of indicators for regulation design and regulation intensity which have been developed in Chapter 3.

4.4 Results

This section presents the results of my empirical estimation of the weak part of the narrowly strong Porter Hypothesis. The discussion starts with an introduction of the formal econometric model, which is a direct application of the research model developed above, including some remarks on the sample and the model variables. The presentation and discussion of the regression results follows immediately thereafter. In addition, this section contains an overview on the robustness tests performed to confirm the validity of the estimated coefficients, and a comparison of the overall results of this study to those of related studies on induced innovation in renewable energy technologies.

The five econometric models to estimate the innovation inducement effect of environmental regulation in wind and solar power technologies are presented below as Equations (4.6) to (4.10). The formulation of these equations takes into account the discussion of the related empirical research presented in Section 4.1. Amongst others, it was pointed out that recent studies, esp. Johnstone et al. (2008), found that the innovation enhancing effect of renewable energy support policies varies considerably for different types of technology. Therefore, I do not only estimate the regulation-innovation relationship for solar and wind energy in aggregation but also individually for each technology.

In all five regression models, the dependent variable is a simple count[78] of annual patent applications on technologies classified as related to wind power (SC_W), solar power (SC_S), or both (SC_SW) filed by domestic applicants with any national or international patent authority[79].

$$SC\_SW_{i,t} = \alpha_i + \beta_1 DKS\_SC\_SW_{i,t} + \beta_2 DTOPAT_{i,t} + \beta_3\, ITOCAPA\_YOY_t + \beta_4 RES\_SW_{i,t} + \sum \beta_{c+4} ClusterEx_{c,i,t} + \varepsilon_{i,t} \quad (4.6)$$

$$SC\_S_{i,t} = \alpha_i + \beta_1 DKS\_SC\_S_{i,t} + \beta_2 DTOPAT_{i,t} + \beta_3\, ITOCAPA\_YOY_t + \beta_4 RES\_S_{i,t} + \sum \beta_{c+4} ClusterEx_{c,i,t} + \varepsilon_{i,t} \quad (4.7)$$

$$SC\_W_{i,t} = \alpha_i + \beta_1 DKS\_SC\_W_{i,t} + \beta_2 DTOPAT_{i,t} + \beta_3\, ITOCAPA\_YOY_t + \beta_4 RES\_W_{i,t} + \sum \beta_{c+4} ClusterEx_{c,i,t} + \varepsilon_{i,t} \quad (4.8)$$

$$SC\_S_{i,t} = \alpha_i + \beta_1 DKS\_SC\_S_{i,t} + \beta_2 DTOPAT_{i,t} + \beta_3\, ITOCAPA\_YOY_t + \beta_4 RES\_S_{i,t} + \sum \beta_{c+4} InstruEx_{c,i,t} + \varepsilon_{i,t} \quad (4.9)$$

$$SC\_W_{i,t} = \alpha_i + \beta_1 DKS\_SC\_W_{i,t} + \beta_2 DTOPAT_{i,t} + \beta_3\, ITOCAPA\_YOY_t + \beta_4 RES\_W_{i,t} + \sum \beta_{c+4} InstruEx_{c,i,t} + \varepsilon_{i,t} \quad (4.10)$$

Moreover, all equations contain fixed terms (α_i) in order to control for unobserved heterogeneity on country level, the domestic stock of patent applications on wind power (DKS_SC_W), solar power (DKS_SC_S), or both (DKS_SC_SW) calculated using simple counts[78], total domestic patents (DTOPAT), the year-on-year percentage change in the global installed electricity generation capacity (ITOCAPA_YOY), and an error term (ε). As for all previous regression models, the indices i and t represent country[80] (1 to 225) and time period (1990 to 2011). The indices c and p indicate the numbering of policy cluster and instruments.

Besides these variables, Equations (4.6) to (4.10) contain one or multiple indicators of environmental regulation design and intensity as developed throughout Chapter 3. To recap, RES_SW stands for the domestic

[78] In order to decide among the four alternative patent count approaches presented in Section 4.3.1, I follow Popp et al. (2011) and select the preferable approach based on its statistical fit with the data sample. Using Equation (4.6) as basis, the regression results presented in Appendix 22 show that the Chi² values of the simple counts (SC/SCw) are higher than those of the family counts (FC/FCw). Similarly, the Chi² values of the unweighted count models (SC/FC) are consistently higher than those of the weighted count models (SCw/FCw). Therefore, I choose the simple count (SC) of patent applications as my preferred measure of wind and solar innovation.

[79] As discussed in Section 4.3.1, solar and wind patents are identified based on the technology codes Y02E 10/5 and Y02E 10/7 respectively.

[80] A list of all countries included in the sample is presented in Appendix 9.

percentage share of electricity generated from solar and wind in total electricity generation. Accordingly, RES_S and RES_W give the technology-specific shares of solar and wind. ClusterEx stands for a set of binary variables indicating the existence of each of the six policy clusters: targets (C_TAR_E), RD&D support (C_RDD_E), quotas (C_QUO_E), feed-in tariffs (C_FIT_E), fiscal incentives (C_FIS_E), and carbon trading (C_GHG_E). Similarly, InstruEx stands for a set of binary variables which indicate the existence of each of the eleven instrument types: renewable energy targets or strategies (TAR_E), research, development, and demonstration programs (RDD_E), renewable energy quotas without certificate trading (QUO_E), renewable energy quotas with certificate trading (REC_E), feed-in tariffs (fixed rate or premium) (FIT_E), net metering (NET_E), public competitive bidding (tendering) (TEN_E), tax credits (investment or production) (TXC_E), tax reductions (carbon, energy, sales, VAT, or other taxes) (TXR_E), public spending, capital subsidies, and low cost loans (PUB_E), and greenhouse gas trading systems (GHG_E).

A formal introduction of all variables listed above including their individual data sources as well the corresponding descriptive statistics are given in Appendix 19 and Appendix 20 respectively. The correlation matrix is presented in Appendix 21.

The models' maximum likelihood estimates are obtained using a negative binomial model for panel data with fixed effects (Hausman, Hall, & Griliches, 1984). Negative binomial models are one of two common approaches to estimate econometric models which rely on counts as dependent variable, as it is the case here. The alternative option would be to estimate the equations using a Poisson model. A prerequisite for the application of this model is, however, that the dependent variables exhibit a Poisson distribution which requires equidispersion. In other words, Poisson-distributed data are characterized by equality between its conditional means and conditional variances. The descriptive statistics presented in Appendix 20 show that this is certainly not the case for any of the dependent variables used in this section. In contrast, a comparison of the means and variances of these variables suggests that the patent counts are overdispersed, i.e. their variances exceed their means. In such cases, negative binomial models are more efficient than Poisson models and are therefore preferred for the analyses carried out in this section (Wooldridge, 2002, Chapter 19).

Table 19 presents the regression results for Equations (4.6) to (4.10). I start the discussion with the coefficient estimates for the three non-regulatory variables. Thereafter, I turn to the core variables on regulation design and intensity. Hereby, the estimates of the regulation effect are first discussed on the aggregated level, i.e. for wind and solar combined and then separately by technology.

Dep. var.	SC_SW[2]	SC_S	SC_W	SC_S	SC_W
Variable	(4.6)	(4.7)	(4.8)	(4.9)	(4.10)
DKS_SC_...[1]	.2332 ***	.4057 ***	.4636 ***	.3865 ***	.5125 ***
DTOPAT	.0021 ***	.0011 **	.0031 ***	-.0009 *	.0029 ***
ITOCAPA_YOY	.4375 ***	.5196 ***	.4448 ***	.5206 ***	.4416 ***
RES_...[1]	.0433 ***	.0902 **	.0420 ***	.0688	.0412 ***
C_TAR_E	.1783 ***	.1309	.1045		
C_RDD_E	.6338 ***	.7787 ***	.5931 ***		
C_QUO_E	.0436	.0408	.0316		
C_FIT_E	.1556 **	.2162 ***	.1428 *		
C_FIS_E	.4047 ***	.5463 ***	.3845 ***		
C_GHG_E	.3119 ***	.5192 ***	.2868 ***		
TAR_E				.1246	.0708
RDD_E				.7769 ***	.5743 ***
QUO_E				.1182	-.3742 **
REC_E				-.0585	.0516
FIT_E				.3687 ***	.2743 ***
NET_E				.0906	.2084 *
TEN_E				.1562 *	.0565
TXC_E				.2000 **	.1102
TXR_E				.0488	-.0662
PUB_E				.4036 ***	.3653 ***
GHG_E				.4395 ***	.2198 **
CONSTANT	-1.772 ***	-2.210 ***	-1.925 ***	-2.190 ***	-1.878 ***
Obs.	2,562	1,999	2,312	1,999	2,312
Groups	122	97	112	97	112
Group size, min.	21	6	6	6	6
Group size, avg.	21	20.61	20.64	20.61	20.64
Group size, max.	21	21	21	21	21
Wald Chi²	2,253 ***	1,895 ***	1,667 ***	1,978 ***	1,840 ***

Notes: Results are estimated using fixed effects negative binomial panel regression with observations grouped by country. *, **, and *** indicate statistical significance at 10%, 5%, and 1% level respectively. | (1) The ... in variables RES_... and DKS_SC_... are placeholders for the suffixes SW (solar and wind energy data), S (solar energy data) and W (wind energy data). (2) Due to convergence problems in maximum likelihood estimation, the more detailed specification using InstruEx indicators cannot be applied if SC_SW is the dependent variable.

Table 19 – Results of regulation-innovation regressions
Source: Own illustration.

The first thing which stands out from the results presented in Table 19 is that the coefficient estimates for the knowledge stocks (DKS_SC_...), domestic total patents (DTOPAT), and global capacity changes (ITOCAPA_YOY) are generally positive and statically highly significant as predicted by theory and demonstrated empirically in previous studies. Moreover, the results show that renewable energy technologies' responsiveness to knowledge stocks (DKS_SC_...) is more pronounced in technology-specific than in aggregated regression models. This finding supports the notion that knowledge spillovers are strong within narrow groups of renewable energy technologies but rather limited between them (Braun et al., 2010), i.e. wind turbine manufacturers benefit more from the existing knowledge in wind than in solar power technologies.

The estimates for total domestic patents (DTOPAT) suggest that the wind turbine industry follows trends in domestic patenting behavior more strongly than the solar panel industry which is less responsive to changes in the propensity to patent. While the reasons for these technology-wise differences are not perfectly clear, their statistical significance suggests that controlling for this effect is important.

Lastly, the coefficient estimates for yearly changes in the global electricity generation capacity (ITOCAPA_YOY) are similar in the aggregated and technology-specific models. This indicates that general changes in business opportunities for the energy equipment industry affect the solar and wind power sectors to a similar extend.

Having discussed the non-regulatory drivers, I proceed with the estimation results on the environmental regulation indicators, which are the key variables in this analysis. To start with the results on the aggregated level, the coefficient estimates for Equation (4.6) suggest that regulation intensity (RES_SW) has a significantly positive impact on the number of patent applications on wind and solar power technologies. However, this effect is quite small in absolute terms. An increase in solar and wind's share in electricity generation by 1 unit (%-point), what is a lot, is estimated to cause a 4.4% ($=e^{0.0433}-1$) increase in annual patent applications.

The results for the policy design indicators show a similar picture and confirm the initial finding that renewable energy support policies have a positive impact on patenting activity. The coefficients for all but one policy cluster are positive and mostly statistically significant at the 1% level. The estimated values suggest that public RD&D programs (C_RDD_E) are the policy cluster with the strongest positive impact on innovation in wind and solar power. Their existence increases patent output by 88% ($=e^{0.6338}-1$).

In addition to RD&D programs (C_RDD_E), the existence of measures from the fiscal incentives (C_FIS_E) and the greenhouse gas trading system cluster (C_GHG_E) are also found to have a strong, positive impact on renewable energy innovation. A reason for the importance of measures from these clusters might be that their underlying mechanisms are very concrete and therefore reduce innovators' business risk. Fiscal incentives do often include subsidies or government purchase programs which have an immediate effect on their beneficiaries. Similarly, the adoption of far-reaching and complex measures like greenhouse gas trading systems signals that governments are highly committed to climate protection and for this reason create long-term business opportunities, which help industry to justify their R&D investments.

So far I have focused in my discussion on the results of Equation (4.6), which explores innovation inducement on an aggregated level. The next step in the discussion is the evaluation of regression models (4.7) to (4.10), which analyze the innovation data on the more detailed technology level. The technology-specific models differ from the aggregate one in two points. First, the dependent variables (SC_S and SC_W) and the corresponding knowledge stocks (DKS_SC_S and DKS_SC_W) have been adjusted to only count the number of annual patent applications on solar *or* wind energy technology by domestic applicants filed with national or international patent authorities. Second, as the estimation process does no longer suffer from convergence issues[81], the technology-specific models are not restricted to the cluster level but can control for the effect of renewable energy support policies on the level of individual policy instruments.

Starting with the solar models, the results of the policy cluster regression (4.7) correspond well to the respective full sample results (4.6). The regulation intensity measures and all policy cluster indicators, except for C_TAR_E and C_QUO_E, carry a positive sign and are highly significant. The sizes of the coefficient values are similar as well.

Against the background of the convergence issues during full sample estimation, the results of Equations (4.9) are of special interest as they show the effect of different renewable energy support policies at a greater level of detail. Based on the aggregated data, it was so far not possible to explore which policy instruments are responsible for the relatively strong innovation inducement effect of the feed-in tariff (C_FIT_E) and the fiscal incentive cluster (C_FIS_E).

Within the feed-in tariff cluster, it are classical fixed and premium rate tariffs (FIT_E) that drive innovation while the more advanced instruments, net metering (NET_E) and tendering (TEN_E), are found to be less innovation inducing. This is surprising as a main objective of

[81] Due to convergence problems in maximum likelihood estimation, the more detailed specification using InstruEx indicators could not be applied when SC_SW was the dependent variable.

these advanced instruments is to impose competitive pressure on equipment producers in order to bring down LCOE.

Within the fiscal incentives cluster, innovation is mainly driven by tax credits (TXC_E) and immediate government interventions like public spending, subsidies, and low cost loans (PUB_E). All these measures have in common that manufacturers of renewable energy equipment can more or less reliably assess the business implications of these measures. Once granted, they ensure at least a certain market success or immediate compensation by the government. Tax reductions (TXR_E) are rather indirect and subject to frequent changes and therefore have a lesser effect on innovation than other measures from this cluster.

Overall, the regression results based on the solar energy data, (4.7) and (4.9), point in the same direction as those based on the full sample (4.6). Yet, it is evident that the technology-specific explanatory variables tend to carry larger coefficient values than the technology-neutral ones. The rank order of policy clusters, however, is again completely identical; research, development, and demonstration programs (C_RDD_E) have the strongest innovation inducement effect of all policy clusters. They are followed by fiscal incentives (C_FIS_E) and greenhouse gas trading systems (C_GHG_E), and already with considerable distance feed-in tariffs (C_FIT_E). The lack of significance of the quotas clusters (C_QUO_E) and the corresponding policy instruments (QUO_E, REC_E) suggests that these measures do not foster innovation in solar energy equipment. One reason for their lack of impact might be that, on the one hand, technology-specific quotas provide little incentive to innovate and, on the other hand, that renewable energy certificates favor more established and therefore price competitive technologies like hydro, biomass, and geothermal.

Turning to the wind energy models, the comparison of technology-specific results, (4.8) and (4.10), to the technology-neutral ones (4.6) yields the same pattern which already became apparent in the analyses of the combined as well as the solar energy sample. RD&D programs (C_RDD_E) provide the strongest incentive to innovate followed by fiscal incentives (C_FIS_E) and greenhouse gas trading (C_GHG_E). On the other hand, the innovation inducements effects of quotas (C_QUO_E) and renewable energy targets (C_TAR_E) are not significant.

Interestingly, a comparison of the estimation results between the solar- and wind-specific analyses shows, first, quite similar patterns in terms of sign, proportional size, and significance levels of the explanatory variables, but also second, the tendency towards larger coefficient values in the solar-specific regressions. The latter effect can be explained by the overall higher number of solar energy patents, which is more than 50% higher than the corresponding number of wind energy patents[82]. Hence, one should be careful to draw premature inferences on the technology-specific effectiveness of policy measures based on coefficient values alone. Overall, the results of the technology-specific models do rather not support the finding of Johnstone et al. (2008) and others that the innovation inducement capacity of renewable energy support policies differs between types of technology.

In order to test the validity of the regression results reported above, I have conducted three sets of robustness tests. The first test is a comparison of results for alternative geographic scopes, which is presented in Appendix 24. The analysis yields consistent estimates for samples including all countries, OECD countries (as done in most studies, e.g. Johnstone et al., 2008), and G20 countries. Irrespective of the general consistency of these results, there are subtle differences in the importance of certain determinants for the overall innovation inducement effect. In OECD countries, the importance of the existing knowledge stock is of particular importance for overall innovation inducement while in G20 countries it is rather regulation intensity, i.e. renewable energy shares. The reasons for these dissimilarities do not become perfectly clear from the data. However, I hypothesize that differences in the type of innovation cause this effect. OECD countries, on the one hand, might be more concerned with developments at the technological forefront, which are largely dependent on access to previous knowledge. G20 countries, on the other hand, which also include many developing economies, might on average concentrate more on application-related innovation, which is driven by the practical know-how from a large installed base.

The second robustness test takes up the issue of alternative approaches to patent counting. As discussed previously, simple counts fit my data best and have therefore been selected as the preferred counting approach. Family counts, in contrast, are preferable based on theory for their reduced tendency to be biased. Hence, in the second robustness test, presented in Appendix 22, I rerun the main regressions of this chapter using family counts as dependent variables and as input factor to calculate the corresponding knowledge stocks. The results of this robustness test show that using simple counts instead of the theoretically preferable family counts did not change the results.

[82] See Table 18 (page 130) for further details.

The third and last robustness test applies an idea developed in Chapter 3. It was argued that the inclusion of policy indicators on the existence of RD&D programs might lead to spurious results as the data underlying this variable are only available for the members of the OCED and some other countries. Moreover, it was argued that especially in their early phases some of the existing greenhouse gas trading systems did not cover emissions from power plants and therefore should not be considered as renewable energy support policy. In order to test whether these issues related to the C_RDD_E and C_GHG_E variables affected regression results, the third robustness test reruns model (4.6), the main regression model of this chapter, without either or both of these variables. The results presented in Appendix 25 suggest that the inclusion of these variables did not affect regression results negatively.

One remark on policy duration effects: In contrast to Chapter 3, this chapter does not go beyond policy existence. From the regression output presented in Appendix 23, it becomes clear that the policy duration indicators, which reflect past and present policy status, are not compatible with this chapter's dependent variables which reflect only present patenting behavior. Hence, the estimated impact of those policy instruments with the longest history, RE targets, RD&D programs, and feed-in tariffs, becomes very large and suppresses the effects of the remaining variables, including the non-regulation variables[83].

The final step in this discussion is to compare the results of the regression models presented throughout this section with the results of previous studies on induced innovation in renewable energy technologies. Table 20 provides a structured overview and compares results in areas where this and earlier studies overlap.

Before I enter into the discussion of the data presented in Table 20, it needs to be stated that the studies analyzed in this overview do not necessarily have the very same research focus and might define policy categories differently. Moreover, the studies differ in their definitions of wind and solar power patents as well as the geographic and temporal scope of their samples. Hence, all similarities and differences discussed below are indicative and should be interpreted accordingly.

83 An alternative to replace the policy existence indicators by policy duration indicators is to take a look at the policy intensity indicators. The results presented in Table 15 (page 107) show a strong deterministic relationship between the complete set of policy duration indicators and regulation intensity. Therefore, the coefficient value of the intensity indicator (RES_...) gives a rough indication of the role of policy duration.

Policy variable	Results of other studies							Result of this study	
	Johnstone et al. (2008)	Braun et al. (2010)	Walz et al. (2011)	Peters et al. (2012)	Böhringer et al. (2014)	Nesta et al. (2014)	Fraction of studies with significantly positive effect		
(a) Regulation intensity on innovation									
RES_S				+			1 / 1	(+)	✓
RES_W			+				1 / 1	+	✓
RES_SW					+		1 / 1	+	✓
(b) Regulation design on solar energy innovation									
TAR								/	
RDD	/	+		+			2 / 3	+	✓
QUO	/	/					0 / 2	/	✓
REC	/	/					0 / 2	/	✓
FIT	/	/			/		0 / 3	+	×
C_FIS	+						1 / 1	+	✓
(c) Regulation design on wind energy innovation									
TAR			+				1 / 1	/	×
RDD	+	(+)	+				2.5 / 3	+	✓
QUO	+	/					1 / 2	-	×
REC	+	(+)					1.5 / 2	/	×
FIT	/	/	/		+		1 / 4	+	(✓)
C_FIS	+		+				2 / 2	+	✓
(d) Regulation design on innovation in all renewable energy technologies									
TAR								+	
RDD	+				+	/	2 / 3	+	✓
QUO	+						1 / 1	1)	
REC	+						1 / 1	1)	
FIT	/				/		0 / 2	1)	
C_FIS	+						1 / 1	+	✓

Notes: (+) and + indicate (partially) significant, positive coefficient values. (-) and - indicate (partially) significant, negative coefficient values. Partially significant results are counted as 0.5. / indicates insignificant coefficient values. ✓, (✓), and × indicate that results between of this and related studies are often, sometimes, or not consistent. Empty cells represent missing values. | (1) Results are not available due to convergence issues in the estimation process.

Table 20 – Result comparison for reg.-innovation regressions
Source: Own illustration.

This research project agrees with previous studies that more intensive regulation as measured in terms of renewable energy shares in electricity generation has a positive impact on patent applications in this field of technology. Moreover, the results of this study confirm the finding of multiple existing studies that research, development, and demonstration programs (RDD) and fiscal incentives (C_FIS) have a strong positive impact on patenting activity.

However, there are also two areas of dissent. First of all, in contrast to Johnstone et al. (2008) and Braun et al. (2010), I do not find a positive impact of renewable energy certificates (REC) on wind energy patents. Similarly, while Johnstone et al. (2008) find that quotas (QUO) foster innovation in wind energy, my results indicate exactly the opposite. Against the background that I have already encountered multiple puzzling issues related to effect of quotas and renewable energy certificates, there is growing evidence that the data on these instruments suffer either from misspecification or unobserved heterogeneity. The analysis of Section 3.3.3 suggests that the latter is more likely.

The second area of dissent is the effectiveness of feed-in tariffs (FIT). While none of the existing studies except for Böhringer et al. (2014) finds a positive effect of feed-in tariffs on innovation in either wind or solar energy, I do find statistically significant effects in both technologies. As a major regulatory instrument, data on the existence of feed-in tariffs are assumed to be among the most reliable. Hence, I would discount the possibility that erroneous policy data cause the difference between this and previous studies. Given that this dissent is more pronounced in solar power, I assume that the reason lies rather in the different patent identification approach than in the policy data. As repeatedly mentioned, a major advancement of this study is the application of the Y02E patent classification system which is assumed more reliable than the conventional IPC system used in all other studies reviewed in Table 20.

Overall, it can be stated that the results presented throughout this section show that the predicted effects are robust to moderate changes in specification, variable definitions, and sample compositions, and fit well with previous empirical research.

4.5 Conclusion

The analysis presented in this chapter fulfills its goal to generate new insights on the relationship between different types and intensities of environmental regulation and innovation in renewable energy technologies.

The key finding with respect to the regulation intensity dimension is that more intense renewable energy support polices induce more innovation. This result holds for aggregated as well as for technology-specific analyses.

The key finding on the regulation design dimension is that renewable energy support policies vary strongly in their ability to induce technical innovation in wind and solar power. The policy instruments with the strongest innovation inducement effect are public RD&D programs, greenhouse gas trading systems, and fiscal incentives. The strong effect of greenhouse gas trading is particularly interesting, because this policy instrument is very much in line with the notion of well-crafted environmental regulation propagated by Porter & van der Linde (1995). Hence, the innovation enhancing effect of greenhouse gas trading systems can certainly be interpreted as supportive evidence for the narrowly strong Porter Hypothesis.

While the above-mentioned results fit well with existing studies, there is also an area of dissent. In contrast to previous studies, I do not find convincing evidence for the notion that the effectiveness of renewable energy support policies varies considerably between different types of technologies. The minor differences in coefficient values and significance levels, which my regressions reveal, could likewise be artefacts of a change in the dependent variable between the aggregated and the technology-specific models.

The most significant advancement of this thesis compared to previous empirical work on regulation-induced renewable energy innovation, however, lies in the data. The comprehensiveness of the regulation data covering 225 countries over a time period ranging from 1990 to 2011 and distinguishing eleven classes of policy instruments is unprecedented in this research area. Moreover, this analysis is first to apply the novel Y02E system to identify renewable energy patents[84]. Therefore, it is reasonable to assume that the quality of patent data exceeds that of previous studies as well.

Regardless the indisputable progress in capturing differences in regulation design, data accuracy remains the main limiting factor of the results presented in this chapter. Although the taxonomy of renewable energy support policies is certainly more detailed and more comprehensive than those of previous studies, it remains a simplification of reality. Hence, no two randomly selected instruments from any of my

[84] Calel & Dechezleprêtre (2012) is a good example for the successful application of the Y02E system on CCMT innovation in general.

eleven policy categories will ever be perfectly identical. Therefore, the policy indicators used in this analysis are subject to a classical heterogeneity problem[85].

In addition to its contributions to the general literature on regulation-induced innovation in renewable energy equipment, this chapter offers two important learnings for the upcoming analysis of the strong part of the narrowly strong Porter Hypothesis. First, the close relationship between environmental regulation and patent applications on solar and wind power technologies makes knowledge stocks an ideal long-term measure of induced innovation for the following induced-innovation-competitiveness regressions. Second, the leading countries in terms of renewable energy innovation do not necessarily develop expertise in all generation technologies. Although technology-wise regression did not reveal the source of these differences, the descriptive statistics show that specialization by technologies certainly exists and is partially very pronounced. Hence, the approach to estimate individual models for solar and wind energy technologies should be applied in the next chapter as well.

85 For more details on the heterogeneity problem, which is prevalent in the regulation data, refer to the concluding discussion of Section 3.3.3.

5 Environmental regulation and renewable energy exports

The general research approach of this thesis is to decompose the narrowly strong Porter Hypothesis in its two main components, which I named the *weak* and the *strong* part, and to analyze them separately in order to better understand each part's underlying mechanism. While the weak part of the narrowly strong Porter Hypothesis was covered in the previous chapter, this chapter concentrates on the strong, or second, part.

The data presented in the introduction (Chapter 0) suggest the assumption that there is a close connection between tightening environmental policies, revolutionary technological advancements, and export success in renewable energy equipment. The existence of such a relationship would imply that renewable energy support policies have two effects: environmental conservation and industrial promotion. Both of which are certainly appealing for policy makers.

The objective of this chapter is to explore this apparent relationship systematically and, hereby, to contribute to research on the narrowly strong Porter Hypothesis. In doing so, I pay careful attention to the results and lessons learned from previous chapters as well as from the existing literature in this field.

In addition, this chapter takes up an idea from lead market theory and asks if countries which adopted environmental regulation early on experience stronger competitiveness effects than their followers. This supplementary analysis will help to answer the question of how sustainable competitive advantages in renewable energy equipment are if they build on domestic support policies.

The structure of the remainder of this chapter resembles that of Chapter 4. Section 5.1 reviews the empirical literature on the narrowly strong Porter Hypothesis with an emphasis on the econometric strategies[86]. Section 5.2 develops the research model and discusses its key variables including their corresponding data sources. Section 5.3 presents and discusses the estimation results. Section 5.4 concludes.

---

86 The results of the related empirical research on the narrowly strong Porter Hypothesis are thoroughly discussed in Section 2.2.4.

5.1 Empirical research on regulation-induced RE exports

In this section, I review the empirical literature on the impact of environmental regulation on countries' export performance in renewable energy equipment. The discussion starts with a recap of key results from the literature review (Chapter 2) which is presented in Section 5.1.1. The purpose of this section, however, is certainly not to restate findings which have already been presented elsewhere in the dissertation but to go beyond what has been done before. For this reason, Section 5.1.2 concentrates on the analysis and evaluation of the research methods which have been applied in studies closely related to this thesis. Hereby, I am equally interested in their modelling approaches, variable definitions, as well as their estimation techniques.

5.1.1 Empirical results and scope of analysis

Out of the eight publications on the narrowly strong Porter Hypothesis which were discussed in the dedicated section of the literature review (2.2.4) four publications have a similar research focus as this thesis: Costantini & Crespi (2008), Costantini & Mazzanti (2012), Cao & Groba (2013), and Groba (2014). Each of these four studies is concerned with the impact of regulation and regulation-induced innovation on the international competitiveness of countries' environmental goods and services sector. Thus, these studies will be most insightful for my review of empirical results and econometric methods.

The remaining four studies on the narrowly strong Porter Hypothesis are not covered for the following reasons: Shrivastava (1995) conducts a case study analysis on a single company and hence is expected to provide limited insights for econometric research in the renewable energy sector. Although Jha (2009) conducts research in this very field, this study is excluded for its too simplistic research approach, a cross-sectional analysis based on a plain linear regression model. Finally, the two studies by Sung & Song (2013, 2014) are not covered here, because they rather focus on multilateral causality between exports, R&D expenditures, and electricity generation from renewables. Yet, the research focus of my thesis is not on the general causal chain but the impact of certain polices.

The group of studies on the effect of environmental regulation in the renewable energy industry and the green sector[87] unanimously finds that increases in policy intensity foster innovation and export in these product groups. Although the contribution of these studies to research on the

[87] Costantini & Crespi (2008), Costantini & Mazzanti (2012), Cao & Groba (2013), and Groba (2014).

narrowly strong Porter Hypothesis in general is undisputed, the discussion of Section 2.4 showed that the significance of their results for the specific situation in the renewable energy sector is partly unclear due to limitations with respect to their respective data samples.

Out of these four studies, Cao & Groba (2014) is the only one which concentrates exclusively on effects in the solar and wind power industry. All other studies define the scope more broadly. While Groba (2013), for instance, includes solar thermal technologies in his sample, Costantini & Crespi's (2008) study covers technologies like hydro power, geothermal, or biomass, too. The problem is that all before-mentioned technologies are already very mature and therefore often do not enjoy the benefits from renewable energy support policies. Two studies extend the technology scope even beyond renewable energies and also include technologies to increase energy efficiency (Costantini & Crespi, 2008) or, in the most extreme case, the entire green sector (Costantini & Mazzanti, 2012). Obviously, the broader the scope is the less significant the results are for specific industries.

With respect to geographic coverage, Section 2.4 stressed that the before-mentioned studies mostly restrict their analyses to mature economies like the EU or OECD countries. The only exception to this pattern is Cao & Groba (2013) which focusses on trade flows from and into China. The data presented in Section 1.3 show[88] that both scope definitions are problematic as developed and developing countries from all regions are very active traders in renewable energy equipment and, hence, should likewise be included in the analysis.

Finally, the discussion showed that all four studies use quite dated samples from today's perspective. The most recent sample ends in 2008 and is therefore already seven years old – a long period of time for an industry which develops as fast as renewable energy equipment[89].

In summary, studies on the narrowly strong Porter Hypothesis found that more and more intense environmental regulation fosters innovation and competitiveness. The significance of these existing results for the renewable energy equipment sector specifically is not very clear, though. The tendency to define the research scope rather broadly and to concentrate on the most advanced industrial countries puts the applicability of their general results on this particular sector into question.

[88] For a preliminary analysis of the export and import patterns in the renewable energy industry, refer to Table 1 (page 11) and Table 2 (page 14).

[89] For the strong growth which the market for renewable energy equipment experienced over the last years, refer to Figure 1 (page 4).

In order to validate the previous findings for the global renewable energy industry, I restrict the analysis of this chapter to solar and wind power, the core technologies in this field. Moreover, I make sure to include all meaningful ex- and importers regardless of their level of economic development and to use the most recent data available to account for the fast-paced change of this industry.

5.1.2 Econometric models and estimation approaches

Leaving aside differences in the research scopes, the empirical strategies of the four studies discussed above are very similar in many respects. In order to derive implications for my own research, this section thoroughly analyzes the key elements of these studies' econometric approaches: overall economic model, detailed model specification, and estimation approach. Table 21 summarizes the results of this evaluation.

With respect to my first dimension of analysis, the overall economic model, consensus between the four studies is highest. All four publications build their empirical work on the gravity model of trade, which was first developed by Tinbergen (1962). The gravity model of trade enjoys great appeal in research on international trade because it is comparably easy to implement, generally fits the data very well, and can be applied in multi-country contexts. In contrast, most other trade models have been developed for a two or sometimes three country world (Anderson, 2010). The basic idea is that bilateral trade flows between two countries are a function of the respective economies' sizes and the ease of conducting trade between them[90]. Hereby, determinants of the ease of trade commonly include geographic distance, cultural similarities, as well as tariffs and non-tariff barriers (e.g. Baldwin & Taglioni, 2006). Due to its indisputable advantages, I follow the example of my predecessors and also apply the gravity model of trade to empirically test the narrowly strong Porter Hypothesis.

The second dimension of my analysis is the model specification. The design of the gravity equation allows researchers to add additional unilateral or bilateral variables to analyze the determinants of trade at greater levels of detail. This feature was also used extensively in the four studies under consideration[91]. The sets of variables usually added in excess of the structural variables of the gravity model include measures of regulation intensity and design, innovation, and other controls.

---

[90] A detailed introduction to the gravity model of trade including its theoretical foundations and theory-conform specification follows in Section 5.2.1.

[91] Costantini & Crespi (2008), Costantini & Mazzanti (2012), Cao & Groba (2013), and Groba (2014).

Concerning the question of which measures of environmental regulation to include, there is less agreement than there was for the decision on the general economic model. The spectrum of regulation intensity indicators ranges from the level of CO_2 emissions, over pollution abatement and control expenditures, to taxes and composite indices. The share of renewables in total domestic electricity generation, which is the preferable measure of regulation intensity in research on the solar and wind power industry[92], is only used in the studies by Cao & Groba (2013) and Groba (2014). With respect to the second dimension of environmental regulation, regulation design, Cao & Groba (2013) and Groba (2014) are again the only studies which take this aspect into account. Costantini & Crespi (2008) and Costantini & Mazzanti (2012), in contrast, just control for regulation intensity.

Innovation indicators are the second major block of explanatory variables. As discussed in the previous chapter on the regulation-innovation relationship, there are two main options to measure innovation. The first approach is input-based and measures R&D expenditures. The second approach is output-based and measures patent applications. In both cases, indicator quality increases in measurement accuracy, i.e. the more granular the expenditure and patent data are the more reliable is the innovation indicator. All publications ensure that the scopes of their innovation measures are well-aligned with their explanatory variables. Interestingly, Cao & Groba (2013) is the only study which measures innovation as knowledge stock. This finding is surprising as knowledge stocks, which capture innovation over multiple years, are clearly superior to current patent applications when it comes to assessing the competitiveness impact of innovation. As the value of new patents needs time to unfold and then stays high for multiple years, controlling for current patent applications alone probably underestimates the competitiveness-enhancing effect of innovation.

In addition to the indicators of environmental regulation and innovation activity which have been applied consistently in each of the studies reviewed, further control variables have been used on an individual basis. Among these additional control variables are measures like the rule of law in importing countries, as indicator of the attractiveness as an export destination (Costantini & Crespi, 2008), or changes in GDP, as an indicator of business cycle effects (Cao & Groba, 2013).

---

92 For the discussion on the preferable measure of regulation intensity in this research area, refer to Section 3.2.3.

Study	Structural variables of gravity model	Reg. intensity indicators	Reg. design indicators	Innovation indicators	Other	Fixed effects	Estimation approach
Costantini & Crespi (2008)	Trade: > Bilateral exports Mass: > GDP (Ex-/Importer) > Pop. (Ex-/Importer) Dist.: > Geo. distance > Colonial ties > Contiguity > Land area	> CO_2 emissions > Public and private PACE > Env. taxes > Public investment in env. protection	> n/a	> Total patents > Env. patents > Total R&D	> FDI > Rule of law	> Exporter (time fixed)	> OLS > GLS > IV
Costantini & Mazzanti (2012)	Trade: > Bilateral exports Mass: > GDP, value (pair) > GDP, similarity (pair) Dist.: > Geo. distance > Euro zone	> Public and private PACE > Env. taxes > Energy taxes > Eco mgmt. and audit schemes	> n/a	> Total patents > Env. patents > Total R&D > Env. R&D	> ETS intro.	> Exporter (time var.) > Importer (time var.) > Ctry. pair (time var.)	2-stage approach: (1st) Probit (2nd) GMM
Cao & Groba (2013)	Trade: > Bilateral exports Mass: > GDP (importer) Dist.: > Geo. distance > Land area > Import tariffs	> Solar power share	Policy existence: > Tax measures > Obligations > Incentive tariffs	> Knowledge stocks on solar power > Solar power R&D exp.	> Delta GDP	> Importer (time fixed) > Ctry. pair (time var.)	> OLS > PPML > NBREG
Groba (2014)	Trade: > Bilateral exports Mass: > GDP, value (pair) > GDP, similarity (pair) Dist.: > Geo. distance > Contiguity > Language > EU > Import tariffs	> Solar power share > Reg. intensity index	Policy existence/ policy duration: > Tax measures > Obligations > Incentive tariffs	> Solar power R&D exp.	> n/a	> Exporter (time fixed) > Importer (time fixed) > Time	> PPML

Table 21 – Methodology of related reg.-competitiveness studies[93]
Source: Own illustration.

93 This overview contains fewer studies than Table 6 (page 52) in the literature review. Shrivastava (1995), Jha (2009), and Sung & Song (2013, 2014) are excluded as they use qualitative methods, too simplistic estimation strategies, or have a different focus.

With regard to my third dimension of analysis, the estimation approach, the differences between the four studies are most pronounced. While all studies include fixed effects in order to control for unobserved heterogeneity in the data, there is absolutely no consensus on which type of fixed effects to apply. The range of fixed effects used in the literature includes importer and exporter effects, pair-wise effects, and time effects. On top of this, importer- and exporter-fixed effects are likewise modeled as time-fixed and time-varying.

The level of dissimilarity is equally high when it comes to the estimation approach. The spectrum of techniques includes linear models such as OLS, GLS, and IV, discrete choice models such as Poisson and negative binomial models, as well as mixed approaches. Costantini & Crespi (2008) and Cao & Groba (2013) use multiple methods in parallel in order to demonstrate the robustness of their results.

All in all, the methodological review of the four publications which are closest to my own research question suggests that the gravity model of trade is the clearly preferred economic model to conduct empirical research on the narrowly strong Porter Hypothesis. With respect to the detailed model specification and estimation approach, the implications from the existing research are ambiguous. The sets of variables and fixed effects included as well as the estimation techniques are just too diverse to provide meaningful guidance for this chapter's econometric strategy. Therefore, these dimensions require special emphasis in the development of the research model, carried out in the next section.

5.2 Research model

The objective of this section is to develop an econometric approach to conduct meaningful empirical research on the impact of environmental regulation on countries' international competitiveness in renewable energy equipment. Following the existing literature, I build my model on the gravity model of trade. However, one of the key implications from the previous section is that, while the gravity model appears to be the dominant approach, there is no commonly accepted way of applying it.

Hence, the first step in the research model development process, presented in Section 5.2.1, is concerned with the history of the gravity model, its foundations in economic theory, and the latest insights on its theory-consistent implementation. Starting from the correctly-specified raw version of the gravity equation, Section 5.2.2 prepares the model for research on the determinants of trade in renewable energy products. Section 0 introduces the data on trade flows in solar and wind power equipment, which are essential for the analyses of this chapter, and conducts first descriptive analyses on the corresponding data sample.

5.2.1 Trade flow estimation using the gravity equation

The gravity equation is one of economists' standard tools to model multinational trade flows. Its first applications in empirical research date back to Tinbergen (1962) and Pöyhönen (1963). The gravity model of economics owes its rather odd name to its resemblance to Isaac Newton's (physical) law of gravitation. The similarities are most obvious if the gravity model of economics is written in its original, multiplicative form, as shown in Equation (5.1) (Deardorff, 1998).

$$X_{i,j,t} = G\frac{Y_{i,t}^{\beta_1}Y_{j,t}^{\beta_2}}{d_{i,j,t}^{\beta_3}}\eta_{i,j,t} \qquad (5.1)$$

The X in Equation (5.1) stands for the flow of goods from exporting country i to importing country j at time t. G is a constant term of proportionality[94]. The Ys are the sizes of the exporting and importing countries' economies or, to stay in in the analogy of the law of gravitation, their economic masses. d stands for the geographic distance between the two countries. η is an error term (Tinbergen, 1962).

A handy feature of the gravity model of economics is that its functional form can be changed from multiplicative to linear by logarithmic transformation. In its log-log formulation, Equation (5.2), the gravity model can be easily estimated using standard econometric techniques such as OLS. This straight-forward formulation is one reason why the gravity equation has become one of the most popular models for empirical studies in international economics as well as in multinational studies of environmental economics (e.g. Beers & Bergh, 1997; Harris et al., 2002; Jug & Mirza, 2005). The second reason is its generally very good statistical fit with the data (Head & Meyer, 2014).

$$\ln X_{i,j,t} = \alpha + \beta_1 \ln Y_{i,t} + \beta_2 \ln Y_{j,t} - \beta_3 \ln d_{i,j,t} + \varepsilon_{i,j,t} \qquad (5.2)$$

$$where\ \alpha = \ln G\ and\ \varepsilon_{i,j,t} = \ln \eta_{i,j,t}$$

[94] The alternative label, gravitational constant, which also appears in the literature, is somehow misleading because it implies that G is the same across all gravity equations. However, unlike the g (9.81 m/s²) from the law of gravitation, this is certainly not the case for the G included in the economic gravity model, which depends amongst other factors on the remaining variables' unit of measurement.

However, many economists have long handled empirical results derived from gravity models with great skepticism – mainly because of the initially missing theoretical foundations. The gravity model was seen as black box which admittedly generated many useful results but remained somehow dubious for its unclear features (Deardorff, 1984).

This view started to change in the late 1970s and 1980s. Anderson (1979) was first to demonstrate that the gravity model is indeed founded on established trade theories. He shows that the standard gravity equation can be derived from a constant elasticity of substitution (CES) model in which goods are differentiated by their country of origin (Armington assumption). Similarly, Bergstrand (1985) derives the gravity equation from a general equilibrium world trade model where international goods are closer substitutes to each other than to domestic goods. In another influential publication, Bergstrand (1989) establishes a connection between the neoclassical Heckscher-Ohlin (H-O) model for inter-industry trade, the increasing return to scale (IRS) model of Helpman-Krugman-Markusen for intra-industry-trade, and the gravity model (Deardorff, 1998).

Regardless its substantiating theoretical foundations, it needed another decade until the gravity equation was widely accepted as an important, theory-consistent empirical instrument to explain and also predict international trade flows (Deardorff, 1998; Evenett & Keller, 2002; Head & Meyer, 2014).

Following the creation of a sound theoretical foundation, researchers' attention shifted towards the development of estimation techniques which are consistent with the theoretically correct formulation of the gravity model. Triggered by the continued appearance of counter-intuitive results from gravity-based research models[95], Anderson & van Wincoop's (2003) paper is certainly among the most influential contributions in this field. The authors show that the log-log formulation, which was still widely applied in empirical studies at that time, is not compatible with the CES-based equation developed by Anderson (1979) and therefore leads to biased estimates (Anderson, 2010).

In their seminal contribution, Anderson & van Wincoop (2003) stress the importance of including what they call multilateral resistance terms (MRT) to ensure consistency with the CES-based gravity model of

[95] The so-called McCallum boarder puzzle on trade patterns between the US and Canada (McCallum, 1995) is a prominent example of such anomalies.

Anderson (1979). They argue that trade flows between pairs of countries do not simply depend on the absolute sizes of these countries' bilateral trade barriers[96] but rather on the sizes of their bilateral trade barriers relative to the sizes of their average barriers to all trade partners. In short, the inclusion of MRTs ensures that the model controls for the effect from changes in countries' bilateral and multilateral trade barriers.

Equation (5.3) states the Anderson & van Wincoop (2003) version of the gravity model, which is also called structural model (e.g. Anderson, 2010). As in the equations stated above, X is the trade flow from i to j at time t, α is a constant term, and the Ys are ex- and importing countries' economic masses. t is a vector of all factors which impact the ease of trade between pairs of countries including but not limited to geographic distance. The respective coefficient (β_3) depends on the elasticity of substitution between domestic and international goods (σ). Π and P are the MRTs of the exporting and importing country. ε is another error term.

$$\ln X_{i,j,t} = \alpha + \beta_1 \ln Y_{i,t} + \beta_2 \ln Y_{j,t} + \beta_3 \ln t_{i,j,t} + \beta_4 \ln \Pi_{i,t} + \beta_5 \ln \mathrm{P}_{j,t} + \varepsilon_{i,j,t} \quad (5.3)$$

$$where\ \beta_3 = 1 - \sigma, with\ \sigma > 1$$

Despite their consistency with theory, MRTs are rarely used in practice because they are unobservable and, in addition, notoriously difficult to estimate (Head & Meyer, 2014). Most empirical research employs an alternative approach and accounts for multilateral resistance using exporter- and importer-fixed effects. An approach with is in line with MRTs, at least for cross-sectional data (Feenstra, 2002; Fally, 2015).

However, as Baldwin & Taglioni (2006) point out[97], the inclusion of simple time-fixed country effects is not sufficient in econometric analyses using panel data. They show that there is a better option which ensures that the model is consistent with theory and at the same time does without the complicated MRTs.

The specification proposed by Baldwin & Taglioni (2006) is presented below as Equation (5.4). Besides the variables introduced earlier, the equation contains three fixed effects: a time-varying exporter effect ($\gamma_{i,t}$), a time-varying importer effect ($\gamma_{j,t}$), and a time-invariant pair effect ($\gamma_{i,j}$). While this approach works perfectly if the research interest is on time-varying bilateral variables like regional trade agreements, the time-

96 Arguing based on barriers to trade or on ease of trade leads to the same results. The two approaches only differ in their points of view.

97 See also Egger & Pfaffermayr (2003) for the correct specification of fixed effects in gravity models for panel data.

varying country effects make it impossible to study the role of country-specific variables, even if they are time-varying[98]. Hence, this approach is not suitable for studies on the narrowly strong Porter Hypothesis, where country-specific policy and innovation indicators are what researchers are most interested it.

$$\ln X_{i,j,t} = \alpha + \beta_1 \ln t_{i,j,t} + \gamma_{i,t} + \gamma_{j,t} + \gamma_{i,j} + \varepsilon_{i,j,t} \quad (5.4)$$

As the first best approach is not available, I apply the second best option and replace the time-varying exporter and importer effects ($\gamma_{i,t}$ and $\gamma_{j,t}$) by their time-fixed equivalents (γ_i and γ_j) and add a time dummy (γ_t) (Egger & Pfaffermayr, 2003). While this approach is not perfectly in line with Anderson & van Wincoop (2003), Equation (5.5) allows me to estimate the impact of country-specific, time-varying indicators, which is not possible based on Equation (5.4). Hence, the final specification of the raw version of my gravity model is given in Equation (5.5).

$$\ln X_{i,j,t} = \alpha + \beta_1 \ln Y_{i,t} + \beta_2 \ln Y_{j,t} + \beta_3 \ln t_{i,j,t} + \gamma_i + \gamma_j + \gamma_{i,j} + \gamma_t + \varepsilon_{i,j,t} \quad (5.5)$$

The literature suggests that the inclusion of time-fixed country effects is a viable alternative for panel studies which cover reasonably short sampling periods (WTO & UNCTAD, 2012). As it is not specified what "reasonably short" means, I will run robustness tests to ensure that the length of my sampling period has no negative consequences for the estimation accuracy.

5.2.2 Formal model specification

As the theory-consistent version of the raw gravity model, Equation (5.4), is not suitable for the empirical analysis conducted in this chapter, the second best option, Equation (5.5), serves as starting point for the specification of the research model. The fact that Equation (5.5) contains time-fixed pair effects, which is uncommon for gravity models[99], simplifies this process. As the pair dummies fully capture the time-fixed component of the ease of trade variable (t), only the time-varying component remains. The challenge is that t itself is unobservable and needs to be estimated from its observable determinants.

---

98 Due to this reason Equation (5.4) does not longer contain measures of countries' economic mass. Their coefficients would be perfectly collinear with the time-varying country effects.

99 Time-fixed pair effects are unsuitable for many gravity-based research projects because they make it impossible to estimate bilateral effects which are not time-varying such as distance or a common border (Baldwin & Taglioni, 2006). As my main interest is on unilateral variables, this limitation does not impact my research negatively.

Scientists who are specialized in empirical applications of the gravity model have proposed a comprehensive set of variables which are known to impact the ease of trade between two countries (Head, Mayer, & Reis, 2010; Head & Meyer, 2014). For the sake of simplicity and as bilateral components of the gravity model are not the focus of my research, I concentrate on those variables which have also been applied in the four regulation-competitiveness studies reviewed in Section 5.1.2.

Equation (5.6), which I call baseline model, is an adjusted specification of the gravity model's raw version (5.5). It includes all structural variables proposed in the related research that are compatible with Equation (5.5).

$$\ln X_{i,j,t} = \alpha + \beta_1 \ln GDP\_ex_{i,t} + \beta_2 \ln GDP\_im_{j,t} + \beta_3 EU_{i,j,t} + \beta_4 EURO_{i,j,t} + \beta_5 TARIFF\_SW_{i,j,t} + \gamma_i + \gamma_j + \gamma_{i,j} + \gamma_t + \varepsilon_{i,j,t} \tag{5.6}$$

Compared to the previous specification, two elements have been modified. First, exporter's and importer's economic sizes ($Y_{j,t}$) and ($Y_{i,t}$) have been replaced by the natural logarithms of their GDPs ($\ln GDP\_ex_{i,t}$) and ($\ln GDP\_im_{j,t}$), the operational equivalents of economic mass. While Costantini & Crespi (2008) do also control for a population effect[100], none of the other studies includes this indicator. I follow the majority of studies and rely on countries' GDP as indicator of economic mass.

The second adjustment is the replacement of the abstract ease of trade indicator (t) by a set of variables which are more readily available. The existing research on the narrowly strong Porter Hypothesis uses a number of different variables for this purpose: geographic distance between the exporting and importing country, a set of dummy variables indicating whether both countries share a common boarder, a common official language, or a common colonial history, import tariff rates, and dummies for EU and euro area membership.

As discussed, the inclusion of time-fixed pair effects allows focusing on the time-varying component of ease of trade (t). Time-fixed effects are captured by the pair dummies. Hence, I follow the previous research and include EU and EURO, a set of two dummy variables which indicates if both countries are members of the European Union and the euro area respectively. Furthermore, I add TARIFF_SW, a measure of the average effective import tariff rates for wind and solar power equipment.

Given the fact that my sample is more global than those of previous studies, it would be very attractive to also control for the impact of other

[100] Costantini & Crespi (2008) also control for land area. This variable cannot be included in the model as it would be perfectly collinear with the country fixed effect (γ_i and γ_j).

regional trade agreements (RTA) besides the EU. While the EU's common market is the world's most integrate trade bloc, joint membership in NAFTA, ASEAN, Mercosur, or other RTAs certainly fosters bilateral trade as well. However, high-quality, of-the-shelf data on RTA membership and other bi- and multilateral trade agreements is only available until 2006 (e.g. the data sample of Head, Mayer, & Reis, 2010). As the strong growth of renewable energy installations and the corresponding increase in trade is very much a phenomenon of the recent past[101], neglecting observations from 2007 onwards seems not to be a viable option, though.

In order to approximate the role of the non-EU RTAs, I have conducted a supplementary analysis of regional trade flows, which is presented in Part (a) of Table 22. First of all, the data show that trade in renewable energy equipment is dominated by Asian and European exporters. While North American countries also play a minor role as export nations, the export volumes from African, Eurasian, Middle Eastern, and South American countries are negligible.

A breakdown of trade flows into intra- and inter-regional shares reveals that intra-regional trade is especially strong in Europe[102]. 85% of European exports stay in the region. For comparison, the corresponding shares of Asian and North American exports are with 34% and 33% much lower. While this analysis is certainly not sufficient to draw inferences on RTAs' effectiveness to promote intra-regional trade, the data do suggest the assumption that the membership in other RTAs is not as important as trade flow determinant as membership in the EU. All in all, while it is certainly not ideal to neglect other RTAs and only control for EU membership, I still prefer this approach to restricting the sample to observation of 2006 or earlier.

Another debatable issue is whether it is reasonable to, at the same time, control for EU and euro area membership. Including both variables does only make sense if trade between euro area members is, everything else equal, considerable more intense than trade between EU countries. There are two arguments in favor of including both indicators. First, the analysis presented in Part (b) of Table 22 shows that intra-euro-area trade is indeed more intense than intra-EU trade. While the euro area, as of 2010, only accounted for 62% of the European GDP, 82% of the euro

---

101 Figure 4 (page 8) illustrates the growth in solar and wind power installations over the last decade. Table 1 (page 11) provides data on the dynamics of trade.

102 The share of intra-regional trade is even higher for South American exporters (90%). However, due to very small export volumes, this effect is not in the focus of analysis.

area's exports in solar and wind energy equipment went to other euro area countries. Second, the regression results of Costantini & Mazzanti (2012) for trade patterns of EU exporters likewise demonstrate that joint membership in the euro zone has a positive impact on trade volumes. Taken together, the results of the analysis presented in Table 22 and the previous discussion suggest that the current specification of the gravity model, Equation (5.6), is reasonable.

(a) Global exports in solar and wind power equipment in 2010

Region	Trade flows in USD bn (2005)			Export shares in %		
	Intra-regional	Inter-regional	Total	Intra-regional	Inter-regional	Total
Africa	0.01	0.16	0.17	6%	94%	100%
Asia & Oceania	16.52	31.72	48.24	34%	66%	100%
Eurasia	0.00	0.04	0.04	9%	91%	100%
Europe	18.47	3.24	21.71	85%	15%	100%
Middle East	0.00	0.01	0.01	41%	59%	100%
North America	1.19	2.44	3.63	33%	67%	100%
South America	0.03	0.00	0.03	90%	10%	100%

(b) Euro area exports in solar and wind power equipment in 2010

Importer:	Exporter: Euro area countries			
	2010 Exports (USD bn 2005)	2010 Exports (%)	2010 GDP (USD bn 2005)	2010 GDP (%)
Europe (non-EU; non-Euro)	0.42	3%	1,374	8%
Europe (EU; non-Euro)	2.25	16%	5,390	31%
Europe (EU; Euro)	11.77	82%	10,903	62%
Total	14.44	100%	17,667	100%

Table 22 – Intra-/ inter-regional trade in solar and wind equipment
Source: Own illustration based on data from UN (2015).

The last step is to add the specific variables needed for research on the narrowly strong Porter Hypothesis and/or the lead market theory.

$$\begin{aligned} &\textit{solar and wind energy exports} \\ &\quad = \textit{baseline gravity model} + \textit{innovation} \\ &\quad + \textit{regulation intensity} + \textit{regulation design} + \varepsilon \end{aligned} \tag{5.7}$$

Equation (5.7) is an extension of the baseline gravity model (5.6) which allows me to test the competitiveness effect of the different innovation and regulation indicators developed throughout Chapters 3 and 4.

5.2.3 Data on trade and its determinants

As the dependent variable of my research model, bilateral exports in solar and wind power equipment (X_SW) are the most important new variable in this chapter. With regard to the data source, I follow the approach of the related publications on the narrowly strong Porter Hypothesis and extract the respective trade data from the United Nations' Comtrade database (UN, 2015).

Just like in the selection process of relevant patent applications, presented in Section 4.3.1, I have discovered considerable differences in the scoping of commodity classes (HS codes) used to capture countries' exports in wind and solar energy equipment. Although these variations are partially attributable to differences in the papers' research questions, a large part is unsystematic and caused by the discretionary selection or omission of commodity classes.

Table 23 provides an overview of the trade flow definitions of those existing empirical studies on the Porter Hypothesis which exclusively or at least partially explore the effects in the renewable energy equipment industry.

Starting with the definition of the commodity classes for wind energy equipment, the analysis of the data presented in Table 23 shows that the difference between this and previous studies is huge. Other authors label on average 3.2 to 5.8 times more exports as related to wind energy than I do. An analysis the HS codes used in previous research shows that the scope of wind power was often defined very generously.

The first HS code 730820, for instance, proposed by Cao & Groba (2013), refers to towers and lattice masts. Although some of the products from this commodity class certainly go into wind power installations, there are also many other applications (e.g. power lines or broadcasting and cell phone towers). The next item on the list is miscellaneous engines and motors. While it is not clear what goes into this commodity class, it is certainly not wind energy equipment. Engines are the opposite of generators (such as wind turbines). They are made to convert electricity or other sources of energy into mechanical energy and not the other way round. Another example of inaccuracies in previous studies' data selection approach is HS code 850239 (other electric generating sets). This 6-digit code belongs to the same 4-digit parent (8502) as HS code 850231, which clearly refers to those generating sets used in wind turbines. This implies that HS code 850239 certainly does not contain any generating sets which should be labelled as wind power exports.

HS code	Description	Global exports (in USD m, current)			Coverage of HS classes by study			
	(a) Wind-energy-related technologies	1990	2000	2010	Costantini & Crespi (2008)	Cao & Groba (2013)	Groba (2014)	This study
730820	Towers and lattice masts [...]	85	382	3,301		x		
841280	Engines and motors, [other]	20	167	758		x		
841290	Parts of engines & motors [...]	236	1,126	5,199		x		
841381	Pumps, [other]	239	1,846	4,144	x	x		
850231	Wind-powered generating sets		505	9,271	x	x		x
850239	Electric generating sets, [other]		893	4,101		x		
850240	Electric rotary converters	70	120	168	x	x		
	Total exports captured in 1990				309	650		
	Total exports captured in 2000				2,471	5,038		505
	Total exports captured in 2010				13,583	26,942		9,271
	(b) Solar-energy-related technologies							
840219	Vapor generating boilers [...]	87	289	568			x	
841911	Instantaneous gas water heaters [...]	143	341	974	x		x	
841919	Instantaneous water heaters, non-electric [...]	86	565	1,812	x		x	
841950	Heat exchange units [...]	651	2,486	7,475	x		x	
850440	Static converters [...]	1,906	16,116	44,002		x	x	
850720	Electric accumulators [...]	369	1,499	4,884		x	x	
854140	Photosensitive semiconductor devices, incl. photovoltaic cells [...]	725	7,227	72,626	x	x	x	x
900290	Lenses, prisms, mirrors and other optical elements, of any material [...]	156	847	1,912			x	
	Total exports captured in 1990				1,605	3,000	4,123	725
	Total exports captured in 2000				10,619	24,842	29,370	7,227
	Total exports captured in 2010				82,887	121,512	134,253	72,626

Notes: Global exports by HS code are taken from the Comtrade database (UN, 2015). Empty cells indicate missing values. Costantini & Crespi (2008) also include energy efficiency technologies in their product definition which are not listed here. Costantini & Mazzanti (2012) is not included in this overview because they go beyond renewable energies and instead cover the entire green-tech sector.

Table 23 – Trade flow definitions of related publications
Source: Own illustration based on data from UN (2015).

I could continue to go down the list without changing the message of this review: The only HS code which can be categorized as wind power equipment with certainty is 850231, wind-powered generating sets. The selection of any of the other codes listed in Part (a) of Table 23 bears a huge risk of reducing measurement accuracy by introducing noise from non-wind-related products. For these reasons, I exclusively rely on HS code 850231 to capture trade in wind energy products.

Regarding solar power equipment, the situation is exactly the same. Previous studies select larger numbers of HS codes and hence run the risk of producing spurious estimation results. On average, they identify 2.6 to 4.0 times the export flows I label as solar-power-related. The first four commodity classes from Part (b) of Table 23, for instance, are (at least remotely) related to solar thermal equipment. Even though it is perfectly acceptable to categorize solar thermal as renewable energy technology, this categorization does not make a lot of sense if the research interest is the impact of renewable energy support policies. Almost all renewable energy support policies target the electricity sector and therefore have absolutely no impact on heating technologies.

Another big commodity class potentially related to solar power is 850440 (static converts). The problem is the same as for the towers and lattice masts in the wind energy discussion. Static converts have many different applications. Although they are part of most photovoltaic installations, it does not become clear from the Comtrade database, how big the share of static converts made for solar power applications really is.

Unfortunately, the main commodity class 854140 (photosensitive semiconductor devices, incl. photovoltaic cells) is an aggregate in itself. While solar PV components probably make up a large part of the trade flows under this HS code, other products such LEDs are certainly not negligible either. Nevertheless, HS code 854140 remains the product group with the highest probability to consist out of solar PV equipment, at least to a large extent. Hence, I will use this commodity class to capture bilateral trade flows in solar-power-related goods.

Having identified the commodity classes which fit my research objectives best (HS codes 850231 and 854140), it's time to take a first look at the trade data. Part (a) of Figure 16 illustrates the development of trade in the product groups defined above. The exponential growth trend fits well with my previous analyses which showed similar growth paths for the proliferation of renewable energy support polices, the number of patent application, and global installed capacities[103]. Within little more than two decades the global trade volume in these technologies increased from about 1 bn USD in 1990 to 77 bn USD in 2011. The only interruption in the otherwise continuous growth trajectory was during the great recession of 2008/2009. In the context of the previous chapters' analyses, this plot of trade flows is another piece of evidence supporting the notion that support policies and the technological advancements they induce have a positive impact on the renewables industry.

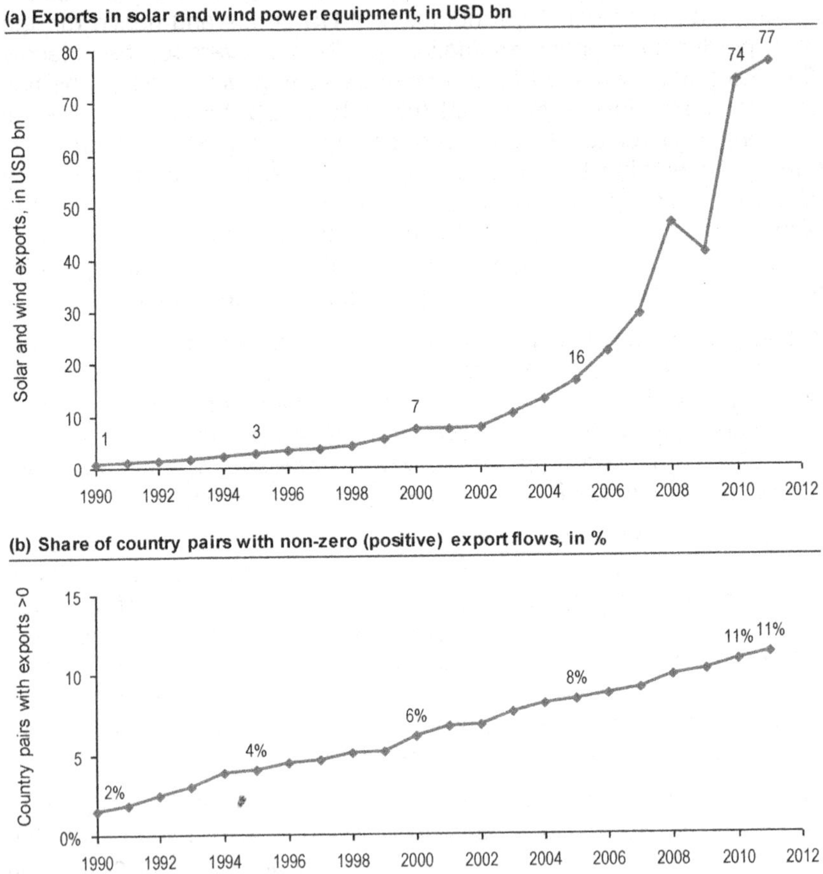

Figure 16 – Trade in solar and wind power equipment
Source: Own illustration based on data from UN (2015).

[103] The increase in the number and variety of renewable energy support policies is illustrated, for example, in Figure 7 (page 86), the growth trend of patent applications on solar and wind power technologies is shown in Figure 15 (page 133), and the development of the installed capacities of these technologies in Figure 1 (page 4).

Another significant factor in trade research based on gravity models is the share of observations with zero trade flows, i.e. no exports of renewable energy equipment from exporting country i to importing country j in a given year t. Part (b) of Figure 16 gives the shares of non-zero observation. As one could have expected, the share of non-zero trade flows is initially very low and only increases gradually; following the trend in global trade volumes. On average, trade flows are equal to zero in about 95% of all potential export-importer-time combinations. The exact share depends on the period of observation. This feature of the data has important implications for the selection of an appropriate estimation approach which is discussed in Section 5.3 below.

Besides the trade flows, estimating the relationship summarized in Equation (5.7) also requires data on the structural variables of the gravity equation, on countries' innovativeness in the relevant technologies, as well as on their environmental policy landscapes.

GDP figures and import tariff rates have been downloaded from the databases of the World Bank (2015a, 2015b). The data on the EU and euro area membership come from the European Commission (2015) and the ECB (2015) respectively. Finally, the data on countries' renewable energy support policies and their innovation output are taken from the previous analyses presented in Chapters 3 and 4.

5.3 Results

This section operationalizes the research model developed above and presents the results of my empirical analysis of the strong part of the narrowly strong Porter Hypothesis. The discussion starts with the selection of an appropriate estimation approach which is covered in Section 5.3.1. Thereafter, Section 5.3.2 presents and discusses the regression results on the relationships between regulation, innovation, and competitiveness as well as the complementary robustness tests. Section 5.3.3 closes with a comparison of my regression results to those of previous empirical research.

5.3.1 Estimation approach

The trade flow analysis of Figure 16 above shows that my data contain many observations where exports are equal to zero. Against this background, estimating Equation (5.6) in its double-log formulation is not an appropriate option. Too many valuable observations would be lost as ln(0) is not defined. Although the loss of observations would not lead to biased estimates if the zeros occurred randomly (statistical zeros) (Head & Meyer, 2014), I can rule out this possibility based on the development of zero trade flows over time. Part (b) of Figure 16 indicates that the share of zero observations is trending (structural zeros), a strong argument against random occurrence.

In gravity research, one of the common approaches used to avoid the loss of information in the presence of structural zeros is to apply count data models (Santos-Silva & Tenreyro, 2006; Head & Meyer, 2014). As export flows can only take non-negative integer values, they comply with the definition of a count.

Generally, there are two options to estimate count data models: the Poisson model and the negative binomial model (Wooldridge, 2002, Chapter 19). Both approaches have been applied in research on the narrowly strong Porter Hypothesis in the renewable energy equipment industry. While Groba (2014) exclusively applies the Poisson model, Cao & Groba (2013) use both. In addition, some publications propose to apply zero-inflated versions of the Poisson and the negative binomial model if the share of zero observations exceeds the shares predicted by their underlying distributions (Burger, van Oort, & Linders, 2009).

However, as pointed out by Head & Meyer (2014), one should be very cautious to apply count data models on pseudo-count data, i.e. variables which while, they fulfill the definition of a count (non-negative integers), are actually continuous. The reason is that the estimation results of some of these models are very sensitive to the scale of the dependent variable (Bosquet & Boulhol, 2010; Head & Meyer, 2014). In the context of this chapter, this means that changing the trade flows' unit of measurement from Euro to billion Euros, for instance, would lead to different coefficient estimates[104]. The only count data model which is found to efficiently produce unbiased estimates if applied to pseudo-count data is the Poisson pseudo-maximum-likelihood estimator (PPML) (Santos-Silva & Tenreyro, 2006). The probability function of the Poisson model is given below as Equation (5.8) (Hill et al., 2012).

$$f(x) = P(X\_SW_{i,j,t} = x\_sw_{i,j,t}) = \frac{exp(-\lambda)\lambda^{x\_sw_{i,j,t}}}{x\_sw_{i,j,t}!}, (x\_sw_{i,j,t} = 0,1,2,\dots) \tag{5.8}$$

$$where\ E(X\_SW_{i,j,t}) = \lambda$$

[104] Unreported test regressions based on the standard negative binomial model (STATA command: nbreg), the zero-inflated Poisson model (STATA command: zip), and the zero-inflated negative binomial model (STATA command: zinb) confirm this behavior. Rescaling the dependent variable causes large changes in the coefficient estimates.

Before Equation (5.6) can be estimated in a PPML framework it has to be raised to the power of e. The resulting regression function is stated below as Equation (5.9).

$$E(X\_SW_{i,j,t}) = exp(\alpha + \beta_1 \ln GDP\_ex_{i,t} + \beta_2 \ln GDP\_im_{j,t} + \beta_3 EU_{i,j,t} + \beta_4 EURO_{i,j,t} + \beta_5 TARIFF\_SW_{i,j,t} + \gamma_i + \gamma_j + \gamma_{i,j} + \gamma_t) \quad (5.9)$$

A specific problem of this research project is that Equation (5.9) has computational requirements which exceed the capacities of the available econometric software package and the underlying hardware by several magnitudes. The inclusion of pair-fixed effect ($\gamma_{i,j}$) alone implies that 2N(N-1) dummy variables have to be estimated. This means that, for my sample of 225 countries[105] over 22 years, the number of dummy variables sums up to 100,800 (2 x 225 x 224)[106].

Fortunately, there is another option to operationalize the gravity model. If Equation (5.9) is estimated using a panel Poisson model, it simplifies to Equation (5.10).

$$E(X\_SW_{i,j,t}) = exp(\alpha_{i,j} + \beta_1 \ln GDP\_ex_{i,t} + \beta_2 \ln GDP\_im_{j,t} + \beta_3 EU_{i,j,t} + \beta_4 EURO_{i,j,t} + \beta_5 TARIFF\_SW_{i,j,t} + \gamma_t) \quad (5.10)$$

As the cross-sectional unit of gravity models of trade is the country pair, the pair-fixed effect dummy ($\gamma_{i,j}$) is no longer required as explicit variable. All time-fixed unobservable heterogeneity on country-pair level is captured by the adjusted cross-sectional intercept ($\alpha_{i,j}$). Moreover, ex- (γ_i) and importer effects (γ_j) also drop out of the regression model because they are invariant within the cross-sections and therefore not estimable in a panel setting.

Because the original STATA command for panel Poisson models (xtpoisson) is prone to convergence problems in maximum likelihood estimation, I draw back on Timothy Simcoe's (2015) xtpqml command which is recommended by Tenreyro (2015) for gravity models controlling for pair-wise effects. The xtpqml command initiates a fixed-effects Poisson quasi-maximum-likelihood regression with robust standard errors, which is based on STATA's original xtpoisson command with

105 A list of all countries included in the sample is presented in Appendix 9.

106 The number of right-hand variables in STATA/IC (version 14) is restricted to 798. Even the most powerful software package STATA/ME does not allow more than 10,998 right-hand variables.

fixed effects (,fe) option but is less affected by the problem of non-convergence.

Before I enter into the estimation of the full model, I formally test the appropriateness of my new baseline gravity model described above. The regression results for Equation (5.10) are presented in Table 24.

Dep. var.	X_SW	X_SW	X_ALL
Variable	(5.10)	(5.11a)	(5.11b)
lnGDP_ex	2.866 ***	2.834 ***	1.237 ***
lnGDP_im	-.1634	-.1807	1.030 ***
EU	1.737 ***	1.752 ***	.5219 ***
EURO	1.218 ***	1.219 ***	.3457 ***
TARIFF_SW	-.0165		
Pair FE (panel)	yes	yes	yes
Time FE	yes	yes	yes
Obs. total	724,724	724,724	724,724
Obs. dropped	603,351	603,351	530,803
Obs. used	121,373	121,373	193,921
Groups	5,651	5,651	9,029
Group size, min.	11	11	11
Group size, avg.	21.5	21.5	21.5
Group size, max.	22	22	22
Wald Chi²	1,236 ***	1,212 ***	8,616 ***
Log likelihood	-9.93e+10	-9.94e+10	-1.48e+13

Notes: Results are estimated using Poisson quasi maximum likelihood regression for panel data with cluster robust standard errors. *, **, and *** indicate statistical significance at 10%, 5%, and 1% level respectively.

Table 24 – Alternative specifications of the baseline gravity model
Source: Own illustration.

The coefficient estimates for EU (EU) and euro area membership (EURO) are positive and statistically highly significant, as predicted by theory and confirmed in empirical research (e.g. Costantini & Mazzanti, 2012; Groba, 2014). The estimates for the economic masses (lnGDP_ex and lnGDP_im), however, lie outside of their common ranges and are on top of that partially not significant[107]. Similarly, the coefficient estimate on the import tariff variable (TARIFF_SW) is very small and not statistically significant either. Hence, I exclude the latter from my regression model. The natural logarithm of the importer's GDP (lnGDP_im), in contrast, remains part of the model irrespective of its insignificance because it is a structural component of the gravity equation and therefore theoretically required. The adjusted version of my baseline model is stated below as Equation (5.11a).

[107] As integral components of the gravity model, the coefficient estimates on ex- and importer's GDP are usually statically highly significant with values around 1 (Head & Meyer, 2014).

$$E(X\_SW_{i,j,t}) = exp(\alpha_{i,j} + \beta_1 \ln GDP\_ex_{i,t} + \beta_2 \ln GDP\_im_{j,t} + \beta_3 EU_{i,j,t} + \beta_4 EURO_{i,j,t} + \gamma_t) \quad (5.11a)$$

$$E(X\_ALL_{i,j,t}) = exp(\alpha_{i,j} + \beta_1 \ln GDP\_ex_{i,t} + \beta_2 \ln GDP\_im_{j,t} + \beta_3 EU_{i,j,t} + \beta_4 EURO_{i,j,t} + \gamma_t) \quad (5.11b)$$

The regression results for Equation (5.11a), presented in the second column of Table 24, show that the exclusion of the import tariff rates (TARIFF_SW) barely affected the estimates on the remaining variables. Unfortunately, this is also the case for the economic masses (lnGDP_ex and lnGDP_im), whose estimates are still unusual for gravity models.

However, these unusual coefficient estimates do not necessarily mean that the model is misspecified or that there is a problem with the data. Generally, it is not uncommon for gravity models using sectoral trade flows[108] that the mass coefficients are considerable different from unity (WTO & UNCTAD, 2012). As the study by Costantini & Crespi (2008) demonstrates, this is also the case in the green-tech sector. The coefficient estimates which they find in their analysis on trade in renewable energy and energy efficiency equipment come very close to those I report in Table 24 above[109]. Hence, it seems reasonable to assume that my estimates on the trade impact of ex- and importer's GDP are not caused by a faulty model or erroneous data but are just typical for trade in renewable energy equipment.

Even though I do not attempt to explore the underlying reasons systematically, I hypothesize that the results on the GDP coefficients, which Costantini & Crespi (2008) and I find, are driven by two effects. On the one hand, the large size and high significance of the exporting country's GDP suggest that only technologically advanced countries with corresponding GDPs qualify as producers of renewable energy equipment. On the other hand, the insignificance of the importing country's GDP indicates that the size of the economy is not necessarily a good proxy for the size of each and every product market. In the specific case of renewable energy equipment, for instance, market size is

108 An alternative term for sectoral trade flows, which is also widely used in the literature, is disaggregated trade flows.

109 Depending on the model specification, their estimated coefficients on the natural log of exporting countries' GDPs are roughly between 2 and 4 while those on the natural log of importing countries' GDPs are around 0.5. Moreover, Costantini & Crespi (2008) report lower significance levels for the importer's GDP than for the exporter's GDP.

probably much more closely related to the presence of renewable energy support policies than to overall economic output[110].

This interpretation of the regression results presented in Table 24 is supported by an alternative reading of the gravity equation. In this reading, the exporter's economic mass ($Y_{i,t}$) indicates its capability to supply certain products, and the importer's economic mass ($Y_{j,t}$) indicates its suitability as a market for these products (Head & Meyer, 2014).

Regardless the fact that GDP coefficients departing from unity are not uncommon in gravity research, I conduct an additional test to confirm the validity of my specification. In this test, I rerun the baseline model with an alternative sample that consists of the very same exporter-importer-time combinations but contains total (X_ALL) instead of solar- and wind-related exports (X_SW), Equations (5.11b).

The application of this neutral data sample yields estimates which are consistent with the typical results of empirical gravity models. Hence, I conclude that Equation (5.11a) properly models multinational trade flows in solar- and wind-energy-equipment and use this specification as basis for my empirical analysis on the narrowly strong Porter Hypothesis.

5.3.2 Regression results

Having selected an appropriate estimation approach and fine-tuned the baseline model, I will now turn to the presentation and discussion of my regression results.

I have compiled six regression models, (5.12) to (5.17), to study the link between regulation, innovation, and competitiveness and thereby shed new light on the narrowly strong Porter Hypothesis and the lead market theory. Each of these six models extends the new baseline gravity model (5.11a) by including additional explanatory variables. To avoid repetition, I will in the following only explain those variables which have not been introduced before as part of baseline gravity model.

Equation (5.12) tests if more intense regulation leads to higher renewable energy exports and if export competitiveness is affected by innovation. Hereby, I again rely on the established approach to proxy the intensity of countries' renewable energy support policies by the share of

[110] The results, presented in Section 5.3.2, provide evidence for the latter argument.

solar and wind in total domestic electricity generation (RES_SW)[111]. I use the domestic stock of wind and solar patents (DKS_SC_SW) as measure of innovation. Knowledge stocks have the advantage that they do not only capture the innovative output of the current but also those of previous periods. In order to control for the impact of the situation in the importing country, I include corresponding indicators for the trade partner as well (RES_SW_im and DKS_SC_SW_im).

$$E(X\_SW_{i,j,t}) = \exp(baseline + \beta_5 DKS\_SC\_SW_{i,t} + \beta_6 RES\_SW_{i,t} + \beta_7 DKS\_SC\_SW\_im_{j,t} + \beta_8 RES\_SW\_im_{j,t}) \tag{5.12}$$

$$E(X\_SW_{i,j,t}) = \exp(baseline + \beta_5 DKS\_SC\_SW_{i,t} + \beta_6 CPV\_E_{i,t} + \beta_7 DKS\_SC\_SW\_im_{j,t} + \beta_8 CPV\_E\_im_{j,t}) \tag{5.13}$$

$$E(X\_SW_{i,j,t}) = \exp(baseline + \beta_5 DKS\_SC\_SW_{i,t} + \sum \beta_{c+5} ClusterEx_{c,i,t} + \beta_{12} DKS\_SC\_SW\_im_{j,t} + \beta_{13} CPV\_E\_im_{j,t}) \tag{5.14}$$

$$E(X\_SW_{i,j,t}) = \exp(baseline + \beta_5 DKS\_SC\_SW_{i,t} + \sum \beta_{p+5} InstruEx_{p,i,t} + \beta_{17} DKS\_SC\_SW\_im_{j,t} + \beta_{18} CPV\_E\_im_{j,t}) \tag{5.15}$$

$$E(X\_SW_{i,j,t}) = \exp(baseline + \beta_5 DKS\_SC\_SW_{i,t} + \beta_6 C\_ANY\_E_{i,t} + \beta_7 C\_ANY\_DP5_{i,t} + \beta_8 C\_ANY\_DP10_{i,t} + \beta_9 C\_ANY\_DP15_{i,t} + \beta_{10} DKS\_SC\_SW\_im_{j,t} + \beta_{11} CPV\_E\_im_{j,t}) \tag{5.16}$$

$$E(X\_SW_{i,j,t}) = \exp(baseline + \beta_5 DKS\_SC\_SW_{i,t} + \sum \beta_{c+5} ClusterEx_{c,i,t} + \sum \beta_{c+11} ClusterDP5_{c,i,t} + \sum \beta_{c+17} ClusterDP10_{c,i,t} + \sum \beta_{c+23} ClusterDP15_{c,i,t} + \beta_{30} DKS\_SC\_SW\_im_{j,t} + \beta_{31} CPV\_E\_im_{j,t}) \tag{5.17}$$

$$where\ baseline = \alpha_{i,j} + \beta_1 \ln GDP\_ex_{i,t} + \beta_2 \ln GDP\_im_{j,t} + \beta_3 EU_{i,j,t} + \beta_4 EURO_{i,j,t} + \gamma_t$$

Equation (5.13) also tests the impact from ex- and importer's regulation intensities and domestic knowledge stocks, but measures regulation intensity differently. I implement a proposal of Johnstone et al. (2008) and proxy regulation intensity using compound variables (CPV_E and CPV_E_im). These variables take a value between 0 and 1 indicating the share of renewable energy support policies, as categorized in Table 7, which have been implemented. All eleven policy instruments have the same weight.

111 Due to convergence issues in the estimation of the maximum likelihood estimator, I cannot implement the suggestion from the previous chapter to analyze solar and wind effects separately.

The next two Equations, (5.14) and (5.15), investigate the competitiveness enhancing effect of exporters' environmental regulation more granularly. Hereby, Equations (5.14) and (5.15) differ from each other in their level of detailing. While Equation (5.14) tests the impact from different policy measures on cluster level (ClusterEx)[112], Equation (5.15) tests the effectiveness of policy instruments on the more detailed instrument level (InstruEx)[113].

Last but not least, Equations (5.16) and (5.17) have been designed to test the hypothesis that countries with a longer history of renewable energy support policies benefit more strongly from the positive effects of such policies than countries which have adopted them more recently. Similar to Equations (5.14) and (5.15), Equations (5.16) and (5.17) just vary in their level of granularity.

Equation (5.16) models policy duration on a general level. C_ANY_E is a dummy variable which indicates whether the country under consideration has adopted at least one of the eleven renewable energy support policies introduced in Section 3.1.4. Similarly, C_ANY_DP5, C_ANY_DP10, C_ANY_DP15 are additional dummy variables which signal the existence of renewable energy support policies for at least five, ten, or fifteen years. Taken together these four indicator variables allow to test for the lead market effect.

Equation (5.17) takes a more detailed approach and models policy duration on cluster level. For this purpose, it includes four sets of dummy variables, ClusterEx, ClusterDP5, ClusterDP10, and ClusterDP15[114]. Their underlying mechanism corresponds to the C_ANY_... variables introduced before. Each variable indicates the existence of policy

---

[112] ClusterEx consists of the following six policy clusters: targets (C_TAR_E), RD&D support (C_RDD_E), quotas (C_QUO_E), feed-in tariffs (C_FIT_E), fiscal incentives (C_FIS_E), and greenhouse gas trading (C_GHG_E).

[113] InstruEx consists of the following eleven policy instruments: renewable energy targets or strategies (TAR_E), research, development, and demonstration programs (RDD_E), renewable energy quotas without certificate trading (QUO_E), renewable energy quotas with certificate trading (REC_E), feed-in tariffs (fixed rate or premium) (FIT_E), net metering (NET_E), public competitive bidding (tendering) (TEN_E), tax credits (investment or production) (TXC_E), tax reductions (carbon, energy, sales, VAT, or other taxes) (TXR_E), public spending, capital subsidies, and low cost loans (PUB_E), and greenhouse gas trading systems (GHG_E).

[114] ClusterEx, DP5, ClusterDP10, and ClusterDP15 each consists of six policy clusters: targets (C_TAR_E, _DP5, _DP10, _DP15), RD&D support (C_RDD_E, _DP5, _DP10, _DP15), quotas (C_QUO_E, _DP5, _DP10, _DP15), feed-in tariffs (C_FIT_E, _DP5, _DP10, _DP15), fiscal incentives (C_FIS_E, _DP5, _DP10, _DP15), and carbon trading (C_GHG_E, _DP5, _DP10, _DP15).

instruments from one of the six clusters for at least one, five, ten, or fifteen years.

The full documentation of all variables included in Equations (5.12) to (5.17) is given in Appendix 26. Descriptive statistics and correlation matrices[115] are presented in Appendix 27 and Appendix 28.

Table 25 summarizes the results of regression models (5.12) to (5.17). Before I enter into the discussion of individual results, it is worth highlighting a finding on the baseline variables, which represent the common core of all six models: The coefficient estimates for this group of variables are reasonably stable across all models. Further, the signs and sizes of coefficient estimates as well as their significance levels remain close to their original values. This indicates that the baseline gravity model (5.11a) is a solid foundation for this chapter's analyses.

With respect to the individual regression models, the results depicted in Table 25 provide supporting evidence for both the narrowly strong Porter Hypothesis and the lead market theory and thereby generate new valuable insights which help to answer two of my key research questions: What is the impact of countries' environmental regulation on their export competitiveness in wind and solar power equipment? And, do early adopters enjoy a lead market effect?

To begin with the two main elements of the Porter Hypothesis, environmental regulation and regulation-induced innovation[116], the regression results of Table 25 show that both contribute positively to countries' renewable energy exports. The regulation intensity indicator (RES_SW) which is part of Equation (5.13) is positive and statistically significant at the 1% level. The coefficient value of RES_SW indicates that each additional unit (%-point) of renewables in the exporter's electricity mix increases bilateral export flows on average by 5.30%[117]. The results of Equation (5.14), which uses the alternative intensity indicator (CPV_E), also suggest the conclusion that exports increase in the intensity of regulation.

---

115 Correlations between both policy clusters and individual policy instruments are positive, often highly positive. However, there is no combination which reaches critical levels (>0.65).

116 The results of the regulation-innovation regressions discussed in Chapter 4 demonstrate that environmental regulation is a significant driver of innovative output in solar and wind power technologies.

117 Incident rate ratio (IRR): 5.30% = $(e^{0.0516} - 1) \times 100\%$.

Dep. var.	X_SW	X_SW	X_SW	X_SW
Variable	(5.12)	(5.13)	(5.14)	(5.15)
lnGDP_ex	3.076 ***	3.043 ***	3.079 ***	3.047 ***
lnGDP_im	.0154	-.2391	.0148	.0067
EU	1.689 ***	1.561 ***	1.195 ***	1.263 ***
EURO	1.044 ***	1.030 ***	.7601 ***	.7301 ***
DKS_SC_SW	.0593	.0867	.1321 *	.1022
RES_SW	.0516 ***			
CPV_E		.9299 **		
C_TAR_E			.2872 *	
C_RDD_E			.1108	
C_QUO_E			.2690 **	
C_FIT_E			.1489	
C_FIS_E			.0490	
C_GHG_E			.9210 ***	
TAR_E				.2744 *
RDD_E				.1013
QUO_E				.4839 ***
REC_E				.1258
FIT_E				-.1924 **
NET_E				.3573 **
TEN_E				.0046
TXC_E				.2144 *
TXR_E				-.0981
PUB_E				.0051
GHG_E				.8215 ***
DKS_SC_SW_im	-.1098 *	-.1039 *	-.0908	-.0935 *
RES_SW_im	.0125			
CPV_E_im		.8265 ***	.6686 ***	.6488 **
Pair FE (panel)	yes	yes	yes	yes
Time FE	yes	yes	yes	yes
Obs. total	724,724	724,724	724,724	724,724
Obs. dropped	603,351	603,351	603,351	603,351
Obs. used	121,373	121,373	121,373	121,373
Groups	5,651	5,651	5,651	5,651
Group size, min.	11	11	11	11
Group size, avg.	21.5	21.5	21.5	21.5
Group size, max.	22	22	22	22
Wald Chi²	1,632 ***	1,383 ***	1,494 ***	1,647 ***
Log likelihood	-9.71e+10	-9.66e+10	-9.30e+10	-9.16e+10

Notes: Results are estimated using Poisson quasi maximum likelihood regression for panel data with cluster robust standard errors. *, **, and *** indicate statistical significance at 10%, 5%, and 1% level respectively.

Table 25 – Results of innovation-/ reg.-competitiveness regressions
Source: Own illustration.

Dep. var.	X_SW	X_SW
Variable	(5.16)	(5.17)
lnGDP_ex	3.182 ***	3.653 ***
lnGDP_im	-.2735	-.0522
EU	1.633 ***	1.101 ***
EURO	.9054 ***	.4787 **
DKS_SC_SW	.093	.1284 *
C_ANY_E	-.1133	
C_ANY_DP5	.2927	
C_ANY_DP10	.3514 **	
C_ANY_DP15	.5564 ***	
C_TAR_E		.1576
C_RDD_E		-.0923
C_QUO_E		.2001 *
C_FIT_E		.2312 **
C_FIS_E		.0859
C_GHG_E		.5538 ***
C_TAR_DP5		-.0658
C_RDD_DP5		.5421 **
C_QUO_DP5		-.0928
C_FIT_DP5		.0574
C_FIS_DP5		.1215
C_GHG_DP5		.3671 *
C_TAR_DP10		.2540
C_RDD_DP10		.3589 **
C_QUO_DP10		.0977
C_FIT_DP10		.1014
C_FIS_DP10		-.2073
C_GHG_DP10		n/a
C_TAR_DP15		.0631
C_RDD_DP15		.1941
C_QUO_DP15		n/a
C_FIT_DP15		-.0959
C_FIS_DP15		.8056 ***
C_GHG_DP15		n/a
DKS_SC_SW_im	-.0935 *	-.079
CPV_E_im	.6488 **	.6523 **
Pair FE (panel)	yes	yes
Time FE	yes	yes
Obs. total	724,724	724,724
Obs. dropped	603,351	603,352
Obs. used	121,373	121,372
Groups	5,651	5,651
Group size, min.	11	11
Group size, avg.	21.5	21.5
Group size, max.	22	22
Wald Chi²	1,314 ***	2,061 ***
Log likelihood	-9.51e+10	-8.91e+10

Notes: Results are estimated using Poisson quasi maximum likelihood regression for panel data with cluster robust standard errors. *, **, and *** indicate statistical significance at 10%, 5%, and 1% level. n/a indicates that var. has been omitted due to missing data.

Table 25 – Results of innovation-/ reg.-competitiveness regressions (cont'd)
Source: Own illustration.

The respective coefficient estimates on the innovation indicator included in all six equations (DKS_SC_SW) point into the same direction but are less significant[118]. Those estimates which are statically significant show that an increase in the domestic knowledge stock in solar and wind power technologies by 1,000 patent applications leads, everything else equal, to a ~14%[119] increase in renewable energy exports. Taken together, the estimates on these variables provide strong support for the narrowly strong Porter Hypothesis and show that policy intensity and innovative output contribute positively to countries' export volumes.

As outlined above, all six regression models also control for the impacts of regulation intensity and innovative output of the importing countries. While there is no evidence that the current share of solar and wind in the importer's electricity mix (RES_SW_im) has a considerable impact on trade flows, the importer's knowledge stock (DKS_SC_SW_im) and the intensity of its renewable energy support policies (CPV_E_im) certainly do have an impact.

The results indicate that import volumes decrease if the domestic knowledge stocks of the importer increases. This is reasonable as the presence of domestic know-how on wind and solar power technologies decreases the need to import these products from abroad. Similarly, the finding that imports increase in the intensity of the importer's policy portfolio is consistent with previous research which suggests that innovation is affected by policy schemes of ex- and importers alike (Peters et al., 2012). In sum, exports tend to flow into countries with a regulatory demand pull and limited capacities to satisfy this demand based on their own technological know-how. These results support my hypothesis from Section 5.3.1 that the small, insignificant coefficient estimates on the importer's GDP indicate that other, more specific factors, e.g. regulation, are more important as determinants of trade in renewable energy equipment than just importer's overall economic size.

So far I have analyzed the effects of the Porter Hypothesis' main elements in general. The discussion of the next two models will show in how far the positive connection between regulation and export success is affected by policy design.

On the cluster level, the coefficient estimates from Equation (5.14) suggest that the existence of renewable energy targets and strategies

---

118 In four out of six cases, the exporter's innovation indicator (DKS_SC_SW) fails to reach the 10% level.

119 IRR for (5.14): 14.12% = $(e^{0.1321} - 1) \times 100\%$; IRR for (5.17): 13.70% = $(e^{0.1284} - 1) \times 100\%$.

(C_TAR_E), renewable energy quotas (C_QUO_E), and especially carbon trading systems (C_GHG_E) foster exports in solar and wind power equipment. The existence of each of these policy instruments increases exports by 31-151% [120]. The coefficient estimates of the remaining three clusters, public research, development, and demonstration programs (C_RDD_E), feed-in tariffs (C_FIT_E), and fiscal incentives (C_FIS_E) are positive but statistical insignificant.

The analysis on the instrument level, conducted based on model (5.15), confirms the results obtained on cluster level. The effects from targets (TAR_E), quotas without renewable energy certificate trading (QUO_E), and greenhouse gas trading systems (GHG_E) remain positive and statistically significant, for QUO_E and GHG_E even at the 1% level. Furthermore, the more detailed analysis on instrument level reveals additional insights which were unobservable on cluster level. The coefficient estimates suggest that classical feed-in-tariffs (FIT_E) have a negative impact on export performance while the related but considerably more advanced net metering regimes (NET_E) [121] foster export competitiveness. In addition, tax credits (TXC_E) are found to have an export-enhancing effect as well.

What is interesting is that with quotas (QUO_E) and tax credits (TXC_E) two conventional policies instruments are found to have strong, positive impacts on export performance [122]. These policy instruments have in common that they affect domestic demand for solar panels and wind turbines very directly. The corresponding increase in installed capacities caused by these instruments, in turn also means increased demand for the domestic renewable energy equipment industry and therefore technological progress through the incorporation of practical experiences from production and operation [123]. Hence, the traditional market pull policies foster export performance as they boost domestic production capacities and accelerate the industrial learning process.

Out of the four market-based instruments, which are most in line with the ideas of the Porter Hypothesis, only net metering (NET_E) and greenhouse gas trading systems (GHG_E) are found to have a positive impact on exports. The remaining two, renewable energy quotas with

---

120 IRR for C_TAR_E: 33.27% = ($e^{0.2872}$ – 1) x 100%; IRR for C_QUO_E: 30.87% = ($e^{0.2690}$ – 1) x 100%; IRR for C_GHG_E: 151.18% = ($e^{0.9210}$ – 1) x 100%.

121 FIT_E and NET_E both belong to the cluster of feed-in tariffs. See Table 7 (page 71) for details.

122 I will show later that this line of argumentation is probably also applicable for the feed-in tariff cluster (C_FIT_E). However, these results are less clear.

123 For details on the principles of market pull policies, refer to Figure 6 (page 65).

certificate trading (REC_E) and tendering (TEN_E), have positive coefficient values as well but fail to reach statistical significance. These results might be interpreted in two directions. On the one hand, one might likewise consider all four variables and read their comparably low significance levels as indication that market features do not automatically increase export competitiveness. But, on the other hand, one might also focus on the coefficient estimate for carbon trading systems (GHG_E), the instrument that comes closest to the idea of well-crafted environmental regulation, and interpret the statistical and economic significance of this very coefficient as supporting evidence for the narrowly strong Porter Hypothesis.

I am more inclined to follow the latter argument. Taking into consideration that carbon trading affects the entire electricity sector, the coefficient value of .8215 is quite remarkable[124]. As I have pointed out before, generating electricity from wind and especially from solar power is often still more expensive[125] than to employ more traditional renewable energy technologies (hydro, biomass, and geothermal). This in mind, it is impressive that wind and solar exports, after all, benefit from the implementation of carbon trading. The most natural explanation for this effect is that those who invest in wind and solar believe in the future potential of these technologies. They presume that wind and solar power might allow them to meet their emission targets more effectively, i.e. less costly, than traditional renewables.

Although the findings related to the narrowly strong Porter Hypothesis are of course very important, the results of Table 25 are not less insightful with respect to the ideas of the lead market theory. The estimates for Equation (5.16) clearly show that while renewable energy support policies are not effective in promoting exports from the very beginning (C_ANY_E), a long tradition of such policies is indeed associated with larger competitiveness effects. Based on the coefficients obtained from the model, export volumes increase by 65% ten to fourteen years after policy adoption (C_ANY_DP10), and even by 140% (C_ANY_DP15) after more than fifteen years[126]. These figures clearly show that countries which had support policies in place for more than fifteen years benefit the most. In sum, the coefficient estimates for (5.16)

---

124 The coefficient estimate of .8215 corresponds to an IRR of 127.39% (= ($e^{0.8215}$ – 1) x 100%).

125 A rough comparison of the levelized cost of electricity is given in Figure 3 (page 7).

126 IRR for C_ANY_E: -10.71% = ($e^{-0.1133}$ – 1) x 100%; IRR for C_ANY_DP5: 34.00% = ($e^{0.2927}$ – 1) x 100%; IRR for C_ANY_DP10: 42.11% = ($e^{0.3514}$ – 1) x 100%; IRR for C_ANY_DP15: 74.44% = ($e^{0.5564}$ – 1) x 100%.

strongly support the notion that early adopters of renewable energy support policies tend to develop into lead markets for these technologies.

Equation (5.17) brings together the ideas of both, the narrowly strong Porter Hypothesis and the lead market theory, and estimates the impact of policy duration for each of the six instrument cluster. The corresponding regression results yield two additional findings. First, the fact that the coefficient on the feed-in tariff cluster (FIT[127]) turned positive suggests that the insignificant or even negative estimates for this important variable found based on Equations (5.14) and (5.15) might be artefacts of unobserved heterogeneity. The high coefficient values and significance levels of feed-in tariffs (FIT) right after their implementation signals that this widely used instrument indeed plays an important role in the early phase of renewable energy support.

Second, the results show that different types of policy instruments are subject to different time lags between implementation and the associated export effects. While quotas (QUO), feed-in tariffs (FIT), and carbon trading (GHG) are found to increase exports quite fast, RD&D programs (RDD) and fiscal incentives (FIS) are associated with considerable time lags. Irrespective of its significance, this result should be interpreted carefully. The analyses of Chapter 4 clearly demonstrate that public RD&D programs (RDD) and fiscal incentives (FIS) are most effective with respect to innovation inducement (technology-push policies). Given the natural time lag between the incentive to innovate, generation of innovative output and export success it is not surprising that the export-enhancing effects of these policies need more time to unfold. Moreover, it is unlikely that the more demand-oriented instruments, like quotas (QUO) and feed-in tariffs (FIT), would be very effective in the very beginning in the absence of previously introduced technology-push policies. In other words, the effectiveness of instruments differs between the early and later phases of renewables support.

Two robustness tests confirm the stability of the findings presented and discussed in this chapter. The first robustness test, presented in Appendix 29, takes up an issue from Section 5.2.1. It was argued there that the second best approach to model the gravity equation, which was applied in this chapter, only leads to unbiased coefficient estimates if the sampling period is reasonably short (WTO & UNCTAD, 2012). Unfortunately, the literature does not specify what is meant by a reasonably short sampling period. Hence, the purpose of the first

---

[127] In the discussion on Eq. (5.17), FIT refers to all variables on the feed-in tariffs cluster: C_FIT_E, _DP5, _DP10, and _DP15. The same applies for the TAR, RDD, QUO, FIS, and GHG cluster.

robustness test is to show that the results of the main model, Equation (5.14), remain unchanged if the sampling period is shortened. As most non-zero observation fall into the more recent past[128], the truncation process starts with the oldest observations. The results of the sample truncation test show that shortening the observation period does not change the overall outcome. The coefficient values and significance levels of all variables included in Equation (5.14) remain stable.

The second robustness test, which has also been applied in the previous two chapters, is the exclusion of the indicators on the existence of RD&D programs (C_RDD_E and RDD_E) and greenhouse gas trading systems (C_GHG_E and GHG_E). It was argued before that these variables might affect regression results due to limited data availability and uncertainties with respect to the exact scope of the underlying policies. The re-estimation of regression models (5.14) and (5.15), documented in Appendix 30 and Appendix 31, suggests that these concerns are unfounded for the analyses of this chapter.

In sum, the robustness tests show that the regression results presented throughout this section are stable and are not affected by moderate changes in model specification or sample composition.

5.3.3 Results in the context of previous research

As in the previous chapter, the last step in the discussion of estimation results is the comparison of my findings with those of existing studies. Table 26 provides a structured overview on those topics where my thesis overlaps with previous studies. Let me state again that the studies included in this overview do not necessarily have the very same research focus as mine and might define policy categories or other variables differently. In addition, these studies use their own definitions of renewable energy exports and might also differ in their geographic and temporal scopes. Hence, all similarities and differences discussed below are indicative and should be interpreted accordingly.

The first and probably most important message from the overview presented in Table 26 is the generally very high level of consistency between the results of this thesis and the existing literature on the relationship between environmental regulation, technological innovation, and export performance in solar and wind power equipment. This is particularly true for the core finding that both exporter's regulation intensity and long-term innovative output contribute positively to export competitiveness, which is supported by 3/4 resp. 2/3 of the other studies.

[128] Refer to Figure 16 (page 168) for the annual shares of zero observations.

Explanatory variable	Results of other studies					Result of this study	
	Costantini & Crespi (2008)	Costantini & Mazzanti (2012)	Cao & Groba (2013)	Groba (2014)	Fraction of studies with significantly positive effect		
(a) Regulation intensity on export competitiveness							
RES_SW/CPV_E			(+)	+	3 / 4	+	✓
Other studies' variable	(+)	+					
(b) Innovation on export competitiveness							
DKS_SC_SW			/		2 / 3	(+)	✓
Other studies' variable	+	+					
(c) Existence of policy instruments on export competitiveness							
QUO_E			(-)	(+)	0.5 / 2	+	(✓)
FIT_E			+	(+)	1.5 / 2	+/-	(✓)
NET_E						+	
C_FIS_E			(-)	/	0 / 2	/	✓
(d) Duration of policy instruments on export competitiveness							
ANY_E/ANY_DP...					0.5 / 1	+	✓
Other studies' variable				(+)			
(e) Importer's regulation intensity on trade volumes							
RES_SW_im/CPV_E_im				+/-	1 / 2	+	(✓)
Other studies' variable	/						

Notes: (+) and + indicate (partially) significant, positive coefficient values. (-) and - indicate (partially) significant, negative coefficient values. Partially significant results are counted as 0.5 in the total column. / indicates insignificant coefficient values. ✓ and (✓) indicate that results between of this and related studies are often or sometimes consistent. Empty cells represent missing values.

Table 26 – Result comparison for reg.-competitiveness regressions
Source: Own illustration.

With respect to the next block, certain policy instruments' impact on export performance, the level of consensus is lower. As Cao & Groba (2013) and Groba (2014) are the only publications which have studied the impact of specific policy instruments on export performance before, the peer group has gotten smaller as well. While Cao & Groba (2013), Groba (2014), and I don't find that fiscal incentives (C_FIS_E) have a positive impact of export volumes, there is only partial agreement on the effectiveness of quotas (QUO_E). Although the results are more difficult to compare, there is also general agreement on the effectiveness of feed-in tariffs (FIT_E/NET_E). While my results for net metering (NET_E) are clearly consistent with the finding of Cao & Groba (2013) and Groba

(2014) that feed-in tariffs foster exports[129], my results for classical feed-in tariffs (FIT_E) are less clear. I found likewise statistically positive and negative results on this instrument. The model specification which yields the positive coefficient estimates seems to be preferable, though.

Previous results on the impact of policy duration on export competitiveness are just available from Groba (2014), who was first to conduct research in this field. Groba (2014) found some evidence that countries with a long history of renewables support benefit most from these policies. The results presented earlier in this chapter confirm his findings on a general as well as on a policy cluster level and, therefore, provide additional empirical evidence for the lead market theory.

Regarding the last category, the trade impact of importer's regulation intensity, the results are again quite mixed. While Costantini & Crespi (2008) suggest that this effect is not statistically significant, Groba (2014) find both, significantly positive and negative coefficients, depending on the intensity measure. Hence, although the previous research provides no valuable insights on the kind of impact which importer's regulation intensity has on trade flows, it at least confirms that it generally has an impact which should be considered and further explored.

In summary, it can be concluded that there is a high level of consensus in those areas where this thesis overlaps with the existing research on the regulation-innovation-competitiveness relationship.

5.4 Conclusion

This chapter has fulfilled its objective to generate new empirical evidence on the strong part of the narrowly strong Porter Hypothesis and the lead market theory for environmental goods and services. To state the main result first, my regressions provide strong supporting evidence for each of these two concepts.

With respect to the narrowly strong Porter Hypothesis, I am able to show that more intensive environmental regulation and larger domestic knowledge stocks drive exports in solar and wind power equipment. Concerning the design dimension, which is of special interest here, two of my findings are of particular importance. First, the data suggest that classical demand-pull policies which have been designed to drive up domestic installations are also a driving force of countries' export performance. Hereby, I find the strongest effects for renewable energy quotas (without certificate trading), tax credits, and to a lesser extent

129 Cao & Groba (2013) and Groba (2014) do not distinguish between classical fixed rate and premium feed-in tariffs (FIT) and net metering (NET).

(classical) feed-in tariffs. Moreover, my results show that, second, greenhouse gas trading systems have a remarkably strong effect on renewable energy exports as well. This finding shows that regulation design does matter and that well-crafted regulation can enhance countries' export competitiveness in solar and wind power technologies.

Concerning the lead market theory, I find that countries with a long history of renewables support tend to export more solar- and wind-power-related goods than countries which have just started to promote these technologies. The data suggest that fifteen years after initial policy adoption, export volumes have, on average, more than doubled relative to countries which did not engage in renewables support.

An additional finding of the analyses presented in this chapter is the strong impact of importers' knowledge stocks and the intensity of their renewable energy support polices. The regression results indicate that both have a considerable effect on trade flows. While increasing levels of know-how in the importing country are found to reduce the propensity to import, intensive political support for renewable energies has the opposite effect and leads to higher import volumes.

These results fit very well with the existing research. Comparison shows high levels of consensus on topics where my dissertation overlaps with previous studies. However, the comparison of results also shows that the significance level of my results tends to be higher.

Two factors might explain the improved significance: a higher data quality and an advanced estimation process. Regarding the quality of data, I again benefit from the very granular and comprehensive policy data and the technology-specific innovation data which I have already applied in previous analyses. This data allow me to capture changes in important export drivers more precisely than previous studies. It also enlarges the temporal and geographic scope. In addition, the trade flow data which are new to this chapter are considerably more targeted towards solar and wind power than their equivalents in previous studies.

From a methodological perspective, the major advancement of this chapter's analyses is the inclusion of pair-wise fixed effects in the specification of the gravity model. According Baldwin & Taglioni (2006) the common approach to control for MRTs based on im- and exporter-fixed effects alone leads to severely biased coefficient estimates if applied on panel data. Costantini & Mazzanti (2012) is the only previous study with a multilateral approach which also includes pair effects[130].

[130] Cao & Groba (2013) include pair dummies, but they do so in simplified, bilateral model.

While data quality is certainly a strength of the analyses presented in this chapter, they are not free of limitations. As pointed out before, my policy design data are subject to unobserved heterogeneity. Moreover, the accuracy of the trade flow data is limited by the coding structure of the Harmonized System, which treats photovoltaic cells, LEDs, and other photosensitive semiconductors as one product group. This lack of granularity might be the reasons why, in my data, >89% of total annual exports are solar-related. While this uneven distribution is not problematic per se, it becomes an issue in this chapter because non-convergence of the maximum likelihood estimator prevents a separate analysis of solar and wind power effects. Hence, the applicability of my results for the wind energy segment is compromised.

6 Summary and overall conclusion

The objective of this dissertation was to study the connection between environmental regulation, technological advancement, and export competitiveness in renewable energy equipment. Hereby, renewable energy equipment was defined as technologies to generate electricity from wind and solar radiation.

A thorough understanding of this relationship and the competitiveness-enhancing features of environmental regulation is very important for policy makers. Prompted by the Kyoto Protocol's binding emission targets, concerns about the long-term consequences of global warming, and finite energy resources, many countries have engaged in the support of renewable energies. In the meantime, renewable energy support policies have developed into a major policy category with corresponding budgetary requirements.

Irrespective of the undisputed benefits which larger shares of renewables in the electricity mix have in the fight against anthropogenic climate change, the current welfare losses associated with this development concern politicians. Governments are anxious to contribute more than others and thereby compromise the competiveness of their own countries. But, this is just one perspective – there is another point of view.

As of 2013, modern renewable energies like hydro, wind, and solar already accounted for ten percent of global electricity generation. At the same time, more than half of the newly commissioned electricity generation capacity used renewable forms of energy, up from less than a quarter just a decade ago. Obviously, this means enormous opportunity for manufacturers of renewable energy equipment. Many governments have realized this and started to give renewable energy support policies another spin. They increasingly appreciate that, if applied correctly, these policies benefit environment and economy alike. The key question is: How to design policy portfolios which foster the creation of an internationally competitive renewable energy equipment industry?

My thesis has answered this question based on the theoretical framework of the narrowly strong Porter Hypothesis (Porter, 1991; Porter & van der Linde, 1995). In essence, the narrowly strong Porter Hypothesis brings together the ideas of induced innovation (Hicks, 1932) and competitive advantage of nations (Porter, 1990), and applies them to the green-tech sector. To a lesser extent, my thesis also builds on the lead market theory for environmental goods and services, which suggests that early adopters of environmental regulation benefit more (Beise, 2001, 2004; Beise & Rennings, 2005).

Following the basic structure of the Porter Hypothesis, my empirical research approach consists of two parts. In the first part, I have conducted a patent analysis to test the impact of environmental regulation on countries' innovative output in solar and wind power technologies. In the second part, I have used a gravity model of trade to estimate the joint impact of environmental regulation and induced innovation on countries' export competitiveness in solar and wind power equipment. The gravity model was also used to conduct the complementary analysis on the lead market theory.

While this doctoral thesis is certainly not first to empirically test the narrowly strong Porter Hypothesis in the renewable energy industry, it advances the existing research in three areas: scope, data quality, and estimation process. The advancements in the scope dimension are twofold. On the one hand, my industry scope is very narrow and only includes manufacturers of solar and wind power technologies. This clear focus reduces the noise from other green-tech sectors. On the other hand, the temporal and geographic scope is very comprehensive and covers 225 countries and territories between 1990 and 2011. Hence, this study is first to go beyond OECD and EU and to test the Porter effect likewise for developing and developed countries. This is of particular importance because of the fact that none of the previous studies included China as an exporting country in a multilateral regression model. Given that China is the world's largest exporter of solar power equipment, its exclusion is a major limitation of earlier publications[131].

Data quality is the area where the advancements of this dissertation are most visible. Richness and accuracy of the data have been improvement along all key elements of the Porter Hypothesis: environmental regulation, technological innovation, and export flows. The level of detail at which environmental regulation was measured is unprecedented in research on the narrowly strong Porter Hypothesis. Besides the obligatory regulation intensity measure, which has been fine-tuned to reflect my narrow industry scope, I distinguish between six clusters and eleven types of policy instruments, which taken together represent all known renewable energy support policies adopted anywhere in the world

[131] Cao & Groba (2013) is the only previous study which included China as exporter. The problem is that this study exclusively concentrates on bilateral trade flows. This means that Cao & Groba (2013) rather explore how regulation affects trade from and into China than international trade.

since 1974. With respect to the remaining two elements, innovation and exports flows, I have not increased the level of detail but the accuracy of the data. Using the novel Y02E classification system, I was able to capture patent applications, my measure of innovative output, more precisely than previous studies which had to rely on the conventional IPC system. The accuracy of trade flow data was improved through a more restrictive selection of commodity classes. In addition, the fact that I have used very recent data should also not be neglected given the speed at which the renewable energy equipment industry develops.

With respect to the third methodological dimension, the estimation approach, my thesis contributes to the literature in two ways. First, I have analyzed the weak and the strong part of the narrowly strong Porter Hypothesis separately in order to demonstrate that an innovation-enhancing effect of environmental regulation, which is critical for the line of argumentation in the strong part, actually exists. Second, I have applied an advanced specification of the gravity model, which controls for multilateral resistance to trade based on pair-wise effects, in all trade flow regressions. This modelling approach ensures that omitted variables on the ease of bilateral trade do not lead to biased estimates.

Based on the procedure described above, this dissertation has reached its objective to shed new light on the politically important relationship between environmental regulation, innovation, and export success in renewable energy equipment. The most important results are summarized in Table 27.

To state the key result first: I have found strong empirical evidence in support of the narrowly strong Porter Hypothesis as well as the lead market theory in my data on the renewable energy equipment industry.

With respect to the main building blocks of the Porter Hypothesis, the data show that more stringent regulation indeed leads to increased innovative outputs in wind and solar power technologies. In contrast to previous studies, though, I found no evidence that this effect differs by technology. Moreover, the results demonstrate that environmental regulation and regulation-induced innovation jointly foster countries' export competitiveness in renewable energy equipment.

As mentioned above, a novelty of this dissertation is its detailed consideration of countries' regulation design. Hence, the corresponding results are of particular importance for the literature on the narrowly strong Porter Hypothesis. The data presented in Part (b) of Table 27 clearly show that the innovation inducing and the competitiveness enhancing aspects of the Porter Hypothesis are driven by different sets of policies. The only policy instrument which strongly fosters both innovation output and export performance is greenhouse gas certificate trading. This special role of carbon trading schemes is of particular interest as this policy instrument comes closest to the original ideas of Porter & van der Linde (1995). Carbon trading fulfills all their criteria of well-crafted environmental regulation: It defines outcomes not methods, it uses market forces, and it is very clear with respect to its scope and its requirements. Hence, the exceptional effectiveness of greenhouse gas certificate trading systems in driving innovation as well as export performance means strong support for the narrowly strong Porter Hypothesis.

Dependent variable	**Innovation**	**Competitiveness**
Explanatory variables	(Step 1)	(Step 2)
(a) Main effects		
Regulation intensity	✓	✓
Innovative output	*n/a*	✓
(b) Effects by instrument clusters		
Renewable energy targets and strategies	✓	✓
RD&D programs	✓	✓
Renewable energy quotas		✓
Feed-in tariffs/Energy production payments	✓	✓
Fiscal incentives	✓	✓
Greenhouse gas certificate trading systems	✓	✓

Notes: Steps 1 and 2 refer to the weak and strong part of the narrowly strong Porter Hypothesis. Large check marks (✓) identify primary drivers with high statistical significance and large coefficient values. Small check marks (✓) identify secondary drivers with medium to high statistical significance and small to medium coefficient values.

Table 27 – Overview: Main drivers of the Porter effect
Source: Own illustration.

Out of the remaining five policy clusters, RD&D programs, and fiscal incentives (with its instruments public spending, capital subsidies, and low-cost loans) are most effective in promoting solar and wind power innovation. Both measures directly address the double externality problem associated with innovation in the renewable energy sector and are therefore very well-suited for getting new technologies off the ground in early stages of development.

In the second step of the narrowly strong Porter Hypothesis, competitiveness enhancement, the key driver besides carbon trading are renewable energy quotas, which are among the strongest demand pull policies. The importance of this instrument highlights how critical domestic demand conditions are for countries' export success.

With respect to the second theory tested in this dissertation, the lead market theory for environmental goods and services, the results show that those countries which have had renewable energy support policies in place for long periods of time benefit considerably more than countries which adopted them just recently. The data suggest that 15 years after policy adoption, export volumes have more than doubled compared to countries not supporting renewables.

The results summarized above have three important implications for the design of effective portfolios of renewable energy support policies. First, their comprehensive effectiveness makes greenhouse gas trading systems the ideal framework policy. Carbon trading increases the renewable energy equipment industry's incentive to innovate as it mutes the pollution externality aspect of the double externality problem; and carbon trading ensures that investments into R&D and new electricity generation capacities are directed towards the most competitive technologies, which will later on be very attractive for the world market.

In addition to a well-crafted framework concept, a good policy portfolio requires, second, a well-balanced mix of supplementary policies. RD&D programs and certain fiscal measures are very effective as technology-push policies in the early stage of development. They help to create first technical know-how in the lab-phase. Quotas and other demand pull policies, in contrast, are very well-suited for the later growth phase. They help to scale up installed capacities and thereby promote the creation of practical know-how which then feeds back into the development process.

Third, the presence of a lead market effect implies that the barriers to enter into the market for renewable energy equipment are getting higher. It increasingly becomes a tough challenge to promote the development of a domestic renewable energy equipment industry. Hence, governments should evaluate carefully if it is still worthwhile to push the development of domestic equipment manufacturers or if it is more promising to concentrate on other parts of the value chain such as parts production, assembly, or maintenance.

Irrespective of it many valuable insights, the empirical results of this doctoral thesis are not free of limitations. Although the improved quality of policy data is one of my important contributions, these data are still far from being perfect. My classification framework assigns each policy instrument to one of eleven categories. Irrespective of the considerably higher level of detail compared to earlier studies, every classification framework remains a simplification of reality and is, therefore, subject to a classical unobserved heterogeneity problem. A closely related problem caused by the high number of policy indicators is multicollinearity. Countries often adopt similar combinations of policy instruments, thus the level correlation between policy variables is generally quite high. Consequently, it is challenging to unmistakably assign changes in the dependent variables to specific policy indicators. However, as policy variables are notoriously difficult to substitute by instrumental variables, there is no straight-forward solution. Another data-related issue compromises the reliability of my export data. The Comtrade database (UN, 2015), which is standard in empirical trade research, is not granular enough to isolate trade in photovoltaics equipment. Trade flows in solar energy related goods are reported in aggregation with other types of photosensitive semiconductors which inevitable increases the level of noise in the data.

Taking into consideration the results as well as the limitations of this research project, the next items on the agenda could be the following. First, the data on export flows in solar and wind power equipment could be improved based on the more detailed 8- and 10-digit HS codes. The challenge of such an approach, however, would be to match these between countries because 8- and 10-digit codes are currently not completely harmonized on a global basis. Second, research could be conducted on the international effect of domestic policy portfolios. In this context, it would be interesting to understand in how far specific domestic policy instruments affect innovation and export activity in other countries. As renewable energy support consumes considerable amounts of financial resources, strong spillover effects would certainly reduce the appeal of the respective policy measures.

Appendix

List of appendices

(a) Cumulative, global end-of-year capacities in GW[1]										
Technology	2004	2005	2006	2007	2008	2009	2010	2011	2012	2013
Solar PV (incl. CSP)	6	7	9	11	17	25	42	72	103	142
Wind power	46	58	73	93	120	158	197	238	283	318
Hydro power	799	815	832	858	875	885	908	933	960	1,000
Other renewables[2]	72	73	76	78	80	85	93	94	95	100
Total	923	953	990	1,040	1,092	1,153	1,240	1,337	1,441	1,560
(b) Global market, in GW/a										
Solar PV (incl. CSP)	1	1	1	2	6	7	17	30	30	40
Wind power	8	12	15	20	27	39	39	41	45	35
Hydro power	19	16	17	26	17	9	23	25	27	40
Other renewables[2]	1	2	2	3	1	5	8	1	1	6
Total	30	31	36	51	51	61	88	97	103	121

(c) Shares in global power plant market, in MW and %				
Technology	2003 (in MW)	2003 (in %)	2013 (in MW)	2013 (in %)
Solar PV (incl. CSP)	1,394	1%	40,662	18%
Wind power	8,365	6%	36,144	16%
Hydro power	19,518	14%	38,403	17%
Other renewables[2]	1,394	1%	2,259	1%
Conventional[3]	108,745	78%	108,432	48%
Total	139,417	100%	225,901	100%

Notes: (1) For the years 2004 to 2012, global capacities at year end have been recalculated based on the total installed capacity at the end of 2013 and annual capacity additions of the years 2004 to 2012. (2) Other renewables include electricity generation from modern biomass and geothermal power. (3) Conventional includes nuclear and fossil-fuel-based (coal gas and oil) power plants.

Appendix 1 – Data table for Figure 1
Source: Own illustration based on data from REN21 (2014a).

(a) Cumulative end-of-year wind power capacity, in MW									
Country	2005	2006	2007	2008	2009	2010	2011	2012	2013
China	1,260	2,599	5,910	12,020	25,805	44,733	62,364	75,324	91,412
United States	9,149	11,575	16,824	25,068	35,086	40,298	46,929	60,007	61,091
Germany	18,415	20,622	22,247	23,903	25,777	27,191	29,071	31,270	34,250
Spain	10,028	11,623	15,145	16,689	19,160	20,623	21,674	22,784	22,959
India	4,430	6,270	7,845	9,655	10,926	13,065	16,084	18,421	20,150
Other	15,809	21,362	25,864	32,962	42,154	51,727	61,928	75,388	88,243
World	59,091	74,051	93,835	120,297	158,908	197,637	238,050	283,194	318,105
(b) Cumulative end-of-year solar power[1] capacity, in MW									
Country	2005	2006	2007	2008	2009	2010	2011	2012	2013[2]
Germany	1,980	2,931	4,205	6,160	9,959	17,370	24,807	32,411	35,411
Italy	38	50	120	458	1,181	3,502	12,923	16,361	18,111
United States	479	624	831	1,169	1,616	2,534	4,431	7,777	11,477
China	*	80	100	140	300	800	3,300	8,300	11,550
Japan	1,422	1,709	1,919	2,144	2,627	3,618	4,914	6,914	9,414
Other	1,193	1,206	2,008	5,773	7,502	12,512	20,094	28,717	52,870
World	5,112	6,600	9,183	15,844	23,185	40,336	70,469	100,480	138,833

Notes: Asterisk (*) indicates that capacity is unknown or marginal, i.e. <1 MW. | (1) Solar power capacities include PV and CSP installations. (2) Solar figures for 2013 are projected.

Appendix 2 – Data table for Figure 4
Source: Own illustration based on data from EPIA (2009, 2011, 2012, 2014) and GWEC (2006, 2008a, 2008b, 2009, 2010, 2011, 2012, 2013).

HS code	Description
(a) Conventional power generation technologies	
84	Nuclear reactors, boilers, machinery and mechanical appliances; parts thereof
8406	Steam turbines and other vapor turbines
840681	Steam turbines and other vapor turbines (excl. for marine propulsion), of an output > 40 MW
840682	Steam turbines and other vapor turbines (excl. for marine propulsion), of an output not > 40 MW
840690	Parts of the steam turbines and other vapor turbines of 8406.10-8406.82
8408	Compression-ignition internal combustion piston engines (diesel or semi-diesel engines).
840890	Internal combustion piston engines (diesel/semi-diesel engines) (excl. of 8408.10 & 8408.20)
8411	Turbo-jets, turbo-propellers and other gas turbines
841181	Gas turbines other than turbo-jets/turbo-propellers, of a power not > 5000 kW
841182	Gas turbines other than turbo-jets/turbo-propellers, of a power > 5000 kW
841199	Parts of the other gas turbines of 8411.81 & 8411.82
85	Electrical machinery and equipment and parts thereof; sound recorders and reproducers, television image and sound recorders and reproducers, and
8502	Electric generating sets and rotary converters
850213	Electric generating sets with C-I internal combustion piston engines (diesel/semi-diesel engines), of an output > 375 kVA
850220	Electric generating sets with spark-ignition internal combustion piston engines
850239	Electric generating sets n.e.s. in 85.02
850240	Electric rotary converters
(b.1) Renewable power generation technologies: Solar	
85	Electrical machinery and equipment and parts thereof; sound recorders and reproducers, television image and sound recorders and reproducers, and parts and accessories of such articles
8541	Diodes, transistors and similar semiconductor devices; photosensitive semiconductor devices, including photovoltaic cells whether or not assembled in modules or made up into panels; light emitting diodes; mounted piezo-electric crystals
854140	Photosensitive semiconductor devices, incl. photovoltaic cells whether/not assembled in modules/made up into panels; light emitting diodes
(b.2) Renewable power generation technologies: Wind	
85	Electrical machinery and equipment and parts thereof; sound recorders and reproducers, television image and sound recorders and reproducers, and parts and accessories of such articles
8502	Electric generating sets and rotary converters
850231	Wind-powered electric generating sets
(b.3) Renewable power generation technologies: Hydro	
84	Nuclear reactors, boilers, machinery and mechanical appliances; parts thereof
8410	Hydraulic turbines, water wheels, and regulators therefor.
841011	Hydraulic turbines & water wheels, of a power not > 1000 kW
841012	Hydraulic turbines & water wheels, of a power > 1000 kW but not > 10000 kW
841013	Hydraulic turbines & water wheels, of a power > 10000 kW
841090	Parts (incl. regulators) of the hydraulic turbines & water wheels of 8410.11-8410.13

Notes: Commodity codes refer to the 2007 version of the Harmonized System.

Appendix 3 – Commodity classes by power generation technology
Source: Own illustration based on information from UN (2015).

Country/Territory	RE targets or strategies	RD&D programs	Quotas		Feed-in tariffs			Fiscal incentives			GHG certificate trading system
			RE quotas with certificate trading system	RE quotas without certificate trading system	Feed-in tariff (fixed or premium; incl. energy prod. payments)	Net metering	Public competitive bidding (tendering)	Tax credits (investment or production)	Tax reduction (carbon, energy, sales, VAT or other taxes)	Public spending, capital subsidies and low-cost loans	
Africa											
Algeria	x				x		x	x			
Angola										x	
Benin	x								x		
Botswana	x								x	x	
Burkina Faso	x				x		x	x	x		
Burundi	x										
Cameroon									x		
Cape Verde	x				x	x	x		x		
Côte d'Ivoire (Ivory Coast)	x								x		
Djibouti	x										
Egypt	x	x			x	x	x		x	x	
Eritrea	x										
Ethiopia	x								x	x	
Gabon	x										
Gambia, The									x		
Ghana	x			x	x				x	x	
Guinea	x								x		
Guinea-Bissau	x								x		
Kenya	x				x		x		x	x	
Lesotho	x				x	x	x	x		x	
Libya	x								x		
Madagascar	x								x		
Malawi	x								x		
Mali	x								x	x	
Mauritania	x										
Mauritius	x				x	x	x			x	
Morocco	x						x			x	
Mozambique	x									x	
Niger	x								x		
Nigeria	x				x				x	x	
Rwanda	x				x				x	x	
Senegal	x		x					x	x		
Seychelles	x									x	

Appendix 4 – RE support policies by country as of 2013
Source: Own illustration based on data from IEA/IRENA (2015), OECD (2015), REN21 (2005, 2006, 2007, 2009, 2010, 2011, 2012, 2013, 2014a, 2014b, 2015).

Country/Territory	RE targets or strategies	RD&D programs	Quotas: RE quotas with certificate trading system	Quotas: RE quotas without certificate trading system	Feed-in tariffs: Feed-in tariff (fixed or premium; incl. energy prod. payments)	Feed-in tariffs: Net metering	Feed-in tariffs: Public competitive bidding (tendering)	Fiscal incentives: Tax credits (investment or production)	Fiscal incentives: Tax reduction (carbon, energy, sales, VAT or other taxes)	Fiscal incentives: Public spending, capital subsidies and low-cost loans	GHG certificate trading system
Africa											
South Africa	x		x			x	x		x	x	
Sudan and South Sudan	x										
Tanzania					x				x	x	
Togo									x		
Tunisia	x					x			x	x	
Uganda	x				x				x	x	
Zambia									x	x	
Zimbabwe	x										
Asia & Oceania											
Australia	x	x		x		x				x	
Bangladesh	x								x	x	
Bhutan	x										
China	x	x	x		x		x	x	x	x	
Fiji	x							x	x		
India	x	x		x	x		x	x	x	x	
Indonesia	x		x		x		x	x	x	x	
Japan	x	x		x	x	x	x			x	
Kiribati	x										
Korea, South	x	x		x		x		x	x	x	
Laos	x										
Malaysia	x		x		x		x		x	x	
Maldives	x						x		x	x	
Marshall Islands	x								x		
Micronesia	x										
Mongolia	x				x		x				
Nauru	x										
Nepal	x						x	x	x	x	
New Zealand	x	x								x	x
Pakistan	x				x	x				x	
Palau	x		x								
Philippines	x		x		x	x	x	x	x	x	
Samoa	x										
Singapore						x	x		x	x	

Appendix 4 – RE support policies by country as of 2013 (cont'd)

Source: Own illustration based on data from IEA/IRENA (2015), OECD (2015), REN21 (2005, 2006, 2007, 2009, 2010, 2011, 2012, 2013, 2014a, 2014b, 2015).

Country/Territory	RE targets or strategies	RD&D programs	Quotas: RE quotas with certificate trading system	Quotas: RE quotas without certificate trading system	Feed-in tariffs: Feed-in tariff (fixed or premium; incl. energy prod. payments)	Feed-in tariffs: Net metering	Feed-in tariffs: Public competitive bidding (tendering)	Fiscal incentives: Tax credits (investment or production)	Fiscal incentives: Tax reduction (carbon, energy, sales, VAT or other taxes)	Fiscal incentives: Public spending, capital subsidies and low-cost loans	GHG certificate trading system
Central & South America											
Solomon Islands	x										
Sri Lanka	x		x		x	x			x	x	
Taiwan	x	x			x						
Thailand	x				x				x	x	
Timor-Leste (East Timor)	x										
Tonga	x										
Vanuatu	x								x		
Vietnam	x			x	x			x	x	x	
Antigua and Barbuda	x										
Argentina	x				x		x	x	x	x	
Bahamas, The	x										
Barbados	x					x			x	x	
Belize	x										
Brazil	x					x	x	x	x	x	
Chile	x		x			x	x		x	x	
Colombia	x								x		
Costa Rica	x						x		x		
Dominica	x										
Dominican Republic	x				x	x	x	x	x	x	
Ecuador					x		x		x	x	
El Salvador					x		x	x	x	x	
Grenada	x					x			x		
Guatemala	x					x	x	x	x		
Guyana	x								x		
Haiti										x	
Honduras	x					x	x	x	x		
Jamaica	x					x	x	x	x		
Nicaragua	x				x				x		
Panama					x	x	x	x	x		
Paraguay									x		
Peru							x	x	x	x	
Saint Kitts and Nevis	x										
Saint Lucia	x					x					

Appendix 4 – RE support policies by country as of 2013 (cont'd)

Source: Own illustration based on data from IEA/IRENA (2015), OECD (2015), REN21 (2005, 2006, 2007, 2009, 2010, 2011, 2012, 2013, 2014a, 2014b, 2015).

Country/Territory	RE targets or strategies	RD&D programs	Quotas: RE quotas with certificate trading system	Quotas: RE quotas without certificate trading system	Feed-in tariffs: Feed-in tariff (fixed or premium; incl. energy prod. payments)	Feed-in tariffs: Net metering	Feed-in tariffs: Public competitive bidding (tendering)	Fiscal incentives: Tax credits (investment or production)	Fiscal incentives: Tax reduction (carbon, energy, sales, VAT or other taxes)	Fiscal incentives: Public spending, capital subsidies and low-cost loans	GHG certificate trading system
Central & South America											
Saint Vincent/Grenadines	x										
Suriname	x										
Trinidad and Tobago	x							x	x		
Uruguay	x				x	x	x		x	x	
Eurasia											
Armenia	x				x						
Azerbaijan	x									x	
Belarus	x	x			x				x	x	
Estonia	x				x					x	x
Kazakhstan	x			x	x				x	x	
Kyrgyzstan			x						x	x	
Latvia	x				x	x	x		x	x	x
Lithuania	x		x		x				x	x	x
Moldova	x				x					x	
Russia	x	x					x			x	
Tajikistan	x										
Ukraine	x	x			x	x			x	x	
Uzbekistan							x				
Europe											
Albania	x			x	x	x	x	x	x	x	
Andorra					x						
Austria	x	x		x	x			x		x	x
Belgium	x	x		x			x	x	x		x
Bosnia and Herzegovina	x				x		x			x	
Bulgaria	x				x					x	x
Croatia	x				x						x
Cyprus	x				x	x	x			x	x
Czech Republic	x	x		x				x	x	x	x
Denmark	x	x		x	x	x	x	x	x	x	x
Finland	x	x		x	x				x	x	x
France	x	x		x	x		x	x	x	x	x
Germany	x	x			x			x	x	x	x
Greece	x				x	x		x	x	x	x

Appendix 4 – RE support policies by country as of 2013 (cont'd)

Source: Own illustration based on data from IEA/IRENA (2015), OECD (2015), REN21 (2005, 2006, 2007, 2009, 2010, 2011, 2012, 2013, 2014a, 2014b, 2015).

Country/Territory	RE targets or strategies	RD&D programs	Quotas: RE quotas with certificate trading system	Quotas: RE quotas without certificate trading system	Feed-in tariffs: Feed-in tariff (fixed or premium; incl. energy prod. payments)	Feed-in tariffs: Net metering	Feed-in tariffs: Public competitive bidding (tendering)	Fiscal incentives: Tax credits (investment or production)	Fiscal incentives: Tax reduction (carbon, energy, sales, VAT or other taxes)	Fiscal incentives: Public spending, capital subsidies and low-cost loans	GHG certificate trading system
Europe											
Hungary	x	x		x	x				x	x	x
Iceland											x
Ireland	x	x		x	x		x			x	x
Italy	x	x		x	x	x	x	x	x	x	x
Kosovo	x										
Luxembourg	x	x			x					x	x
Macedonia	x				x						
Malta	x				x	x	x		x	x	x
Montenegro	x				x						
Netherlands	x	x		x	x	x		x	x	x	x
Norway	x	x		x	x		x		x	x	x
Poland	x	x		x			x		x	x	x
Portugal	x	x	x		x	x	x		x		x
Romania	x			x						x	x
Serbia	x				x					x	
Slovakia	x	x		x	x				x	x	x
Slovenia	x			x	x		x	x	x	x	x
Spain	x	x		x	x	x	x	x		x	x
Sweden	x	x		x				x	x	x	x
Switzerland	x	x			x				x	x	
Turkey	x				x					x	
United Kingdom	x	x		x	x				x	x	x
Middle East											
Bahrain										x	
Iran	x	x			x			x		x	
Iraq	x										
Israel	x	x	x		x		x		x	x	
Jordan	x	x			x	x	x		x	x	
Kuwait	x						x				
Lebanon	x					x			x		
Palestinian Territories	x				x	x			x		
Qatar	x										
Saudi Arabia	x										

Appendix 4 – RE support policies by country as of 2013 (cont'd)
Source: Own illustration based on data from IEA/IRENA (2015), OECD (2015), and REN21 (2005, 2006, 2007, 2009, 2010, 2011, 2012, 2013, 2014a, 2014b, 2015).

Country/Territory	RE targets or strategies	RD&D programs	Quotas		Feed-in tariffs			Fiscal incentives			GHG certificate trading system
			RE quotas with certificate trading system	RE quotas without certificate trading system	Feed-in tariff (fixed or premium; incl. energy prod. payments)	Net metering	Public competitive bidding (tendering)	Tax credits (investment or production)	Tax reduction (carbon, energy, sales, VAT or other taxes)	Public spending, capital subsidies and low-cost loans	
Middle East											
Syria	x				x	x	x	x			
Yemen	x										
North America											
Canada		x					x	x	x	x	
Mexico	x	x				x	x	x		x	
United States		x			x		x	x	x	x	

Notes: x indicates that at least one policy from a given policy category has been enacted into law and is still active. Some of these policies might only apply on a regional level (e.g. states). Local level policies (e.g. counties, cities) are not considered in this overview. Moreover, this table shows only renewable energy policies which promote electricity generation from wind and/or solar. However, policies are not necessarily restricted to these two technologies and might at the same time also support other renewables such as geothermal power.

Appendix 4 – RE support policies by country as of 2013 (cont'd)
Source: Own illustration based on data from IEA/IRENA (2015), OECD (2015), and REN21 (2005, 2006, 2007, 2009, 2010, 2011, 2012, 2013, 2014a, 2014b, 2015).

			Quotas		Feed-in tariffs			Fiscal incentives			
Country/Territory	RE targets or strategies	RD&D programs	RE quotas with certificate trading system	RE quotas without certificate trading system	Feed-in tariff (fixed or premium; incl. energy prod. payments)	Net metering	Public competitive bidding (tendering)	Tax credits (investment or production)	Tax reduction (carbon, energy, sales, VAT or other taxes)	Public spending, capital subsidies and low-cost loans	GHG certificate trading system
Africa											
Algeria	x				x						
Botswana	x								x	x	
Burkina Faso	x										
Cape Verde	x										
Egypt	x	x			x		x		x	x	
Ethiopia	x								x	x	
Gabon	x										
Gambia, The									x		
Ghana	x			x					x	x	
Kenya	x				x				x		
Libya	x										
Madagascar	x										
Malawi	x										
Mali	x								x	x	
Mauritius	x				x	x				x	
Morocco	x						x			x	
Mozambique	x									x	
Namibia	x										
Niger	x										
Nigeria	x				x						
Rwanda	x								x	x	
Senegal	x							x			
Seychelles										x	
South Africa	x			x	x		x			x	
Tanzania					x				x	x	
Tunisia	x								x	x	
Uganda	x								x	x	
Zambia									x		
Asia & Oceania											
Australia	x	x		x		x				x	
Bangladesh	x									x	
China	x		x		x		x			x	
Fiji	x										

Appendix 5 – RE support policies by country as of 2010
Source: Own illustration based on data from IEA/IRENA (2015), OECD (2015), and REN21 (2005, 2006, 2007, 2009, 2010, 2011, 2012, 2013, 2014a, 2014b, 2015).

Country/Territory	RE targets or strategies	RD&D programs	Quotas: RE quotas with certificate trading system	Quotas: RE quotas without certificate trading system	Feed-in tariffs: Feed-in tariff (fixed or premium; incl. energy prod. payments)	Feed-in tariffs: Net metering	Feed-in tariffs: Public competitive bidding (tendering)	Fiscal incentives: Tax credits (investment or production)	Fiscal incentives: Tax reduction (carbon, energy, sales, VAT or other taxes)	Fiscal incentives: Public spending, capital subsidies and low-cost loans	GHG certificate trading system
Asia & Oceania											
India	x	x		x	x		x	x	x	x	
Indonesia	x				x		x	x	x	x	
Japan	x	x		x	x	x				x	
Korea, South	x	x		x	x			x	x	x	
Malaysia	x				x					x	
Maldives	x								x	x	
Marshall Islands									x		
Mongolia	x				x		x				
Nepal	x						x	x	x	x	
New Zealand	x	x								x	x
Pakistan	x				x	x				x	
Philippines	x		x		x	x	x	x	x	x	
Samoa	x										
Singapore										x	
Sri Lanka	x				x						
Taiwan	x	x			x						
Thailand	x				x				x	x	
Tonga	x										
Vietnam	x							x	x	x	
Central & South America											
Argentina	x				x		x	x	x	x	
Bolivia									x		
Brazil	x						x		x	x	
Chile	x		x						x	x	
Colombia	x									x	
Costa Rica					x						
Dominican Republic	x				x			x	x	x	
Ecuador					x						
El Salvador					x		x	x	x	x	
Guatemala						x	x	x	x		
Honduras							x	x	x		
Jamaica	x										
Nicaragua	x				x			x	x		

Appendix 5 – RE support policies by country as of 2010 (cont'd)
Source: Own illustration based on data from IEA/IRENA (2015), OECD (2015), and REN21 (2005, 2006, 2007, 2009, 2010, 2011, 2012, 2013, 2014a, 2014b, 2015).

Country/Territory	RE targets or strategies	RD&D programs	Quotas: RE quotas with certificate trading system	Quotas: RE quotas without certificate trading system	Feed-in tariffs: Feed-in tariff (fixed or premium; incl. energy prod. payments)	Feed-in tariffs: Net metering	Feed-in tariffs: Public competitive bidding (tendering)	Fiscal incentives: Tax credits (investment or production)	Fiscal incentives: Tax reduction (carbon, energy, sales, VAT or other taxes)	Fiscal incentives: Public spending, capital subsidies and low-cost loans	GHG certificate trading system
Central & South America											
Panama					x		x				
Peru	x				x		x	x	x		
Trinidad and Tobago								x	x	x	
Uruguay	x		x				x		x		
Eurasia											
Armenia	x				x						
Azerbaijan	x										
Belarus	x								x	x	
Estonia	x				x				x	x	x
Kazakhstan				x	x				x	x	
Kyrgyzstan			x						x	x	
Latvia	x				x		x		x	x	x
Lithuania	x				x				x	x	x
Moldova	x				x				x	x	
Russia	x	x		x						x	
Ukraine	x	x			x				x		
Europe											
Albania	x				x						
Austria	x	x		x	x			x		x	x
Belgium	x	x		x		x		x	x	x	x
Bosnia and Herzegovina					x		x				
Bulgaria	x				x				x	x	x
Croatia	x				x					x	
Cyprus	x				x		x			x	x
Czech Republic	x	x		x	x			x	x	x	x
Denmark	x	x		x	x	x	x	x	x	x	x
Finland	x	x		x	x				x	x	x
France	x	x		x	x		x	x	x	x	x
Germany	x	x			x			x	x	x	x
Greece	x	x			x			x		x	x
Hungary	x	x		x	x				x	x	x
Iceland											x

Appendix 5 – RE support policies by country as of 2010 (cont'd)
Source: Own illustration based on data from IEA/IRENA (2015), OECD (2015), and REN21 (2005, 2006, 2007, 2009, 2010, 2011, 2012, 2013, 2014a, 2014b, 2015).

Country/Territory	RE targets or strategies	RD&D programs	Quotas: RE quotas with certificate trading system	Quotas: RE quotas without certificate trading system	Feed-in tariffs: Feed-in tariff (fixed or premium; incl. energy prod. payments)	Feed-in tariffs: Net metering	Feed-in tariffs: Public competitive bidding (tendering)	Fiscal incentives: Tax credits (investment or production)	Fiscal incentives: Tax reduction (carbon, energy, sales, VAT or other taxes)	Fiscal incentives: Public spending, capital subsidies and low-cost loans	GHG certificate trading system
Europe											
Ireland	x	x		x	x		x			x	x
Italy	x	x		x	x	x	x	x	x	x	x
Luxembourg	x	x			x					x	x
Macedonia					x					x	
Malta	x				x	x			x	x	x
Montenegro	x				x						
Netherlands	x	x		x	x			x	x	x	x
Norway	x	x		x	x				x	x	x
Poland	x	x		x			x		x	x	x
Portugal	x		x		x	x	x	x	x	x	x
Romania	x			x					x	x	x
Serbia	x				x						
Slovakia	x	x			x				x	x	x
Slovenia	x			x	x		x	x	x	x	x
Spain	x	x			x		x	x	x	x	x
Sweden	x	x		x	x			x	x	x	x
Switzerland	x	x			x				x	x	
Turkey	x				x						
United Kingdom	x	x		x	x				x	x	x
Middle East											
Iran	x				x			x			
Israel	x	x			x		x		x		
Jordan	x	x				x			x		
Kuwait	x										
Lebanon	x										
Palestinian Territories	x								x		
Syria	x										
Yemen	x										

Appendix 5 – RE support policies by country as of 2010 (cont'd)
Source: Own illustration based on data from IEA/IRENA (2015), OECD (2015), and REN21 (2005, 2006, 2007, 2009, 2010, 2011, 2012, 2013, 2014a, 2014b, 2015).

Country/Territory	RE targets or strategies	RD&D programs	Quotas: RE quotas with certificate trading system	Quotas: RE quotas without certificate trading system	Feed-in tariffs: Feed-in tariff (fixed or premium; incl. energy prod. payments)	Feed-in tariffs: Net metering	Feed-in tariffs: Public competitive bidding (tendering)	Fiscal incentives: Tax credits (investment or production)	Fiscal incentives: Tax reduction (carbon, energy, sales, VAT or other taxes)	Fiscal incentives: Public spending, capital subsidies and low-cost loans	GHG certificate trading system
North America											
Canada	x	x				x	x	x	x	x	
Mexico	x	x				x	x	x		x	
United States		x		x	x		x	x	x	x	

Notes: x indicates that at least one policy from a given policy category has been enacted into law and is still active. Some of these policies might only apply on a regional level (e.g. states). Local level policies (e.g. counties, cities) are not considered in this overview. Moreover, this table shows only renewable energy policies which promote electricity generation from wind and/or solar. However, policies are not necessarily restricted to these two technologies and might at the same time also support other renewables such as geothermal power.

Appendix 5 – RE support policies by country as of 2010 (cont'd)
Source: Own illustration based on data from IEA/IRENA (2015), OECD (2015), and REN21 (2005, 2006, 2007, 2009, 2010, 2011, 2012, 2013, 2014a, 2014b, 2015).

Country/Territory	RE targets or strategies	RD&D programs	Quotas: RE quotas with certificate trading system	Quotas: RE quotas without certificate trading system	Feed-in tariffs: Feed-in tariff (fixed or premium; incl. energy prod. payments)	Feed-in tariffs: Net metering	Feed-in tariffs: Public competitive bidding (tendering)	Fiscal incentives: Tax credits (investment or production)	Fiscal incentives: Tax reduction (carbon, energy, sales, VAT or other taxes)	Fiscal incentives: Public spending, capital subsidies and low-cost loans	GHG certificate trading system
Africa											
Algeria					x						
Botswana	x	x								x	
Egypt	x										
Ghana									x	x	
Mali	x									x	
Morocco	x							x			
Nigeria	x										
South Africa	x										
Tunisia									x		
Uganda	x									x	
Asia & Oceania											
Australia	x	x		x						x	
Bangladesh	x										
Cambodia										x	
China	x				x		x	x	x	x	
India	x						x	x	x	x	
Indonesia	x				x						
Japan	x	x		x		x				x	
Korea, South	x	x			x				x	x	
Malaysia	x										
Mongolia										x	
New Zealand	x	x								x	
Pakistan	x										
Philippines	x							x	x	x	
Sri Lanka					x						
Thailand	x		x			x				x	
Central & South America											
Argentina					x					x	
Brazil	x				x		x			x	
Chile										x	
Costa Rica					x						
Dominican Republic	x										
Ecuador					x						

Appendix 6 – RE support policies by country as of 2005
Source: Own illustration based on data from IEA/IRENA (2015), OECD (2015), and REN21 (2005, 2006, 2007, 2009, 2010, 2011, 2012, 2013, 2014a, 2014b, 2015).

Country/Territory	RE targets or strategies	RD&D programs	Quotas: RE quotas with certificate trading system	Quotas: RE quotas without certificate trading system	Feed-in tariffs: Feed-in tariff (fixed or premium; incl. energy prod. payments)	Feed-in tariffs: Net metering	Feed-in tariffs: Public competitive bidding (tendering)	Fiscal incentives: Tax credits (investment or production)	Fiscal incentives: Tax reduction (carbon, energy, sales, VAT or other taxes)	Fiscal incentives: Public spending, capital subsidies and low-cost loans	GHG certificate trading system
Eurasia											
Guatemala								x	x		
Nicaragua					x			x			
Eurasia											
Armenia					x						
Azerbaijan	x										
Estonia	x				x				x		x
Latvia	x				x					x	x
Lithuania	x				x			x		x	x
Russia	x	x									
Ukraine	x	x									
Europe											
Austria	x	x		x	x			x		x	x
Belgium	x			x		x		x		x	x
Croatia	x										
Cyprus	x				x					x	x
Czech Republic	x	x		x	x	x		x	x	x	x
Denmark	x	x		x	x	x		x			x
Finland	x	x		x	x				x	x	x
France	x	x		x	x		x	x	x	x	x
Germany	x	x			x			x	x	x	x
Greece	x	x			x			x		x	x
Hungary	x	x		x	x				x	x	x
Ireland	x	x		x	x		x	x		x	x
Italy	x	x		x	x	x		x		x	x
Luxembourg	x	x			x			x	x	x	x
Malta	x								x		x
Montenegro	x										
Netherlands	x	x		x	x			x	x	x	x
Norway	x	x		x			x	x		x	x
Poland	x		x				x		x	x	x
Portugal	x				x			x	x	x	x
Slovakia	x				x			x		x	x
Slovenia	x				x						x

Appendix 6 – RE support policies by country as of 2005 (cont'd)
Source: Own illustration based on data from IEA/IRENA (2015), OECD (2015), and REN21 (2005, 2006, 2007, 2009, 2010, 2011, 2012, 2013, 2014a, 2014b, 2015).

Country/Territory	RE targets or strategies	RD&D programs	Quotas: RE quotas with certificate trading system	Quotas: RE quotas without certificate trading system	Feed-in tariffs: Feed-in tariff (fixed or premium; incl. energy prod. payments)	Feed-in tariffs: Net metering	Feed-in tariffs: Public competitive bidding (tendering)	Fiscal incentives: Tax credits (investment or production)	Fiscal incentives: Tax reduction (carbon, energy, sales, VAT or other taxes)	Fiscal incentives: Public spending, capital subsidies and low-cost loans	GHG certificate trading system
Europe											
Spain	x	x			x			x		x	x
Sweden	x	x		x	x			x	x	x	x
Switzerland	x	x			x						
Turkey	x				x					x	
United Kingdom	x	x		x	x				x	x	x
Middle East											
Iran	x										
Israel	x				x						
Jordan	x										
North America											
Canada	x	x						x	x	x	
Mexico						x		x			
United States	x	x			x			x		x	

Notes: x indicates that at least one policy from a given policy category has been enacted into law and is still active. Some of these policies might only apply on a regional level (e.g. states). Local level policies (e.g. counties, cities) are not considered in this overview. Moreover, this table shows only renewable energy policies which promote electricity generation from wind and/or solar. However, policies are not necessarily restricted to these two technologies and might at the same time also support other renewables such as geothermal power.

Appendix 6 – RE support policies by country as of 2005 (cont'd)
Source: Own illustration based on data from IEA/IRENA (2015), OECD (2015), and REN21 (2005, 2006, 2007, 2009, 2010, 2011, 2012, 2013, 2014a, 2014b, 2015).

Country/Territory	RE targets or strategies	RD&D programs	Quotas		Feed-in tariffs			Fiscal incentives			GHG certificate trading system
			RE quotas with certificate trading system	RE quotas without certificate trading system	Feed-in tariff (fixed or premium; incl. energy prod. payments)	Net metering	Public competitive bidding (tendering)	Tax credits (investment or production)	Tax reduction (carbon, energy, sales, VAT or other taxes)	Public spending, capital subsidies and low-cost loans	
Africa											
Botswana	x									x	
Ghana									x	x	
Mali										x	
Tunisia									x		
Asia & Oceania											
Australia		x								x	
Bangladesh	x										
Japan		x									
Korea, South	x										
Mongolia										x	
New Zealand		x									
Philippines	x									x	
Sri Lanka					x						
Central & South America											
Argentina										x	
Eurasia											
Ukraine	x	x									
Europe											
Austria		x									
Belgium			x								
Denmark		x			x	x					
Finland	x	x			x						
France		x									
Germany		x			x					x	
Greece		x			x						
Hungary	x	x								x	
Italy		x	x		x						
Luxembourg		x			x				x	x	
Netherlands		x			x				x		
Norway		x			x						
Portugal		x			x						
Slovenia					x						
Spain	x	x			x						

Appendix 7 – RE support policies by country as of 2000

Source: Own illustration based on data from IEA/IRENA (2015), OECD (2015), and REN21 (2005, 2006, 2007, 2009, 2010, 2011, 2012, 2013, 2014a, 2014b, 2015).

			Quotas		Feed-in tariffs			Fiscal incentives			
Country/Territory	RE targets or strategies	RD&D programs	RE quotas with certificate trading system	RE quotas without certificate trading system	Feed-in tariff (fixed or premium; incl. energy prod. payments)	Net metering	Public competitive bidding (tendering)	Tax credits (investment or production)	Tax reduction (carbon, energy, sales, VAT or other taxes)	Public spending, capital subsidies and low-cost loans	GHG certificate trading system
Europe											
Sweden		x			x						
Switzerland		x			x						
Turkey		x									
United Kingdom		x									
North America											
Canada		x									
United States		x						x		x	

Notes: x indicates that at least one policy from a given policy category has been enacted into law and is still active. Some of these policies might only apply on a regional level (e.g. states). Local level policies (e.g. counties, cities) are not considered in this overview. Moreover, this table shows only renewable energy policies which promote electricity generation from wind and/or solar. However, policies are not necessarily restricted to these two technologies and might at the same time also support other renewables such as geothermal power.

Appendix 7 – RE support policies by country as of 2000 (cont'd)

Source: Own illustration based on data from IEA/IRENA (2015), OECD (2015), and REN21 (2005, 2006, 2007, 2009, 2010, 2011, 2012, 2013, 2014a, 2014b, 2015).

			Quotas		Feed-in tariffs			Fiscal incentives			
Country/Territory	RE targets or strategies	RD&D programs	RE quotas with certificate trading system	RE quotas without certificate trading system	Feed-in tariff (fixed or premium; incl. energy prod. payments)	Net metering	Public competitive bidding (tendering)	Tax credits (investment or production)	Tax reduction (carbon, energy, sales, VAT or other taxes)	Public spending, capital subsidies and low-cost loans	GHG certificate trading system
Asia & Oceania											
Australia		x									
Japan		x									
Korea, South	x										
New Zealand		x									
Europe											
Austria		x									
Denmark		x									
Finland		x									
France		x									
Germany		x			x					x	
Ireland		x									
Italy		x									
Netherlands		x									
Norway		x									
Portugal		x									
Spain		x									
Sweden		x									
Switzerland		x									
United Kingdom		x									
North America											
Canada		x									
United States		x			x			x			

Notes: x indicates that at least one policy from a given policy category has been enacted into law and is still active. Some of these policies might only apply on a regional level (e.g. states). Local level policies (e.g. counties, cities) are not considered in this overview. Moreover, this table shows only renewable energy policies which promote electricity generation from wind and/or solar. However, policies are not necessarily restricted to these two technologies and might at the same time also support other renewables such as geothermal power.

Appendix 8 – RE support policies by country as of 1990

Source: Own illustration based on data from IEA/IRENA (2015), OECD (2015), and REN21 (2005, 2006, 2007, 2009, 2010, 2011, 2012, 2013, 2014a, 2014b, 2015).

Country/Territory	GDP per capita			Energy intensity per capita			Primary energy ex-/importer		
	'10	'00	'90	'10	'00	'90	'10	'00	'90
Africa									
Algeria	2	3	3	2	2	3	Ex	Ex	Ex
Angola	2	2	2	2	1	1	Ex	Ex	Ex
Benin	1	1	1	1	1	1	Im	Im	Ex
Botswana	3	3	3	2	2	2	Im	Im	Im
Burkina Faso	1	1	1	1	1	1	Im	Im	Im
Burundi	1	1	1	1	1	1	Im	Im	Im
Cameroon	2	2	2	1	1	1	Ex	Ex	Ex
Cape Verde	2	2	2	1	1	1	Im	Im	Im
Central African Republic	1	1	1	1	1	1	Im	Im	Im
Chad	1	1	1	1	1	1	Ex	Im	Im
Comoros	1	1	2	1	1	1	Im	Im	Im
Congo (Brazzaville)	2	2	2	2	1	2	Ex	Ex	Ex
Congo (Kinshasa)	1	1	1	1	1	1	Ex	Ex	Ex
Côte d'Ivoire	1	2	2	1	1	1	Ex	Im	Im
Djibouti	2	2	2	2	2	3	Im	Im	Im
Egypt	2	2	2	2	2	2	Ex	Ex	Ex
Equatorial Guinea	4	3	2	3	1	1	Ex	Ex	Im
Eritrea	1	1		1	1		Im	Im	
Ethiopia	1	1	1	1	1	1	Im	Im	Im
Gabon	3	3	3	2	2	3	Ex	Ex	Ex
Gambia, The	1	1	1	1	1	1	Im	Im	Im
Ghana	1	1	1	1	1	1	Im	Im	Im
Guinea	2	2	2	1	1	1	Im	Im	Im
Guinea-Bissau	1	1	1	1	1	1	Im	Im	Im
Kenya	1	1	1	1	1	1	Im	Im	Im
Lesotho	1	1	1	1	1	1	Im	Im	Im
Liberia	1	1	1	1	1	1	Im	Im	Im
Libya	3	3	3	4	3	4	Ex	Ex	Ex
Madagascar	1	1	1	1	1	1	Im	Im	Im
Malawi	1	1	1	1	1	1	Im	Im	Im
Mali	1	1	1	1	1	1	Im	Im	Im
Mauritania	1	1	1	1	2	1	Im	Im	Im
Mauritius	4	3	3	2	2	2	Im	Im	Im
Morocco	2	2	2	2	2	2	Im	Im	Im
Mozambique	1	1	1	1	1	1	Ex	Im	Im
Namibia	2	2	3	2	2	2	Im	Im	Im
Niger	1	1	1	1	1	1	Im	Im	Im
Nigeria	1	1	1	1	1	1	Ex	Ex	Ex

Appendix 9 – List of countries with cluster values
Source: Own illustration based on data from EIA (2015).

Country/Territory	GDP per capita			Energy intensity per capita			Primary energy ex-/importer		
	'10	'00	'90	'10	'00	'90	'10	'00	'90
Africa									
Reunion	3	3	3	3	3	3	Im	Im	Im
Rwanda	1	1	1	1	1	1	Im	Im	Im
Saint Helena				2	2	2	Im	Im	Im
Sao Tome and Principe	1	1	1	1	1	2	Im	Im	Im
Senegal	1	1	1	1	1	1	Im	Im	Im
Seychelles	4	4	4	4	3	3	Im	Im	Im
Sierra Leone	1	1	2	1	1	1	Im	Im	Im
Somalia	1	1	1	1	1	1	Im	Im	Im
South Africa	3	3	3	3	3	3	Ex	Ex	Ex
Sudan and South Sudan	1	1	1	1	1	1	Ex	Ex	Im
Swaziland	2	3	3	1	2	2	Im	Im	Im
Tanzania	1	1	1	1	1	1	Im	Im	Im
Togo	1	1	1	1	1	1	Im	Im	Im
Tunisia	3	3	2	2	2	2	Im	Im	Ex
Uganda	1	1	1	1	1	1	Im	Im	Im
Western Sahara				1	1	2	Im	Im	Im
Zambia	1	1	1	1	1	2	Im	Im	Im
Zimbabwe	1	2	2	2	2	2	Im	Im	Im
Asia & Oceania									
Afghanistan	1	1	1	1	1	1	Im	Im	Im
American Samoa	3	3	3	4	4	4	Im	Im	Im
Australia	4	4	4	4	4	4	Ex	Ex	Ex
Bangladesh	2	1	1	1	1	1	Im	Im	Im
Bhutan	2	2	1	3	2	2	Ex	Ex	Ex
Brunei	3	4	4	4	4	4	Ex	Ex	Ex
Burma (Myanmar)	2	1	1	1	1	1	Ex	Im	Im
Cambodia	2	1	1	1	1	1	Im	Im	Im
China	2	2	1	3	2	2	Im	Im	Ex
Cook Islands				3	3	2	Im	Im	Im
Fiji	2	2	2	2	2	2	Im	Im	Im
French Polynesia				3	2	3	Im	Im	Im
Guam	4	4	4	4	4	4	Im	Im	Im
Hawaiian Trade Zone									
Hong Kong	4	4	4	4	3	3	Im	Im	Im
India	2	1	1	2	2	2	Im	Im	Im
Indonesia	2	2	2	2	2	2	Ex	Ex	Ex
Japan	4	4	4	4	4	4	Im	Im	Im
Kiribati	2	3	2	1	1	1	Im	Im	Im
Korea, North	1	2	2	2	2	3	Ex	Im	Im

Appendix 9 – List of countries with cluster values (cont'd)
Source: Own illustration based on data from EIA (2015).

Country/Territory	GDP per capita			Energy intensity per capita			Primary energy ex-/importer		
	'10	'00	'90	'10	'00	'90	'10	'00	'90
Asia & Oceania									
Korea, South	4	3	3	4	4	3	Im	Im	Im
Laos	2	1	1	1	1	1	Ex	Ex	Im
Macau	4	4	4	2	3	3	Im	Im	Im
Malaysia	3	3	3	3	3	3	Ex	Ex	Ex
Maldives	2	2	2	2	2	1	Im	Im	Im
Mongolia	2	1	2	2	2	3	Ex	Im	Im
Nauru				4	4	4	Im	Im	Im
Nepal	1	1	1	1	1	1	Im	Im	Im
New Caledonia				4	4	4	Im	Im	Im
New Zealand	4	4	4	4	4	4	Im	Im	Im
Niue				2	2	2	Im	Im	Im
Pakistan	2	2	2	2	2	2	Im	Im	Im
Papua New Guinea	1	1	1	1	1	2	Ex	Ex	Im
Philippines	2	2	2	1	2	2	Im	Im	Im
Samoa	2	2	2	2	2	2	Im	Im	Im
Singapore	4	4	4	4	4	4	Im	Im	Im
Solomon Islands	1	2	2	1	1	1	Im	Im	Im
Sri Lanka	2	2	2	1	1	1	Im	Im	Im
Taiwan	4	4	3	4	4	3	Im	Im	Im
Thailand	3	2	2	3	2	2	Im	Im	Im
Timor-Leste (East Timor)	1			1			Ex		
Tonga	2	2	2	2	2	2	Im	Im	Im
US Pacific Islands							Im	Im	Im
Vanuatu	2	2	2	1	1	2	Im	Im	Im
Vietnam	1	1	1	2	1	1	Ex	Ex	Ex
Wake Island							Im	Im	Im
Central & South America									
Antarctica							Im	Im	Im
Antigua and Barbuda	3	4	4	3	3	3	Im	Im	Im
Argentina	3	3	3	3	3	3	Im	Ex	Ex
Aruba	3	4	4	4	4	4	Im	Im	Im
Bahamas, The	4	4	4	4	4	4	Im	Im	Im
Barbados	4	4	4	3	3	3	Im	Im	Im
Belize	3	3	3	2	2	2	Ex	Im	Im
Bolivia	2	2	2	2	2	2	Ex	Ex	Ex
Brazil	3	3	3	2	3	3	Im	Im	Im
Cayman Islands	4	4	4	4	4	4	Im	Im	Im
Chile	3	3	3	3	3	3	Im	Im	Im

Appendix 9 – List of countries with cluster values (cont'd)
Source: Own illustration based on data from EIA (2015).

Country/Territory	GDP per capita			Energy intensity per capita			Primary energy ex-/importer		
	'10	'00	'90	'10	'00	'90	'10	'00	'90
Central & South America									
Colombia	2	2	2	2	2	2	Ex	Ex	Ex
Costa Rica	3	3	3	2	2	2	Im	Im	Im
Cuba	1	1	1	2	2	3	Im	Im	Im
Dominica	3	3	3	2	2	2	Im	Im	Im
Dominican Republic	3	2	2	2	2	2	Im	Im	Im
Ecuador	2	2	2	2	2	2	Ex	Ex	Ex
El Salvador	2	2	2	2	2	2	Im	Im	Im
Falkland Islands				4	4	4	Im	Im	Im
French Guiana	3	3	3	3	3	3	Im	Im	Im
Grenada	3	3	3	2	2	2	Im	Im	Im
Guadeloupe				3	3	3	Im	Im	Im
Guatemala	2	2	2	2	2	2	Im	Im	Im
Guyana		2	2		2	2	Im	Im	Im
Haiti	1	2	2	1	1	1	Im	Im	Im
Honduras	2	2	2	2	2	2	Im	Im	Im
Jamaica	2	3	3	2	3	3	Im	Im	Im
Martinique	4	4	4	3	3	3	Im	Im	Im
Montserrat				4	4	3	Im	Im	Im
Netherlands Antilles	3	3	4	4	4	4	Im	Im	Im
Nicaragua	1	1	1	1	2	2	Im	Im	Im
Panama	3	3	3	3	3	3	Im	Im	Im
Paraguay	2	2	2	3	3	3	Ex	Ex	Ex
Peru	3	2	2	2	2	2	Im	Im	Ex
Puerto Rico	4	4	4	3	3	3	Im	Im	Im
Saint Kitts and Nevis	3	3	3	3	2	2	Im	Im	Im
Saint Lucia	3	3	3	2	2	2	Im	Im	Im
St. Vincent/Grenadines	3	3	3	2	2	2	Im	Im	Im
Suriname	2	2		3	3	3	Ex	Ex	Im
Trinidad and Tobago	4	3	3	4	4	4	Ex	Ex	Ex
Turks & Caicos Islands				3	2	1	Im	Im	
Uruguay	3	3	3	3	3	3	Im	Im	Im
Venezuela	3	3	3	3	3	3	Ex	Ex	Ex
Virgin Islands, US	4	4	4	4	4	4	Im	Im	Im
Virgin Islands, British				3	2	3	Im	Im	Im
Eurasia									
Azerbaijan	3	2		3	3		Ex	Ex	
Belarus	3	3		3	3		Im	Im	
Estonia	3	3		3	3		Im	Im	
Former USSR			3			4			Ex
Georgia	2	2		2	2		Im	Im	

Appendix 9 – List of countries with cluster values (cont'd)
Source: Own illustration based on data from EIA (2015).

Country/Territory	GDP per capita			Energy intensity per capita			Primary energy ex-/importer		
	'10	'00	'90	'10	'00	'90	'10	'00	'90
Eurasia									
Kazakhstan	3	2		3	3		Ex	Ex	
Kyrgyzstan	1	1		2	3		Im	Im	
Latvia	3	3		3	3		Im	Im	
Lithuania	3	3		3	3		Im	Im	
Moldova	1	1		2	2		Im	Im	
Russia	3	3		4	4		Ex	Ex	
Tajikistan	1	1		2	2		Im	Im	
Turkmenistan	2	2		4	3		Ex	Ex	
Ukraine	2	2		3	3		Im	Im	
Uzbekistan	1	1		3	3		Ex	Ex	
Europe									
Albania	2	2	2	2	2	2	Im	Im	Ex
Austria	4	4	4	4	4	4	Im	Im	Im
Belgium	4	4	4	4	4	4	Im	Im	Im
Bosnia and Herzegovina	2	2		3	3		Im	Im	
Bulgaria	3	3	3	3	3	4	Im	Im	Im
Croatia	3	3		3	3		Im	Im	
Cyprus	3	4	3	3	3	3	Im	Im	Im
Czech Republic	4	3		4	4		Im	Im	
Denmark	4	4	4	4	4	4	Ex	Ex	Im
Faroe Islands				4	4	4	Im	Im	Im
Finland	4	4	4	4	4	4	Im	Im	Im
Former Czechoslovakia			3			4			Im
Former Serbia and Mont.		2			3			Im	
Former Yugoslavia						3			Im
France	4	4	4	4	4	4	Im	Im	Im
Germany	4	4		4	4		Im	Im	
Germany, East						4			Im
Germany, West			4			4			Im
Gibraltar				4	4	4	Im	Im	Im
Greece	4	4	4	3	4	3	Im	Im	Im
Hungary	3	3		3	3	3	Im	Im	Im
Iceland	4	4		4	4	4	Im	Im	Im
Ireland	4	4	4	3	4	3	Im	Im	Im
Italy	4	4	4	3	4	4	Im	Im	Im
Kosovo	1			3			Im		
Luxembourg	4	4	4	4	4	4	Im	Im	Im
Macedonia	3	3		3	3		Im	Im	

Appendix 9 – List of countries with cluster values (cont'd)
Source: Own illustration based on data from EIA (2015).

Country/Territory	GDP per capita			Energy intensity per capita			Primary energy ex-/importer		
	'10	'00	'90	'10	'00	'90	'10	'00	'90
Europe									
Malta	4	4	3	4	3	3	Im	Im	Im
Montenegro	2			3			Im		
Netherlands	4	4	4	4	4	4	Im	Im	Im
Norway	4	4	4	4	4	4	Ex	Ex	Ex
Poland	3	3	3	3	3	3	Im	Im	Im
Portugal	4	4	4	3	3	3	Im	Im	Im
Romania	3	3	3	3	3	4	Im	Im	Im
Serbia	3			3			Im		
Slovakia	4	3		4	4		Im	Im	
Slovenia	4	4		4	4		Im	Im	
Spain	4	4	4	3	4	3	Im	Im	Im
Sweden	4	4	4	4	4	4	Im	Im	Im
Switzerland	4	4	4	4	4	4	Im	Im	Im
Turkey	3	3	3	2	3	2	Im	Im	Im
United Kingdom	4	4	4	4	4	4	Im	Ex	Im
Armenia	2	2		2	3		Im	Im	
Middle East									
Bahrain	3	4	3	4	4	4	Im	Ex	Ex
Iran	3	3	3	3	3	3	Ex	Ex	Ex
Iraq	2	3	3	2	3	3	Ex	Ex	Ex
Israel	4	4	3	3	4	3	Im	Im	Im
Jordan	2	2	2	2	3	3	Im	Im	Im
Kuwait	4	4	4	4	4	4	Ex	Ex	Ex
Lebanon	3	3	2	3	3	2	Im	Im	Im
Oman	4	4	4	4	4	3	Ex	Ex	Ex
Palestinian Territories	1	1		1	1		Im	Im	
Qatar	4	4	4	4	4	4	Ex	Ex	Ex
Saudi Arabia	4	4	4	4	4	4	Ex	Ex	Ex
Syria	2	2	2	2	3	3	Ex	Ex	Ex
United Arab Emirates	4	4	4	4	4	4	Ex	Ex	Ex
Yemen	2	2	1	2	2	2	Ex	Ex	Ex

Notes: 1, 2, 3 and 4 refer to the 1st, 2nd, 3rd, and 4th quartile of each indicator's country ranking. Country rankings and quartiles are recalculated for every year. GDP values are translated into 2005 USD (PPP). Energy intensity is calculated as the ratio of national primary energy consumption and population. Countries in which primary energy production exceeds (falls short of) primary energy consumption are classified as primary energy exporters (ex) (importers (im)). Empty cells indicate missing data.

Appendix 9 – List of countries with cluster values (cont'd)
Source: Own illustration based on data from EIA (2015).

Country/Territory	GDP per capita			Energy intensity per capita			Primary energy ex-/importer		
	'10	'00	'90	'10	'00	'90	'10	'00	'90
North America									
Bermuda	4	4	4	4	3	4	Im	Im	Im
Canada	4	4	4	4	4	4	Ex	Ex	Ex
Greenland				4	4	4	Im	Im	Im
Mexico	3	3	3	3	3	3	Ex	Ex	Ex
St. Pierre and Miquelon				4	4	4	Im	Im	Im
United States	4	4	4	4	4	4	Im	Im	Im

Notes: 1, 2, 3 and 4 refer to the 1st, 2nd, 3rd, and 4th quartile of each indicator's country ranking. Country rankings and quartiles are recalculated for every year. GDP values are translated into 2005 USD (PPP). Energy intensity is calculated as the ratio of national primary energy consumption and population. Countries in which primary energy production exceeds (falls short of) primary energy consumption are classified as primary energy exporters (ex) (importers (im)). Empty cells indicate missing data.

Appendix 9 – List of countries with cluster values (cont'd)
Source: Own illustration based on data from EIA (2015).

Variable	Description	Unit	Source
(a) Regulation intensity measures			
lnRES_SW	(natural logarithm of) aggregated share of solar and wind in total electricity generation	(ln) %-points	EIA Int. Energy Statistics (EIA, 2015)
lnRES_TeH	(natural logarithm of) aggregated share of all non-hydro renewable energy technologies in total electricity generation	(ln) %-points	
lnREC_SWTW	(natural logarithm of) aggregated share of solar and wind in total electricity generation capacity	(ln) %-points	
lnREC_TeH	(natural logarithm of) aggregated share of all non-hydro renewable energy technologies in total electricity generation capacity	(ln) %-points	
(b) Regulation design indicators			
C_TAR_E	Dummy variable indicating the existence of at least one policy from the targets cluster[1)] (1 = cluster exists)	-	IEA/IRENA, OECD, REN21 (see Appendix 4 to Appendix 8)
C_TAR_D	Count variable giving the number of years in which at least one policy from the targets cluster[1)] has been active	years	
C_TAR_D2	Square of C_TAR_D	$years^2$	
C_RDD_E	Dummy variable indicating the existence of at least one policy from the research, development, and demonstration programs cluster[1)] (1 = cluster exists)	-	see above
C_RDD_D	Count variable giving the number of years in which at least one policy from the research, development, and demonstration programs cluster[1)] has been active	years	
C_RDD_D2	Square of C_RDD_D	$years^2$	
C_QUO_E	Dummy variable indicating the existence of at least one policy from the quotas cluster[1)] (1 = cluster exists)	-	see above
C_QUO_D	Count variable giving the number of years in which at least one policy from the quotas cluster[1)] has been active	years	
C_QUO_D2	Square of C_QUO_D	$years^2$	

Appendix 10 – Variable definitions for reg.-intensity regr.
Source: Own illustration.

Variable	Description	Unit	Source
(b) Regulation design indicators			
C_FIT_E	Dummy variable indicating the existence of at least one policy from the feed-in tariffs cluster[1)] (1 = cluster exists)	-	see above
C_FIT_D	Count variable giving the number of years in which at least one policy from the feed-in tariffs cluster[1)] has been active	years	
C_FIT_D2	Square of C_FIT_D	years²	
C_FIS_E	Dummy variable indicating the existence of at least one policy from the fiscal incentives cluster[1)] (1 = cluster exists)	-	see above
C_FIS_D	Count variable giving the number of years in which at least one policy from the fiscal incentives cluster[1)] has been active	years	
C_FIS_D2	Square of C_FIS_D	years²	
C_GHG_E	Dummy variable indicating the existence of at least one policy from the greenhouse gas trading systems cluster[1)] (1 = cluster exists)	-	see above
C_GHG_D	Count variable giving the number of years in which at least one policy from the greenhouse gas trading systems cluster[1)] has been active	years	
C_GHG_D2	Square of C_GHG_D	years²	
TAR_E	Dummy variable indicating the existence of renewable energy targets or strategies (1 = policy exists)	-	see above
TAR_D	Count variable giving the number of years the renewable energy targets or strategies policy has been active	years	
TAR_D2	Square of TAR_D	years²	
RDD_E	Dummy variable indicating the existence of research, development, and demonstration programs (1 = policy exists)	-	see above
RDD_D	Count variable giving the number of years the research, development, and demonstration programs have been active	years	
RDD_D2	Square of RDD_D	years²	
QUO_E	Dummy variable indicating the existence of renewable energy quotas (1 = policy exists)	-	see above
QUO_D	Count variable giving the number of years the renewable energy quotas have been active	years	
QUO_D2	Square of QUO_D	years²	

Appendix 10 – Variable definitions (cont'd)
Source: Own illustration.

Variable	Description	Unit	Source
(b) Regulation design indicators			
REC_E	Dummy variable indicating the existence of renewable energy quotas with certificate trading systems (1 = policy exists)	-	see above
REC_D	Count variable giving the number of years the renewable energy quotas with certificate trading systems have been active	years	
REC_D2	Square of REC_D	$years^2$	
FIT_E	Dummy variable indicating the existence of fixed rate or premium feed-in tariffs (incl. energy production payments) (1 = policy exists)	-	see above
FIT_D	Count variable giving the number of years the fixed rate or premium feed-in tariffs (incl. energy production payments) have been active	years	
FIT_D2	Square of FIT_D	$years^2$	
NET_E	Dummy variable indicating the existence of net metering (1 = policy exists)	-	see above
NET_D	Count variable giving the number of years the net metering policy has been active	years	
NET_D2	Square of NET_D	$years^2$	
TEN_E	Dummy variable indicating the existence of public competitive bidding (tendering) (1 = policy exists)	-	see above
TEN_D	Count variable giving the number of years the public competitive bidding (tendering) policy has been active	years	
TEN_D2	Square of TEN_D	$years^2$	
TXC_E	Dummy variable indicating the existence of investment or production tax credits (1 = policy exists)	-	see above
TXC_D	Count variable giving the number of years the investment or production tax credits policy has been active	years	
TXC_D2	Square of TXC_D	$years^2$	
TXR_E	Dummy variable indicating the existence of tax reductions for carbon, energy, sales, VAT, or other taxes (1 = policy exists)	-	see above
TXR_D	Count variable giving the number of years the tax reductions for carbon, energy, sales, VAT, or other taxes have been active	years	
TXR_D2	Square of TXR_D	$years^2$	

Appendix 10 – Variable definitions (cont'd)
Source: Own illustration.

Variable	Description	Unit	Source
(b) Regulation design indicators			
PUB_E	Dummy variable indicating the existence of public spending, capital subsidies, or low-cost loans (1 = policy exists)	-	see above
PUB_D	Count variable giving the number of years the public spending, capital subsidies, or low-cost loans policies have been active	years	
PUB_D2	Square of PUB_D	$years^2$	
GHG_E	Dummy variable indicating the existence of greenhouse gas certificate trading systems (1 = policy exists)	-	see above
GHG_D	Count variable giving the number of years the greenhouse gas certificate trading systems have been active	years	
GHG_D2	Square of GHG_D	$years^2$	

Notes: (1) For the allocation of policy instruments to clusters, refer to Table 7 (page 71).

Appendix 10 – Variable definitions (cont'd)
Source: Own illustration.

(a) Histogram & normal quantile plot of Eq. (3.1) residuals pre-transformation: RES_SW

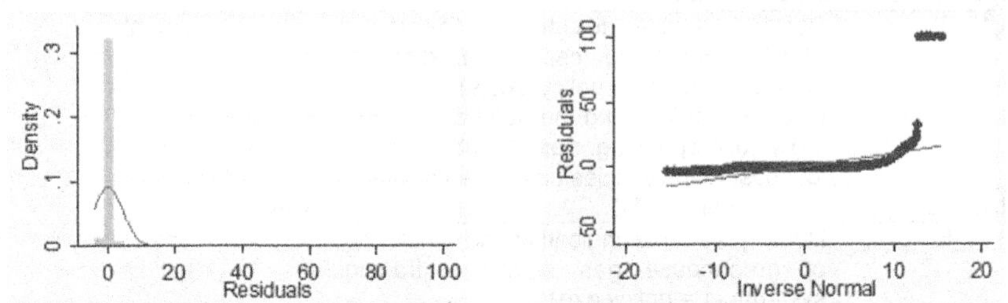

(b) Histogram & normal quantile plot of Eq. (3.1) residuals post-transformation: lnRES_SW

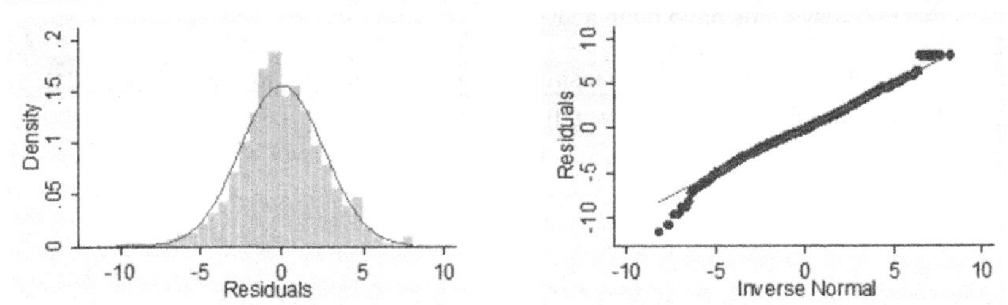

(c) Histogram & normal quantile plot of Eq. (3.3) residuals pre-transformation: REC_SWTW

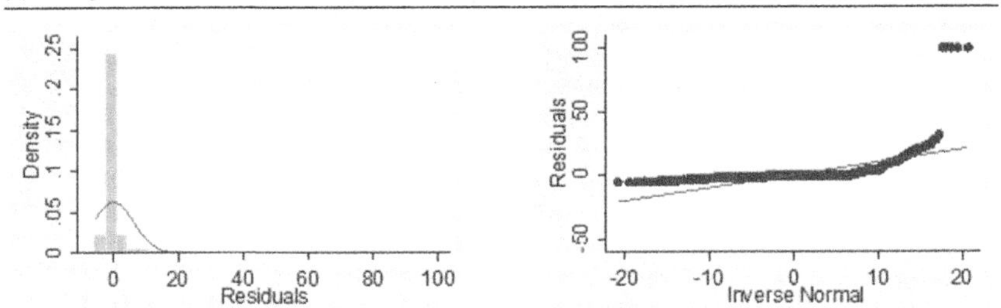

(d) Histogram & normal quantile plot of Eq. (3.3) residuals post-transformation: lnREC_SWTW

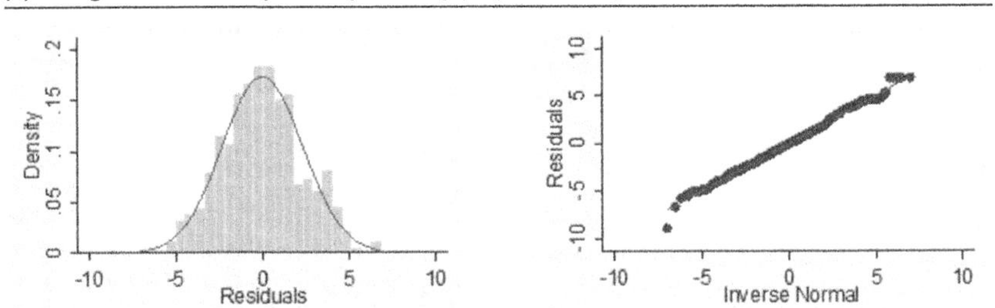

Appendix 11 – Histograms and plots for Eq. (3.1-3.3)
Source: Own illustration.

(a) Individual policy instruments

	(1)	(2)	(3)	(4)	(5)	(6)	(7)	(8)	(9)	(10)	(11)
(1) TAR_D	1.00										
(2) RDD_D	.43	1.00									
(3) QUO_D	.23	.21	1.00								
(4) REC_D	.44	.52	.29	1.00							
(5) FIT_D	.50	.67	.21	.40	1.00						
(6) NET_D	.27	.27	.31	.44	.27	1.00					
(7) TEN_D	.36	.20	.34	.34	.32	.23	1.00				
(8) TXC_D	.31	.55	.14	.28	.62	.21	.29	1.00			
(9) TXR_D	.48	.36	.20	.40	.46	.20	.33	.32	1.00		
(10) PUB_D	.50	.52	.30	.45	.61	.23	.39	.50	.61	1.00	
(11) GHG_D	.51	.44	.22	.64	.58	.29	.41	.33	.52	.54	1.00
(12) TAR_D2	.99	.33	.13	.32	.36	.16	.22	.20	.37	.42	.34
(13) RDD_D2	.36	.93	.16	.43	.58	.23	.18	.61	.32	.48	.36
(14) QUO_D2	.19	.17	.94	.23	.20	.25	.36	.13	.17	.26	.20
(15) REC_D2	.39	.47	.24	.96	.35	.43	.29	.26	.37	.41	.63
(16) FIT_D2	.40	.65	.18	.33	.93	.26	.24	.69	.39	.58	.52
(17) NET_D2	.20	.24	.18	.41	.26	.91	.24	.16	.15	.17	.27
(18) TEN_D2	.30	.15	.32	.32	.26	.15	.93	.23	.29	.33	.36
(19) TXC_D2	.11	.42	.03	.08	.45	.05	.09	.88	.09	.34	.09
(20) TXR_D2	.32	.28	.11	.29	.36	.11	.18	.24	.91	.51	.41
(21) PUB_D2	.45	.44	.21	.31	.55	.14	.25	.46	.54	.91	.44
(22) GHG_D2	.48	.39	.20	.62	.53	.28	.41	.32	.50	.51	.97

	(12)	(13	(14)	(15)	(16)	(17)	(18)	(19)	(20)	(21)	(22)
(12) TAR_D2	1.00										
(13) RDD_D2	.25	1.00									
(14) QUO_D2	.11	.13	1.00								
(15) REC_D2	.29	.40	.18	1.00							
(16) FIT_D2	.28	.63	.19	.30	1.00						
(17) NET_D2	.11	.21	.16	.42	.27	1.00					
(18) TEN_D2	.18	.13	.36	.28	.18	.18	1.00				
(19) TXC_D2	.06	.54	.03	.07	.58	.04	.06	1.00			
(20) TXR_D2	.24	.25	.10	.28	.33	.08	.17	.06	1.00		
(21) PUB_D2	.33	.43	.19	.30	.60	.09	.22	.36	.50	1.00	
(22) GHG_D2	.34	.33	.18	.64	.50	.27	.38	.09	.40	.44	1.00

(b) Clusters of policy instruments

	(23)	(24)	(25)	(26)	(27)	(28)	(29)	(30)	(31)	(32)	(33)
(23) C_TAR	1.00										
(24) C_RDD	.43	1.00									
(25) C_QUO	.45	.51	1.00								
(26) C_FIT	.53	.68	.47	1.00							
(27) C_FIS	.54	.57	.42	.70	1.00						
(28) C_GHG	.51	.44	.62	.60	.48	1.00					
(29) C_TAR_D2	.88	.33	.31	.37	.36	.34	1.00				
(30) C_RDD_D2	.36	.93	.42	.60	.56	.36	.25	1.00			
(31) C_QUO_D2	.38	.46	.94	.41	.35	.58	.26	.39	1.00		
(32) C_FIT_D2	.42	.67	.38	.93	.69	.54	.29	.64	.35	1.00	
(33) C_FIS_D2	.30	.51	.21	.59	.87	.27	.20	.57	.18	.70	1.00
(34) C_GHG_D2	.48	.39	.59	.56	.45	.97	.34	.33	.59	.52	.27

Appendix 12 – Correlation matrix for duration-intensity regr.
Source: Own illustration.

Dep. var.	lnRES_TeH	lnREC_TeH	lnRES_TeH	lnREC_TeH
Variable	(3.1a)	(3.2a)	(3.3a)	(3.4a)
C_TAR_E	.1203	.4354 **		
C_RDD_E	.4932 **	.7795 ***		
C_QUO_E	.1140	.2175		
C_FIT_E	.6038 ***	.6005 ***		
C_FIS_E	.5129 ***	.3741 ***		
C_GHG_E	.8336 ***	.9081 ***		
TAR_E			.1642	.4601 **
RDD_E			.4674 **	.7330 ***
QUO_E			.3477	.3367
REC_E			-.1204	.3240
FIT_E			.5816 ***	.4473 ***
NET_E			-.1431	.0233
TEN_E			.3562 *	.6386 ***
TXC_E			-.3490 **	-.1715
TXR_E			.3342 ***	.2710 **
PUB_E			.5905 ***	.3345 **
GHG_E			.8241 ***	.8622 ***
CONST	-.4368 ***	-.7668 ***	-.4275 ***	-.7226 ***
F	25.33 ***	36.84 ***	18.23 ***	26.41 ***
R^2	0.31	0.37	0.34	0.39
Obs.	2,065	1,910	2,065	1,910
Groups	128	135	128	135

Notes: Results are estimated using fixed effects (within) regression with observation grouped by country. *, **, and *** indicate statistical significance at 10%, 5%, and 1% level respectively. Statistical significance is based on cluster-robust standard errors.

Appendix 13 – Rob. test existence-intensity regr.: non-hydro
Source: Own illustration.

Dep. var.	lnRES_TeH	lnREC_TeH	lnRES_TeH	lnREC_TeH
Variable	(3.5a)	(3.6a)	(3.7a)	(3.8a)
C_TAR_D	.1484 **	.1874 **		
C_RDD_D	.0062	.0840 **		
C_QUO_D	.0059	-.0114		
C_FIT_D	.1544 ***	.1058 **		
C_FIS_D	.0238	.0963 *		
C_GHG_D	.1544	.1033		
TAR_D			.1407 **	.1929 ***
RDD_D			.0352	.1309 ***
QUO_D			.6052 **	-.1288
REC_D			-.1224	-.0527
FIT_D			.1457 ***	.0657
NET_D			-.0573	.0299
TEN_D			-.0437	.2441 **
TXC_D			-.0442	-.0434
TXR_D			.0713	.1304 **
PUB_D			.0591	.0706
GHG_D			.2233 **	.1090
C_TAR_D2	.0001	-.0053 **		
C_RDD_D2	-.0008	-.0025 *		
C_QUO_D2	-.0078	-.0055		
C_FIT_D2	-.0071 ***	-.0064 ***		
C_FIS_D2	-.0002	-.0006		
C_GHG_D2	-.0044	-.0007		
TAR_D2			.0004	-.0061 **
RDD_D2			-.0014	-.0035 **
QUO_D2			-.1098 **	.0475
REC_D2			-.0037	-.0058
FIT_D2			-.0058 ***	-.0049 **
NET_D2			.0051	-.0074
TEN_D2			.0114	-.0237 *
TXC_D2			.0026	.0022
TXR_D2			-.0106 *	-.0067 **
PUB_D2			-.0032	-.0022
GHG_D2			-.0041	.0010
CONST	-.3092 ***	-.6583 ***	-.3555 ***	-.6752 ***
F	15.21 ***	19.34 ***	20.94 ***	24.12 ***
R^2	0.36	0.40	0.39	0.42
Obs.	2,065	1,910	2,065	1,910
Groups	128	135	128	135

Notes: Results are estimated using fixed effects (within) regression with observation grouped by country. *, **, and *** indicate statistical significance at 10%, 5%, and 1% level respectively. Statistical significance is based on cluster-robust standard errors.

Appendix 14 – Rob. test duration-intensity regr.: non-hydro
Source: Own illustration.

Dep. var.	lnRES_SW	lnREC_SWTW	lnRES_SW	lnREC_SWTW
Variable	(3.1b)	(3.2b)	(3.3b)	(3.4b)
C_TAR_E	1.083 ***	.4180 **		
C_RDD_E	.2909	.6402 **		
C_QUO_E	1.129 ***	.9134 ***		
C_FIT_E	1.021 ***	.4332 *		
C_FIS_E	.8145 ***	.4258 *		
TAR_E			.9527 ***	.4157 **
RDD_E			.2735	.2475
QUO_E			1.001 ***	.4677
REC_E			.8639 **	.8933 *
FIT_E			.8231 ***	.0750
NET_E			.1175	-.3129
TEN_E			.3676	1.087 ***
TXC_E			.0931	-.3003
TXR_E			.5824 ***	.6365 ***
PUB_E			.8722 ***	.3083
CONST	-3.520 ***	-1.748 ***	-3.475 ***	-1.622 ***
F	61.94 ***	10.03 ***	32.26 ***	8.00 ***
R^2	0.50	0.15	0.51	0.26
Obs.	1,426	793	1,426	793
Groups	109	124	109	124

Notes: Results are estimated using fixed effects (within) regression with observation grouped by country. *, **, and *** indicate statistical significance at 10%, 5%, and 1% level respectively. Statistical significance is based on cluster-robust standard errors.

Appendix 15 – Robustness test existence-intensity regr.: ex GHG
Source: Own illustration.

Dep. var.	lnRES_SW	lnREC_SWTW	lnRES_SW	lnREC_SWTW
Variable	(3.5b)	(3.6b)	(3.7b)	(3.8b)
C_TAR_D	.2607 ***	.0973		
C_RDD_D	.2126 ***	-.1600		
C_QUO_D	-.0162	.0831		
C_FIT_D	.2570 ***	.2289 *		
C_FIS_D	.0876	.2273 *		
TAR_D			.2556 ***	.1929 **
RDD_D			.2816 ***	-.0708
QUO_D			.5903 **	.4449
REC_D			-.2916 **	.0951
FIT_D			.1828 **	1.589
NET_D			.0786	-.0823
TEN_D			.0897	.1351
TXC_D			.0471	-.0785
TXR_D			.1755 **	.2212 **
PUB_D			.1255 *	.1725 *
C_TAR_D2	-.0060 ***	-.0011		
C_RDD_D2	-.0024	-.0009		
C_QUO_D2	-.0030	-.0054		
C_FIT_D2	-.0135 ***	-.0034		
C_FIS_D2	-.0001	-.0014		
TAR_D2			-.0061 **	-.0026
RDD_D2			-.0038 **	-.0022
QUO_D2			-.0550	-.0678
REC_D2			.0161	-.0061
FIT_D2			-.0120 ***	-.0053
NET_D2			-.0098	.0045
TEN_D2			-.0123	-.0250
TXC_D2			.0003	.0044 *
TXR_D2			-.0188 ***	-.0104 **
PUB_D2			-.0018	-.0018
CONST	-3.881 ***	-1.811 ***	-3.990 ***	-1.900 ***
F	40.18 ***	18.33 ***	143.59 ***	9.94 ***
R^2	0.64	0.48	0.68	0.50
Obs.	1,426	793	1,426	793
Groups	109	124	109	124

Notes: Results are estimated using fixed effects (within) regression with observation grouped by country. *, **, and *** indicate statistical significance at 10%, 5%, and 1% level respectively. Statistical significance is based on cluster-robust standard errors.

Appendix 16 – Rob. test for duration-intensity regr.: ex GHG
Source: Own illustration.

Dep. var.	lnRES_SW	lnREC_SWTW	lnRES_SW	lnREC_SWTW
Variable	(3.1c)	(3.2c)	(3.3c)	(3.4c)
C_TAR_E	.8098 ***	.3842 *		
C_QUO_E	.7632 ***	.8503 ***		
C_FIT_E	1.136 ***	.4719 **		
C_FIS_E	.7043 ***	.4708 *		
C_GHG_E	1.185 ***	1.893 ***		
TAR_E			.7919 ***	.3818 **
QUO_E			.9250 **	.3803
REC_E			.4824	.7600 **
FIT_E			.8772 ***	.0541
NET_E			.2606	-.2715
TEN_E			.3933	1.155 ***
TXC_E			-.0523	-.3098
TXR_E			.4951 **	.6506 ***
PUB_E			.8200 ***	.2536
GHG_E			1.042 ***	1.911 ***
CONST	-3.419 ***	-2.086 ***	-3.379 ***	-2.003 ***
F	68.26 ***	16.28 ***	37.15 ***	9.88 ***
R^2	0.52	0.17	0.53	0.28
Obs.	1,426	793	1,426	793
Groups	109	124	109	124

Notes: Results are estimated using fixed effects (within) regression with observation grouped by country. *, **, and *** indicate statistical significance at 10%, 5%, and 1% level respectively. Statistical significance is based on cluster-robust standard errors.

Appendix 17 – Rob. test for existence-intensity regr.: ex RDD
Source: Own illustration.

Dep. var.	lnRES_SW	lnREC_SWTW	lnRES_SW	lnREC_SWTW
Variable	(3.5c)	(3.6c)	(3.7c)	(3.8c)
C_TAR_D	.2557 ***	.0830		
C_QUO_D	.1235	.0935		
C_FIT_D	.3499 ***	.2068 **		
C_FIS_D	.0742	.2068 *		
C_GHG_D	-.0131	.0830		
TAR_D			.2713 ***	.1732 **
QUO_D			.7967 ***	.5571
REC_D			.0333	.0888
FIT_D			.3300 ***	.2089 **
NET_D			.0995	-.0618
TEN_D			-.0495	.1119
TXC_D			.0521	-.0835
TXR_D			.0949	.2128 **
PUB_D			.1352 *	.1566 *
GHG_D			.0112	.0252
C_TAR_D2	-.0048 *	-.0035		
C_QUO_D2	-.0083	-.0141		
C_FIT_D2	-.0123 ***	-.0071 *		
C_FIS_D2	.0005	-.0023		
C_GHG_D2	-.0012	-.0037		
TAR_D2			-.0051 *	-.0039
QUO_D2			-.0925 *	-.0780
REC_D2			-.0129	-.0162
FIT_D2			-.0139 ***	-.0094 **
NET_D2			-.0079	.0051
TEN_D2			-.0082	-.0222
TXC_D2			.0007	.0036
TXR_D2			-.0168 ***	-.0105 **
PUB_D2			-.0009	-.0036
GHG_D2			.0115	.0077
CONST	-3.478 ***	-2.415 ***	-3.498 ***	-2.253 ***
F	42.19 ***	16.07 ***	80.76 ***	8.82 ***
R^2	0.61	0.46	0.63	0.49
Obs.	1,426	793	1,426	793
Groups	109	124	109	124

Notes: Results are estimated using fixed effects (within) regression with observation grouped by country. *, **, and *** indicate statistical significance at 10%, 5%, and 1% level respectively. Statistical significance is based on cluster-robust standard errors.

Appendix 18 – Rob. test for duration-intensity regr.: ex RDD
Source: Own illustration.

Variable	Description	Unit	Source
(a) Innovation measures			
count_S[1)]	count of patent applications on solar power (Y02E 10/5) by domestic applicants	patent applications	EPO PATSTAT (EPO, 2015)
count_W[1)]	count of patent applications on wind power (Y02E 10/7) by domestic applicants	patent applications	
count_SW[1)]	count of patent applications on solar (Y02E 10/5) or wind power (Y02E 10/7) by domestic applicants	patent applications	
(b) Knowledge stocks			
DKS_*count_S*[1)]	stock of domestic patent applications on solar power (Y02E 10/5)	1,000 patent applications	calculated
DKS_*count_W*[1)]	stock of domestic patent applications on wind power (Y02E 10/7)	1,000 patent applications	
DKS_*count_SW*[1)]	stock of domestic patent applications on solar (Y02E 10/5) or wind power (Y02E 10/7)	1,000 patent applications	
(c) Changes in generation capacities			
ITOCAPA_YOY	year-on-year change in total global electricity generation capacity (all conventional and renewable energy technologies)	%-points	EIA Int. Energy Statistics (EIA, 2015)
(d) Total patents			
DTOPAT	simple count of total patent applications by domestic applicants on any technology except solar and wind power	1,000 patent applications	EPO PATSTAT (EPO, 2015)

Notes: (1) The term 'count' included in the innovation and knowledge stock measures is a placeholder for the four alternative approaches to count patent applications: simple count (SC), family count (FC), size-weighted simple count (SCw), and size-weighted family count (FCw).

Appendix 19 – Variable definitions for reg.-innovation regr.
Source: Own illustration.

Variable	Description	Unit	Source
(e) Regulation intensity measures			
RES_S	share of solar in total electricity generation	%-points	EIA Int. Energy Statistics (EIA, 2015)
RES_W	share of wind in total electricity generation	%-points	
RES_SW	aggregated share of solar and wind in total electricity generation	%-points	
(f) Regulation design indicators			
C_TAR_... C_RDD_... C_QUO_... C_FIT_... C_FIS_... C_GHG_... TAR_... RDD_... QUO_... REC_... FIT_... NET_... TEN_... TXC_... TXR_... PUB_... GHG_...	see Appendix 10		

Appendix 19 – Variable definitions for reg.-innovation regr (cont'd)
Source: Own illustration.

Variable	Obs.	Mean	Std. Dev.	Min	Max
(a) Innovation measures					
SC_S	4,950	8.435	79.78	0	1,978
SC_W	4,950	6.877	50.41	0	1,011
SC_SW	4,950	15.31	124.4	0	2,840
FC_SW	4,950	8.291	70.94	0	1,603
SCw_SW	4,950	45.23	353.6	0	7,469
FCw_SW	4,950	38.21	310.3	0	6,583
(b) Knowledge stocks					
DKS_SC_S	4,950	.0174	.0142	0	3.700
DKS_SC_W	4,950	.0152	.0101	0	2.375
DKS_SC_SW	4,950	.0325	.0228	0	5.637
DKS_FC_SW	4,950	.0165	.0134	0	3.734
DKS_SCw_SW	4,950	.0992	.0743	0	18.86
DKS_FCw_SW	4,950	.0742	.0653	0	16.95
(c) Changes in generation capacities					
ITOCAPA_YOY	4,725	3.183	.9887	1.53	4.71
(d) Total patents					
DTOPAT	4,950	5.980	38.27	0	715.7
(e) Regulation intensity measures					
RES_S	4,636	.0167	.1370	0	3.77
RES_W	4,636	.4617	4.172	0	100.0
RES_SW	4,950	.4482	4.054	0	100.0
(f) Regulation design indicators					
C_TAR_E	4,950	.1436	.3508	0	1
C_RDD_E	4,950	.1087	.3113	0	1
C_QUO_E	4,950	.0398	.1955	0	1
C_FIT_E	4,950	.1305	.3369	0	1
C_FIS_E	4,950	.1356	.3428	0	1
C_GHG_E	4,950	.0402	.1965	0	1
TAR_E	4,950	.1436	.3508	0	1
RDD_E	4,950	.1087	.3113	0	1
QUO_E	4,950	.0089	.0939	0	1
REC_E	4,950	.0309	.1731	0	1
FIT_E	4,950	.1176	.3221	0	1
NET_E	4,950	.0186	.1351	0	1
TEN_E	4,950	.0275	.1635	0	1
TXC_E	4,950	.0543	.2267	0	1
TXR_E	4,950	.0735	.2610	0	1
PUB_E	4,950	.1125	.3160	0	1
GHG_E	4,950	.0402	.1965	0	1

Appendix 20 – Descriptive statistics for reg.-innovation regr.
Source: Own illustration.

	(1)	(2)	(3)	(4)	(5)	(6)	(7)	(8)	(9)	(10)	(11)	(12)	(13)
(1) SC_S	1.00												
(2) SC_W	.81	1.00											
(3) SC_SW	.97	.93	1.00										
(4) FC_SW	.90	.81	.90	1.00									
(5) SCw_SW	.92	.87	.94	.99	1.00								
(6) FCw_SW	.86	.80	.88	.99	.99	1.00							
(7) DKS_SC_S	.92	.76	.90	.93	.93	.91	1.00						
(8) DKS_SC_W	.70	.89	.81	.76	.80	.77	.77	1.00					
(9) DKS_SC_SW	.88	.87	.92	.91	.93	.90	.96	.92	1.00				
(10) DKS_FC_SW	.84	.75	.84	.96	.94	.95	.96	.75	.92	1.00			
(11) DKS_SCw_SW	.84	.81	.87	.96	.95	.96	.95	.84	.96	.98	1.00		
(12) DKS_FCw_SW	.81	.77	.83	.96	.94	.96	.91	.77	.91	.98	.98	1.00	
(13) ITOCAPA_YOY	.10	.12	.11	.11	.11	.11	.09	.12	.11	.10	.11	.12	1.00
(14) DTOPAT	.74	.64	.74	.79	.81	.81	.86	.62	.81	.81	.82	.78	.06
(15) RES_S	.19	.29	.24	.26	.27	.27	.22	.32	.28	.27	.30	.30	.12
(16) RES_W	.04	.14	.08	.10	.11	.11	.05	.14	.09	.09	.11	.11	.11
(17) RES_SW	.05	.15	.09	.11	.12	.12	.06	.15	.10	.11	.12	.12	.12
(18) C_TAR_E	.17	.23	.20	.19	.20	.19	.16	.22	.20	.17	.19	.18	.40
(19) C_RDD_E	.27	.30	.29	.31	.33	.33	.32	.31	.34	.33	.35	.31	.05
(20) C_QUO_E	.19	.23	.22	.23	.23	.23	.20	.24	.23	.23	.23	.23	.21
(21) C_FIT_E	.22	.28	.25	.24	.26	.26	.22	.29	.26	.23	.25	.24	.30
(22) C_FIS_E	.21	.28	.25	.24	.27	.26	.24	.30	.28	.25	.27	.25	.35
(23) C_GHG_E	.07	.20	.12	.15	.16	.16	.08	.21	.14	.14	.17	.17	.22
(24) TAR_E	.17	.23	.20	.19	.20	.19	.16	.22	.20	.17	.19	.18	.40
(25) RDD_E	.27	.30	.29	.31	.33	.33	.32	.31	.34	.33	.35	.31	.05
(26) QUO_E	.04	.10	.07	.03	.04	.03	.06	.15	.10	.03	.04	.02	.09
(27) REC_E	.19	.21	.21	.24	.24	.25	.20	.19	.20	.24	.24	.25	.19
(28) FIT_E	.21	.28	.25	.23	.26	.25	.20	.29	.25	.21	.24	.22	.27
(29) NET_E	.15	.13	.15	.19	.19	.20	.16	.10	.14	.19	.18	.19	.15
(30) TEN_E	.07	.20	.12	.10	.11	.10	.07	.21	.13	.09	.10	.09	.21
(31) TXC_E	.26	.34	.31	.28	.31	.29	.28	.33	.32	.27	.31	.28	.23
(32) TXR_E	.15	.26	.20	.17	.19	.17	.14	.25	.20	.16	.19	.18	.30
(33) PUB_E	.24	.31	.28	.27	.29	.28	.26	.32	.30	.27	.30	.28	.31
(34) GHG_E	.07	.20	.12	.15	.16	.16	.08	.21	.14	.14	.17	.17	.22

Appendix 21 – Correlation matrix for main reg.-innovation regr.
Source: Own illustration.

	(14)	(15)	(16)	(17)	(18)	(19)	(20)	(21)	(22)	(23)	(24)	(25)	(26)
(14) DTOPAT	1.00												
(15) RES_S	.11	1.00											
(16) RES_W	.04	.13	1.00										
(17) RES_SW	.04	.18	1.00	1.00									
(18) C_TAR_E	.16	.17	.11	.12	1.00								
(19) C_RDD_E	.39	.19	.14	.15	.35	1.00							
(20) C_QUO_E	.17	.13	.13	.14	.43	.41	1.00						
(21) C_FIT_E	.24	.18	.16	.16	.57	.50	.44	1.00					
(22) C_FIS_E	.28	.17	.13	.14	.65	.39	.48	.61	1.00				
(23) C_GHG_E	.06	.30	.20	.22	.49	.34	.52	.47	.49	1.00			
(24) TAR_E	.16	.17	.11	.12	1.00	.35	.43	.57	.65	.49	1.00		
(25) RDD_E	.39	.19	.14	.15	.35	1.00	.41	.50	.39	.34	.35	1.00	
(26) QUO_E	.04	.02	.02	.02	.12	.04	.46	.17	.17	.06	.12	.04	1.00
(27) REC_E	.17	.14	.14	.14	.42	.44	.88	.40	.45	.56	.42	.44	-.02
(28) FIT_E	.23	.17	.16	.17	.51	.48	.36	.94	.53	.45	.51	.48	.12
(29) NET_E	.12	.11	.14	.14	.28	.20	.35	.35	.30	.21	.28	.20	.13
(30) TEN_E	.06	.16	.14	.15	.36	.16	.37	.43	.40	.32	.36	.16	.26
(31) TXC_E	.32	.23	.15	.16	.45	.33	.40	.49	.60	.44	.45	.33	.08
(32) TXR_E	.12	.20	.12	.13	.50	.28	.42	.49	.71	.44	.50	.28	.18
(33) PUB_E	.30	.19	.14	.14	.63	.40	.51	.56	.90	.51	.63	.40	.18
(34) GHG_E	.06	.30	.20	.22	.49	.34	.52	.47	.49	1.00	.49	.34	.06

	(27)	(28)	(29)	(30)	(31)	(32)	(33)	(34)
(27) REC_E	1.00							
(28) FIT_E	.35	1.00						
(29) NET_E	.33	.20	1.00					
(30) TEN_E	.28	.32	.22	1.00				
(31) TXC_E	.41	.42	.30	.41	1.00			
(32) TXR_E	.38	.43	.21	.38	.49	1.00		
(33) PUB_E	.48	.50	.27	.39	.51	.57	1.00	
(34) GHG_E	.56	.45	.21	.32	.44	.44	.51	1.00

Appendix 21 – Correlation matrix for main reg.-innovation regr (cont'd)
Source: Own illustration.

Dep. var.	SC_SW	SCw_SW	FC_SW	FCw_SW
Variable	(4.6)	(4.6a)	(4.6b)	(4.6c)
DKS_..._SW[1)]	.2332 ***	.0569 ***	.3082 ***	.0432 ***
DTOPAT	.0021 ***	.0036 ***	.0026 ***	.0042 ***
ITOCAPA_YOY	.4375 ***	.3236 ***	.4898 ***	.3596 ***
RES_SW	.0433 ***	.0324 ***	.0469 ***	.0252 ***
C_TAR_E	.1783 ***	.2452 ***	.1840 **	.1876 **
C_RDD_E	.6338 ***	1.175 ***	.9784 ***	1.754 ***
C_QUO_E	.0436	.0765	-.0004	.1093
C_FIT_E	.1556 **	.1788 **	.2037 ***	.1653 *
C_FIS_E	.4047 ***	.3973 ***	.3813 ***	.3810 ***
C_GHG_E	.3119 ***	.3951 ***	.5013 ***	.4455 ***
CONSTANT	-1.772 ***	-2.575 ***	-2.443 ***	-3.516 ***
Obs.	2,562	2,562	2,289	2,289
Groups	122	122	109	109
Group size, min.	21	21	21	21
Group size, avg.	21	21	21	21
Group size, max.	21	21	21	21
Wald Chi²	2,253 ***	2,144 ***	2,202 ***	2,067 ***

Notes: Results are estimated using fixed effects negative binomial panel regression with observations grouped by country. *, **, and *** indicate statistical significance at 10%, 5%, and 1% level respectively. | (1) The ... in variable DKS_..._SW is a placeholders for the suffixes SC (simple count), SCw (simple count, size weighted), FC (family count), and FCw (family county, size weighted).

Appendix 22 – Rob. test for reg.-innovation regr.: alternative counts
Source: Own illustration.

Dep. var.	SC_SW	SC_S	SC_W	SC_S	SC_W
Variable	(4.6d)	(4.7a)	(4.8a)	(4.9a)	(4.10a)
DKS_SC_...[1]	.0270	.0385	.0919	.0745	.1517 **
DTOPAT	.0017 ***	.0009 *	.0029 ***	.0013 **	.0025 ***
ITOCAPA_YOY	.3477 ***	.3749 ***	.3271 ***	.3458 ***	.3210 ***
RES_...[1]	.0067	-.1267 **	.0128	-.1960 ***	-.0033
C_TAR_D	.0743 ***	.0891 ***	.0776 ***		
C_RDD_D	.0674 ***	.0756 ***	.0664 ***		
C_QUO_D	.0032	-.0241	.0177		
C_FIT_D	.0508 ***	.0513 ***	.0549 ***		
C_FIS_D	-.0159	-.0125	-.0338 **		
C_GHG_D	-.0157	.0229	-.0329 *		
TAR_D				.0791 ***	.0721 ***
RDD_D				.0874 ***	.0832 ***
QUO_D				.0501	.0363
REC_D				-.0767 ***	-.0241
FIT_D				.0374 ***	.0384 ***
NET_D				.0749 ***	.0721 ***
TEN_D				.0544 **	.0182
TXC_D				-.0205	-.0298 **
TXR_D				.0192	-.0443 **
PUB_D				-.0102	.0001
GHG_D				.0612 **	.0088
CONSTANT	-1.358 ***	-1.733 ***	-1.412 ***	-1.646 ***	-1.426 ***
Obs.	2,562	1,999	2,312	1,999	2,312
Groups	122	97	112	97	112
Group size, min.	21	6	6	6	6
Group size, avg.	21	20.61	20.64	20.61	20.64
Group size, max.	21	21	21	21	21
Wald Chi^2	3,319 ***	2,370 ***	2,556 ***	2,417 ***	2,629 ***

Notes: Results are estimated using fixed effects negative binomial panel regression with observations grouped by country. *, **, and *** indicate statistical significance at 10%, 5%, and 1% level respectively. | (1) The ... in variables RES_... and DKS_SC_... are placeholders for the suffixes SW (solar and wind energy data), S (solar energy data) and W (wind energy data).

Appendix 23 – Rob. test for reg.-innovation regr.: policy duration
Source: Own illustration.

Dep. var.	SC_S	SC_S	SC_S	SC_W	SC_W	SC_W
Country scope	All	OECD	G20	All	OECD	G20
Variable	(4.7b)	(4.7c)	(4.7d)	(4.9b)	(4.9c)	(4.9d)
DKS_SC_...[1)]	.4057 ***	.4282 ***	.4898 ***	.4636 ***	.5946 ***	.3007 **
DTOPAT	.0011 **	.0015 **	.0011 *	.0031 ***	.0028 ***	.0026 ***
ITOCAPA_YOY	.5196 ***	.3985 ***	.3769 ***	.4448 ***	.4331 ***	.4478 ***
RES_...[1)]	.0902 **	.1076 ***	0.504	0.420 ***	.0356 ***	.0953 **
C_TAR_E	.1309	.0451	.1707	.1045	.0794	-.0118
C_RDD_E	.7787 ***	.4764 ***	.9065 ***	.5931 ***	.2314 **	.6542 ***
C_QUO_E	.0408	.0156	-.0005	.0316	.0099	.1175
C_FIT_E	.2162 ***	.2111 **	.1951 *	.1428 *	.2136 ***	.2422 **
C_FIS_E	.5463 ***	.6531 ***	.6163 ***	.3845 ***	.4363 ***	.4959 ***
C_GHG_E	.5193 ***	.6630 ***	.5258 ***	.2868 ***	.2715 ***	.2272
CONSTANT	-2.210 ***	-1.482 ***	-1.711 ***	-1.925 ***	-1.428 ***	-1.845 ***
Obs.	1,999	666	398	2,312	708	419
Groups	97	32	19	112	34	20
Group size, min.	6	19	20	6	19	20
Group size, avg.	20.61	20.81	20.95	20.64	20.82	20.95
Group size, max.	21	21	21	21	21	21
Wald Chi²	1,895 ***	1,584 ***	1,285 ***	1,667 ***	1,536 ***	1,028 ***

Notes: Results are estimated using fixed effects negative binomial panel regression with observations grouped by country. *, **, and *** indicate statistical significance at 10%, 5%, and 1% level respectively. | (1) The ... in variables RES_... and DKS_SC_... are placeholders for the suffixes S (solar energy data) and W (wind energy data).

Appendix 24 – Rob. test for reg.-innovation regr.: country clusters
Source: Own illustration.

Dep. var.	SC_SW	SC_SW	SC_SW	SC_SW
Variable	(4.6)	(4.6e)	(4.6f)	(4.6g)
DKS_SC_SW	.2332 ***	.2408 ***	.2229 ***	.2268 ***
DTOPAT	.0021 ***	.0018 ***	.0025 ***	.0022 ***
ITOCAPA_YOY	.4375 ***	.4627 ***	.4381 ***	.4608 ***
RES_SW	.0434 ***	.0500 ***	.0451 ***	.0519 ***
C_TAR_E	.1783 ***	.2835 ***	.1707 **	.2690 ***
C_RDD_E	.6338 ***	.6241 ***		
C_QUO_E	.0436	.1016	.0772	.1335 *
C_FIT_E	.1556 **	.1127 *	.2659 ***	.2285 ***
C_FIS_E	.4047 ***	.4147 ***	.3888 ***	.3979 ***
C_GHG_E	.3119 ***		.3085 ***	
CONSTANT	-1.772 ***	-1.856 ***	-1.548 ***	-1.628 ***
Obs.	2,562	2,562	2,562	2,562
Groups	122	122	122	122
Group size, min.	21	21	21	21
Group size, avg.	21	21	21	21
Group size, max.	21	21	21	21
Wald Chi²	2,253 ***	2,115 ***	1,974 ***	1,874 ***

Notes: Results are estimated using fixed effects negative binomial panel regression with observations grouped by country. *, **, and *** indicate statistical significance at 10%, 5%, and 1% level respectively.

Appendix 25 – Rob. test for reg.-innovation regr.: ex RDD/GHG
Source: Own illustration.

Variable	Description	Unit	Source
(a) Competitiveness measures			
X_ALL	Bilateral exports (all commodity classes)	USD (2005, PPP)	UN (2015)
X_SW	Bilateral exports of solar (HS 854140) and wind energy equipment (HS 850231), after re-exports	USD (2005, PPP)	
(b) Structural elements of the basic gravity equation			
lnGDP_ex	(natural logarithm of) the gross domestic product of exporting country	USD (2005, PPP)	World Bank (2015a)
lnGDP_im	(natural logarithm of) the gross domestic product of importing country	USD (2005, PPP)	World Bank (2015a)
EU	Dummy variable indicating that exporting and importing country are members of the European Union (1 = EU members)	-	European Commission (2015)
EURO	Dummy variable indicating that exporting and importing country are members of the euro area (1 = euro area members)	-	ECB (2015)
TARIFF_SW	Trade-value-weighted effective tariff rates (AHS) on solar (HS 854140) and wind energy equipment (HS 850231)	%	World Bank (2015b)
(c) Regulation intensity measures			
RES_SW	aggregated share of solar and wind in total electricity generation	%-points	EIA Int. Energy Statistics (EIA, 2015)
RES_SW_im	RES_SW for importing country		
CPV_E	Composite variables indicating the share of RE support policies, as categorized in Table 7, which have been implemented; all instruments have the same weight	-	IEA/IRENA, OECD, REN21 (see Appendix 4 to Appendix 8)
CPV_E_im	CPV_E for importing country		
(d) Regulation design indicators			
C_TAR_... C_RDD_... C_QUO_... C_FIT_... C_FIS_... C_GHG_...	see Appendix 10		

Appendix 26 – Variable definitions for reg.-competitiveness regr.
Source: Own illustration.

Variable	Description	Unit	Source
(d) Regulation design indicators			
TAR_... RDD_... QUO_... REC_... FIT_... NET_... TEN_... TXC_... TXR_... PUB_... GHG_...	see Appendix 10		
C_ANY_E	Dummy variable indicating the existence of any of the eleven types of RE support policies as categorized in Table 7 (1 = any policy exists)	-	IEA/IRENA, OECD, REN21 (see Appendix 4 to Appendix 8)
C_ANY_DP5	Dummy variable indicating the existence of any policy instrument over at least five years (1 = (C_ANY_E=1) in five or more previous years)	-	
C_ANY_DP10	Dummy variable indicating the existence of any policy instrument over at least ten years (1 = (C_ANY_E=1) in ten or more previous years)	-	
C_ANY_DP15	Dummy variable indicating the existence of any policy instrument over at least fifteen years (1 = (C_ANY_E=1) in fifteen or more previous years)	-	
C_*cluster*_E[1)]	Dummy variable indicating the existence of a cluster as categorized in Table 7 (1 = cluster exists)	-	IEA/IRENA, OECD, REN21 (see Appendix 4 to Appendix 8)
C_*cluster*_DP5[1)]	Dummy variable indicating the existence of a cluster over at least five years (1 = (C_*cluster*_E[1)]=1) in five or more previous years)	-	
C_*cluster*_DP10[1)]	Dummy variable indicating the existence of a cluster over at least ten years (1 = (C_*cluster*_E[1)]=1) in ten or more previous years)	-	
C_*cluster*_DP15[1)]	Dummy variable indicating the existence of a cluster over at least fifteen years (1 = (C_*cluster*_E[1)]=1) in fifteen or more previous years)	-	
(e) Innovation measures			
DKS_SC_SW	stock of domestic patent applications on solar (Y02E 10/5) or wind power (Y02E 10/7)	1,000 patent applica-tions	calculated from EPO PATSTAT (EPO, 2015)
DKS_SC_SW_im	DKS_SC_SW for importing country		

Notes: (1) 'Cluster' is a placeholder for: TAR, RDD, QUO, FIT, FIS, and GHG.

Appendix 26 – Variable definitions for reg.-competitiveness regr. (cont'd)
Source: Own illustration.

Variable	Obs.	Mean	Std. Dev.	Min	Max
(a) Dependent variables					
X_ALL	724,724	2.08e+08	3.10e+09	0	4.54e+11
X_SW	724,724	5.20e+05	2.28e+07	0	7.64e+09
(b) Explanatory variables – Gravity model					
lnGDP_ex	659,745	2.894	2.367	-2.74	9.53
lnGDP_im	659,745	2.894	2.367	-2.74	9.53
EU	724,724	.0108	.1036	0	1
EURO	724,724	.0029	.0541	0	1
TARIFF_SW	724,724	.0518	.9418	0	36
(c) Explanatory variables – Environmental regulation and innovation					
DKS_SC_SW	724,724	.0401	.0245	0	5.636
DKS_SC_SW_im	724,724	.0401	.0245	0	5.636
RES_SW	724,724	.3602	1.658	0	29.02
RES_SW_im	724,724	.3602	1.658	0	29.02
CPV_E	724,724	.0818	.1697	0	0.91
CPV_E_im	724,724	.0818	.1697	0	0.91
C_TAR_E	724,724	.1736	.3787	0	1
C_RDD_E	724,724	.1344	.3410	0	1
C_QUO_E	724,724	.0492	.2163	0	1
C_FIT_E	724,724	.1601	.3667	0	1
C_FIS_E	724,724	.1668	.3728	0	1
C_GHG_E	724,724	.0497	.2173	0	1
TAR_E	724,724	.1736	.3787	0	1
RDD_E	724,724	.1344	.3410	0	1
QUO_E	724,724	.0110	.1043	0	1
REC_E	724,724	.0382	.1917	0	1
FIT_E	724,724	.1441	.3512	0	1
NET_E	724,724	.0230	.1498	0	1
TEN_E	724,724	.0340	.1811	0	1
TXC_E	724,724	.0672	.2503	0	1
TXR_E	724,724	.0902	.2864	0	1
PUB_E	724,724	.1386	.3455	0	1
GHG_E	724,724	.0497	.2173	0	1
C_TAR_DP5	724,724	.0792	.2700	0	1
C_RDD_DP5	724,724	.1099	.3128	0	1
C_QUO_DP5	724,724	.0207	.1425	0	1
C_FIT_DP5	724,724	.0907	.2871	0	1
C_FIS_DP5	724,724	.0852	.2791	0	1
C_GHG_DP5	724,724	.0197	.1391	0	1
C_TAR_DP10	724,724	.0165	.1273	0	1
C_RDD_DP10	724,724	.0717	.2580	0	1
C_QUO_DP10	724,724	.0025	.0499	0	1
C_FIT_DP10	724,724	.0380	.1911	0	1
C_FIS_DP10	724,724	.0275	.1635	0	1
C_GHG_DP10	724,724	0	0	0	0
C_TAR_DP15	724,724	.0062	.0788	0	1
C_RDD_DP15	724,724	.0422	.2011	0	1
C_QUO_DP15	724,724	0	0	0	0
C_FIT_DP15	724,724	.0160	.1254	0	1
C_FIS_DP15	724,724	.0110	.1043	0	1
C_GHG_DP15	724,724	0	0	0	0
C_ANY_E	724,724	.2930	.4551	0	1
C_ANY_DP5	724,724	.1843	.3877	0	1
C_ANY_DP10	724,724	.0984	.2979	0	1
C_ANY_DP15	724,724	.0529	.2239	0	1

Appendix 27 – Descriptive statistics for reg.-innovation regr.
Source: Own illustration.

	(1)	(2)	(3)	(4)	(5)	(6)	(7)	(8)	(9)	(10)	(11)	(12)	(13)
(1) EXP_SW	1.00												
(2) lnGDP_ex	.05	1.00											
(3) lnGDP_im	.04	.00	1.00										
(4) EU	.05	.12	.12	1.00									
(5) EURO	.05	.07	.07	.52	1.00								
(6) DKS_SC_SW	.13	.34	.01	.05	.05	1.00							
(7) DKS_SC_SW_im	.10	.01	.34	.05	.05	.02	1.00						
(8) RES_SW	.04	.19	.02	.16	.11	.21	.03	1.00					
(9) RES_SW_im	.04	.02	.19	.16	.11	.03	.21	.03	1.00				
(10) CPV_E	.05	.50	.04	.24	.14	.34	.07	.46	.09	1.00			
(11) CPV_E_im	.05	.04	.51	.24	.14	.07	.34	.09	.46	.24	1.00		
(12) TAR_E	.04	.35	.04	.15	.09	.18	.08	.27	.10	.77	.27	1.00	
(13) RDD_E	.03	.57	.00	.18	.11	.32	.01	.31	.01	.60	.03	.32	1.00
(14) QUO_E	.05	.13	.01	.03	.02	.10	.02	.05	.02	.21	.05	.12	.03
(15) REC_E	.03	.29	.02	.17	.10	.20	.04	.29	.05	.65	.13	.42	.43
(16) FIT_E	.04	.41	.03	.19	.12	.24	.05	.35	.06	.72	.16	.49	.45
(17) NET_E	.03	.18	.02	.07	.04	.14	.03	.29	.04	.41	.10	.28	.19
(18) TEN_E	.04	.22	.02	.09	.06	.13	.05	.31	.06	.54	.15	.35	.15
(19) TXC_E	.04	.33	.03	.14	.11	.32	.04	.32	.06	.69	.16	.45	.31
(20) TXR_E	.03	.24	.03	.15	.08	.19	.07	.27	.08	.70	.21	.49	.26
(21) PUB_E	.04	.38	.03	.16	.10	.30	.06	.31	.08	.81	.20	.63	.38
(22) GHG_E	.02	.23	.03	.27	.15	.14	.04	.44	.06	.69	.16	.49	.33
(23) C_TAR_E	.04	.35	.04	.15	.09	.18	.08	.27	.10	.77	.27	1.00	.32
(24) C_RDD_E	.03	.57	.00	.18	.11	.32	.01	.31	.01	.60	.03	.32	1.00
(25) C_QUO_E	.05	.32	.02	.17	.10	.23	.04	.28	.05	.68	.14	.43	.40
(26) C_FIT_E	.04	.44	.03	.19	.12	.25	.06	.35	.07	.79	.19	.55	.47
(27) C_FIS_E	.04	.39	.04	.16	.10	.28	.07	.30	.09	.82	.23	.64	.37
(28) C_GHG_E	.02	.23	.03	.27	.15	.14	.04	.44	.06	.69	.16	.49	.33

	(14)	(15)	(16)	(17)	(18)	(19)	(20)	(21)	(22)	(23)	(24)	(25)	(26)
(14) QUO_E	1.00												
(15) REC_E	-.02	1.00											
(16) FIT_E	.11	.34	1.00										
(17) NET_E	.13	.33	.19	1.00									
(18) TEN_E	.26	.28	.31	.21	1.00								
(19) TXC_E	.07	.40	.42	.29	.40	1.00							
(20) TXR_E	.17	.37	.43	.21	.38	.49	1.00						
(21) PUB_E	.17	.47	.49	.27	.39	.50	.56	1.00					
(22) GHG_E	.05	.56	.44	.20	.31	.44	.44	.51	1.00				
(23) C_TAR_E	.12	.42	.49	.28	.35	.45	.49	.63	.49	1.00			
(24) C_RDD_E	.03	.43	.45	.19	.15	.31	.26	.38	.33	.32	1.00		
(25) C_QUO_E	.46	.88	.36	.35	.37	.39	.41	.50	.52	.43	.40	1.00	
(26) C_FIT_E	.16	.40	.94	.35	.43	.48	.48	.55	.47	.55	.47	.43	1.00
(27) C_FIS_E	.16	.44	.52	.29	.39	.59	.70	.90	.49	.64	.37	.47	.60
(28) C_GHG_E	.05	.56	.44	.20	.31	.44	.44	.51	1.00	.49	.33	.52	.47

	(27)	(28)
(27) C_FIS_E	1.00	
(28) C_GHG_E	.49	1.00

Appendix 28 – Correlation matrix for reg.-competitiveness regr.
Source: Own illustration.

	(1)	(2)	(3)	(4)	(5)	(6)	(7)	(29)	(30)	(31)	(32)	(33)	(34)
(1) EXP_SW	1.00												
(2) lnGDP_ex	.05	1.00											
(3) lnGDP_im	.04	.00	1.00										
(4) EU	.05	.12	.12	1.00									
(5) EURO	.05	.07	.07	.52	1.00								
(6) DKS_SC_SW	.13	.34	.01	.05	.05	1.00							
(7) DKS_SC_SW_im	.10	.01	.34	.05	.05	.02	1.00						
(29) C_ANY_E	.03	.54	.03	.16	.08	.22	.06	1.00					
(30) C_TAR_E	.04	.35	.04	.15	.09	.18	.08	.70	1.00				
(31) C_RDD_E	.03	.57	.00	.18	.11	.32	.01	.60	.32	1.00			
(32) C_QUO_E	.05	.32	.02	.17	.10	.23	.04	.35	.43	.40	1.00		
(33) C_FIT_E	.04	.44	.03	.19	.12	.25	.06	.67	.55	.47	.43	1.00	
(34) C_FIS_E	.04	.39	.04	.16	.10	.28	.07	.69	.64	.37	.47	.60	1.00
(35) C_GHG_E	.02	.23	.03	.27	.15	.14	.04	.35	.49	.33	.52	.47	.49
(36) C_ANY_DP5	.04	.53	.03	.18	.11	.29	.05	.72	.59	.64	.43	.64	.62
(37) C_TAR_DP5	.04	.30	.03	.13	.10	.26	.07	.45	.63	.34	.37	.45	.50
(38) C_RDD_DP5	.03	.53	.01	.19	.13	.35	.01	.53	.35	.81	.44	.48	.40
(39) C_QUO_DP5	.04	.23	.02	.14	.09	.17	.04	.22	.31	.34	.63	.30	.32
(40) C_FIT_DP5	.05	.40	.03	.20	.14	.36	.05	.49	.47	.48	.43	.70	.51
(41) C_FIS_DP5	.05	.32	.03	.14	.10	.35	.05	.46	.47	.35	.41	.45	.65
(42) C_GHG_DP5	.02	.15	.02	.18	.14	.14	.05	.22	.31	.24	.36	.32	.31
(43) C_ANY_DP10	.04	.45	.02	.16	.13	.35	.04	.51	.48	.61	.49	.50	.49
(44) C_TAR_DP10	.01	.13	.01	.04	.04	.10	.02	.20	.28	.20	.16	.16	.19
(45) C_RDD_DP10	.04	.45	.01	.16	.14	.38	.02	.43	.35	.67	.45	.46	.40
(46) C_QUO_DP10	.01	.09	.01	.05	.05	.04	.02	.08	.11	.13	.22	.11	.11
(47) C_FIT_DP10	.03	.31	.02	.15	.13	.40	.03	.30	.30	.40	.31	.41	.35
(48) C_FIS_DP10	.03	.22	.01	.07	.06	.38	.03	.26	.25	.26	.20	.22	.37
(49) C_ANY_DP15	.04	.38	.02	.14	.11	.42	.03	.36	.42	.53	.47	.39	.46
(50) C_TAR_DP15	.01	.10	.01	.02	.02	.14	.02	.12	.17	.15	.08	.15	.15
(51) C_RDD_DP15	.04	.37	.02	.12	.09	.41	.02	.32	.36	.53	.45	.33	.40
(52) C_FIT_DP15	.04	.25	.01	.09	.09	.48	.02	.20	.19	.31	.12	.23	.26
(53) C_FIS_DP15	.04	.20	.01	.05	.05	.52	.01	.16	.13	.22	.04	.15	.23

	(35)	(36)	(37)	(38)	(39)	(40)	(41)	(42)	(43)	(44)	(45)	(46)	(47)
(35) C_GHG_E	1.00												
(36) C_ANY_DP5	.42	1.00											
(37) C_TAR_DP5	.45	.61	1.00										
(38) C_RDD_DP5	.39	.73	.35	1.00									
(39) C_QUO_DP5	.49	.30	.40	.38	1.00								
(40) C_FIT_DP5	.56	.66	.46	.54	.37	1.00							
(41) C_FIS_DP5	.47	.64	.56	.39	.42	.54	1.00						
(42) C_GHG_DP5	.62	.29	.48	.26	.51	.43	.45	1.00					
(43) C_ANY_DP10	.42	.69	.47	.73	.38	.58	.51	.31	1.00				
(44) C_TAR_DP10	.13	.27	.44	.21	.10	.15	.16	.12	.39	1.00			
(45) C_RDD_DP10	.43	.58	.33	.79	.41	.55	.38	.30	.84	.20	1.00		
(46) C_QUO_DP10	.17	.10	.17	.14	.34	.12	.16	.24	.15	.03	.18	1.00	
(47) C_FIT_DP10	.45	.41	.32	.48	.32	.63	.41	.41	.60	.14	.60	.12	1.00
(48) C_FIS_DP10	.21	.35	.26	.30	.18	.33	.55	.19	.51	.17	.32	.11	.44
(49) C_ANY_DP15	.48	.49	.43	.62	.46	.50	.44	.35	.71	.30	.75	.21	.57
(50) C_TAR_DP15	.07	.16	.27	.15	.08	.12	.10	.08	.24	.61	.11	.00	.12
(51) C_RDD_DP15	.43	.44	.32	.60	.45	.45	.38	.29	.63	.15	.75	.16	.56
(52) C_FIT_DP15	.28	.26	.22	.35	.16	.40	.34	.28	.38	.06	.45	.15	.64
(53) C_FIS_DP15	.15	.22	.16	.26	.05	.28	.34	.16	.32	.06	.32	-.01	.45

Appendix 28 – Correlation matrix for reg.-competitiveness (cont'd)
Source: Own illustration.

	(48)	(49)	(50)	(51)	(52)	(53)
(48) C_FIS_DP10	1.00					
(49) C_ANY_DP15	.36	1.00				
(50) C_TAR_DP15	.02	.33	1.00			
(51) C_RDD_DP15	.32	.89	.14	1.00		
(52) C_FIT_DP15	.42	.54	.04	.55	1.00	
(53) C_FIS_DP15	.63	.44	.02	.39	.67	1.00

Notes: The correlation matrix is restricted to those variable combinations which are actually applied in the regression models of Chapter 5 and the corresponding appendices. The presentation of all 1,431 potential combinations (N(N-1)/2+N) would consume too much space.

Appendix 28 – Correlation matrix for reg.-competitiveness regr. (cont'd)
Source: Own illustration.

Dep. var.	X_SW	X_SW	X_SW
Sample period	1990-2011	1993-2011	1996-2011
Variable	(5.14a)	(5.14b)	(5.14c)
lnGDP_ex	3.079 ***	3.349 ***	3.476 ***
lnGDP_im	.0148	-.2337	-.5706
EU	1.195 ***	1.182 ***	1.083 ***
EURO	.7601 ***	.6614 ***	.5271 **
DKS_SC_SW	.1321 *	.1208 *	.0729
C_TAR_E	.2872 *	.2137	.0852
C_RDD_E	.1108	.1299	-.0614
C_QUO_E	.2690 **	.2111 *	.1819
C_FIT_E	.1489	.1517	.1795
C_FIS_E	.0490	.0230	-.1504
C_GHG_E	.9210 ***	.9230 ***	.7814 ***
DKS_SC_SW_im	-.0908	-.103 *	-.1284 *
CPV_E_10	.6686 ***	.5575 *	.0842
Pair FE (panel)	yes	yes	yes
Time FE	yes	yes	yes
Obs. total	724,724	494,130	329,420
Obs. dropped	603,351	410,959	275,980
Obs. used	121,373	83,171	53,440
Groups	5,651	5,565	5,359
Group size, min.	11	11	6
Group size, avg.	21.5	14.9	10.0
Group size, max.	22	15	11
Wald Chi^2	1,494 ***	1,172 ***	693.7 ***
Log likelihood	-9.30e+10	-8.32e+10	-6.58e+10

Notes: Results are estimated using Poisson quasi maximum likelihood regression for panel data with cluster robust standard errors. *, **, and *** indicate statistical significance at 10%, 5%, and 1% level respectively.

Appendix 29 – Rob. test for baseline gravity model: sampling period
Source: Own illustration.

Dep. var.	X_SW	X_SW	X_SW	X_SW
Variable	(5.14d)	(5.14e)	(5.14f)	(5.14g)
lnGDP_ex	3.079 ***	3.088 ***	2.738 ***	2.747 ***
lnGDP_im	.0148	.0178	-.2204	-.2160
EU	1.195 ***	1.212 ***	1.567 ***	1.588 ***
EURO	.7601 ***	.7575 ***	1.052 ***	1.048 ***
DKS_SC_SW	.1321 *	.1275 *	.0561	.0505
C_TAR_E	.2872 *	.2741 *	.3961 **	.3788 **
C_RDD_E	.1108		.1224	
C_QUO_E	.2690 **	.2677 **	.3298 ***	.3272 ***
C_FIT_E	.1489	.1542	-.1459	-.1383
C_FIS_E	.0490	.0453	-.0473	-.0531
C_GHG_E	.9210 ***	.9216 ***		
DKS_SC_SW_im	-.0908	-.0889	-.1015 *	-.0994
CPV_E_im	.6686 ***	.6682 **	.8670 ***	.8673 ***
Pair FE (panel)	yes	yes	yes	yes
Time FE	yes	yes	yes	yes
Obs. total	724,724	724,724	724,724	724,724
Obs. dropped	603,351	603,351	603,351	603,351
Obs. used	121,373	121,373	121,373	121,373
Groups	5,651	5,651	5,651	5,651
Group size, min.	11	11	11	11
Group size, avg.	21.5	21.5	21.5	21.5
Group size, max.	22	22	22	22
Wald Chi^2	1,494 ***	1,464 ***	1,440 ***	1,407 ***
Log likelihood	-9.30e+10	-9.31e+10	-9.60e+10	-9.60e+10

Notes: Results are estimated using Poisson quasi maximum likelihood regression for panel data with cluster robust standard errors. *, **, and *** indicate statistical significance at 10%, 5%, and 1% level respectively.

Appendix 30 – Rob. test for reg.-competitiveness regr.: ex RDD/GHG (for cluster existence indicators)

Source: Own illustration.

Dep. var.	X_SW	X_SW	X_SW	X_SW
Variable	(5.15a)	(5.15b)	(5.15c)	(5.15d)
lnGDP_ex	3.047 ***	3.084 ***	2.801 ***	2.825 ***
lnGDP_im	.0067	.0083	-.1555	-.1536
EU	1.263 ***	1.278 ***	1.624 ***	1.634 ***
EURO	.7301 ***	.7268 ***	.9514 ***	.9488 ***
DKS_SC_SW	.1022	.0976	.0668	.0638
TAR_E	.2744 *	.2653	.4260 ***	.4191 **
RDD_E	.1013		.0626	
QUO_E	.4839 ***	.4722 ***	.4742 ***	.4669 ***
REC_E	.1258	.1314	.1873	.1902
FIT_E	-.1924 **	-.1914 **	-.3437 ***	-.3426 ***
NET_E	.3573 **	.3619 **	.1746	.1787
TEN_E	.0046	.0015	.0663	.0639
TXC_E	.2144 *	.2204 *	.2946 ***	.2981 **
TXR_E	-.0981	-.0930	-.0774	-.0741
PUB_E	.0051	.0007	-.0634	-.0666
GHG_E	.8215 ***	.8185 ***		
DKS_SC_SW_im	-.0935 *	-.0919	-.1011 *	-.1 *
CPV_E_im	.6488 **	.6497 **	.7956 ***	.7962 ***
Pair FE (panel)	yes	yes	yes	yes
Time FE	yes	yes	yes	yes
Obs. total	724,724	724,724	724,724	724,724
Obs. dropped	603,351	603,351	603,351	603,351
Obs. used	121,373	121,373	121,373	121,373
Groups	5,651	5,651	5,651	5,651
Group size, min.	11	11	11	11
Group size, avg.	21.5	21.5	21.5	21.5
Group size, max.	22	22	22	22
Wald Chi²	1,647 ***	1,614 ***	1,588 ***	1,528 ***
Log likelihood	-9.16e+10	-9.17e+10	-9.39e+10	-9.39e+10

Notes: Results are estimated using Poisson quasi maximum likelihood regression for panel data with cluster robust standard errors. *, **, and *** indicate statistical significance at 10%, 5%, and 1% level respectively.

Appendix 31 – Rob. test for reg.-competitiveness regr.: ex RDD/GHG (for instrument existence indicators)
Source: Own illustration.

Bibliography

Alpay, E., Buccola, S., & Kerkvliet, J. (2002). Productivity Growth and Environmental Regulation in Mexican and US Food Manufacturing. *American Journal of Agricultural Economics, 84*(4), 887–901.

Ambec, S., & Barla, P. (2006). Can Environmental Regulations be Good for Business?: An Assessment of the Porter Hypothesis. *Energy Studies Review, 14*(2), 42–62.

Ambec, S., Cohen, M. A., Elgie, S., & Lanoie, P. (2011). *The Porter Hypothesis at 20: Can Environmental Regulation Enhance Innovation and Competitiveness?* (RFF Discussion Papers No. 11-01). Washington, DC.

Ambec, S., Cohen, M. A., Elgie, S., & Lanoie, P. (2013). The Porter Hypothesis at 20: Can Environmental Regulation Enhance Innovation and Competitiveness? *Review of Environmental Economics and Policy, 7*(1), 2–22.

Ambec, S., & Lanoie, P. (2008). Does It Pay to Be Green? A Systematic Overview. *Academy of Management Perspectives, November*, 45–61.

Anderson, J. E. (1979). A Theoretical Foundation for the Gravity Equation. *American Economic Review, 69*(1), 106–116.

Anderson, J. E. (2010). *The Gravity Model* (NBER Working Paper Series No. 16576). Cambridge, MA.

Anderson, J. E., & van Wincoop, E. (2003). Gravity with Gravitas: A Solution to the Border Puzzle. *American Economic Review, 93*(1), 170–192.

Arundel, A. (2001). The relative effectiveness of patents and secrecy for appropriation. *Research Policy, 30*(4), 611–624.

Bahar, H., & Egeland, J, Steenblik, R. (2013). *Domestic Incentive Measures for Renewable Energy With Possible Trade Implications* (OECD Trade and Environment Working Papers No. 2013/01).

Baldwin, R., & Taglioni, D. (2006). *Gravity for Dummies and Dummies for Gravity Equations* (NBER Working Paper Series No. 12516). Cambridge, MA.

Barbera, A. J., & McConnell, V. D. (1990). The Impact of Environmental Regulations on Industry Productivity: Direct and Indirect Effects. *Journal of Environmental Economics and Management, 18*(1), 50–65.

Barrett, S. (1991). Environmental Regulation For Competitive Advantage. *Business Strategy Review, 2*(1), 1–15.

Beers, C. van, & van den Bergh, J. C. (1997). An Empirical Multi-Country Analysis of the Impact of Environmental Regulations on Foreign Trade Flows. *KYKLOS, 50*(1), 29–46.

Beise, M. (2001). *Lead Markets: Country Specific Success Factors of the Global Diffusion of Innovations. ZEW Economic Studies: Vol. 14*. Heidelberg, New York: Springer Science & Business Media.

Beise, M. (2004). Lead markets: country-specific drivers of the global diffusion of innovations. *Research Policy, 33*(6-7), 997–1018.

Beise, M., & Rennings, K. (2005). Lead markets and regulation: a framework for analyzing the international diffusion of environmental innovations. *Ecological Economics, 52*(1), 5–17.

Bergstrand, J. H. (1985). The Gravity Equation in International Trade: Some Microeconomic Foundations and Empirical Evidence. *The Review of Economics and Statistics, 67*(3), 474–481.

Bergstrand, J. H. (1989). The Generalized Gravity Equation, Monopolistic Competition, and the Factor-Proportions Theory in International Trade. *The Review of Economics and Statistics, 71*(1), 143–153.

Berman, E., & Bui, L. T. (2001). Environmental Regulation and Productivity: Evidence from Oil Refineries. *Review of Economics and Statistics, 83*(3), 498–510.

Böhringer, C., Cuntz, A., Harhoff, D., & Otoo, E. A. (2014). *The Impacts of Feed-in Tariffs on Innovation: Empirical Evidence from Germany* (Oldenburg Discussion Papers in Economics No. V - 363 - 14). Oldenburg.

Bosquet, C., & Boulhol, H. (2010). *Scale-dependence of the Negative Binomial Pseudo-Maximum Likelihood Estimator* (Document de Travail GREQAM No. 2010-39). Aix-Marseille.

Bougette, P., & Charlier, C. (2014). *Renewable Energy, Subsidies, and the WTO: Where Has the 'Green' Gone?* (GREDEG Working Papers Series No. 2014-20).

Boyd, G. A., & McClelland, J. D. (1999). The Impact of Environmental Constraints on Productivity Improvement in Integrated Paper Plants. *Journal of Environmental Economics and Management, 38*(2), 121–142.

Brännlund, R., Färe, R., & Grosskopf, S. (1995). Environmental Regulation and Profitability: An Application to Swedish Pulp and Paper Mills. *Environmental and Resource Economics, 6,* 23–36.

Brännlund, R., & Lundgren, T. (2009). Environmental policy without costs?: A review of the Porter hypothesis. *International Review of Environmental and Resource Economics, 3*(2), 75–117.

Braun, F. G., Schmidt-Ehmcke, J., & Zloczysti, P. (2010). *Innovative Activity in Wind and Solar Technology: Empirical Evidence on Knowledge Spillovers Using Patent Data* (DIW Discussion Papers No. 993). Berlin.

Brunel, C., & Levinson, A. (2013). *Measuring Environmental Regulatory Stringency* (OECD Trade and Environment Working Papers No. 2013/05). OECD Publishing.

Brunnermeier, S. B., & Cohen, M. A. (2003). Determinants of environmental innovation in US manufacturing industries. *Journal of Environmental Economics and Management, 45*(2), 278–293.

Burger, M., van Oort, F., & Linders, G.-J. (2009). On the Specification of the Gravity Model of Trade: Zeros, Excess Zeros and Zero-inflated Estimation. *Spatial Economic Analysis, 4*(2), 167–190.

Burtraw, D. (2000). *Innovation Under the Tradable Sulfur Dioxide Emission Permits Program in the U.S. Electricity Sector* (RFF Discussion Papers No. 00-38). Washington, DC.

Cagatay, S., & Mihci, H. (2006). Degree of environmental stringency and the impact on trade patterns. *Journal of Economic Studies, 33*(1), 30–51.

Calel, R., & Dechezleprêtre, A. (2012). *Environmental Policy and Directed Technological Change: Evidence from the European carbon market* (Nota di Lavoro No. 22.2012). Milano.

Cao, J., & Groba, F. (2013). *Chinese Renewable Energy Technology Exports: The Role of Policy, Innovation and Markets* (DIW Discussion Papers No. 1263). Berlin.

Charnovitz, S., & Fischer, C. (2014). *Canada - Renewable Energy: Implications for WTO Law on Green and Not-so-Green Subsidies* (Nota di Lavoro No. 94.2014). Milano.

Cohen, W., Goto, A., Nagata, A., Nelson, R. R., & Walsh, J. P. (2002). R&D spillovers, patents and the incentives to innovate in Japan and the United States. *Research Policy, 31*(8-9), 1349–1367.

Cohen, W., Nelson, R., & Walsh, J. (2000). *Protecting Their Intellectual Assets: Appropriability Conditions and Why U.S. Manufacturing Firms Patent (or Not)* (NBER Working Paper Series No. 7552). Cambridge, MA.

Copeland, B. R., & Taylor, S. M. (2003). *Trade and the Environment: Theory and Evidence*. Princeton: Princeton University Press.

Costantini, V., & Crespi, F. (2008). Environmental regulation and the export dynamics of energy technologies. *Ecological Economics, 66*(2-3), 447–460.

Costantini, V., & Mazzanti, M. (2012). On the green and innovative side of trade competitiveness? The impact of environmental policies and innovation on EU exports. *Research Policy, 41*(1), 132–153.

Crespi, F. (2013). Environmental Policy and Induced Technological Change in European Industries. In V. Costantini & M. Mazzanti (Eds.), *The Dynamics of Environmental and Economic Systems* (pp. 143–157). Dordrecht: Springer Netherlands.

Dasgupta, S., Mody, A., Roy, S., & Wheeler, D. (2001). Environmental Regulation and Development:: A Cross-country Empirical Analysis. *Oxford Development Studies, 29*(2), 173–187.

Deardorff, A. V. (1984). Chapter 10 Testing Trade Theories and Predicting Trade Flows. In *Handbook of International Economics. Handbook of International Economics* (pp. 467–517). Elsevier.

Deardorff, A. V. (1998). Determinants of Bilateral Trade: Does Gravity Work in a Neoclassical World? In J. A. Frankel (Ed.), *The Regionalization of the World Economy* (pp. 7–32). Chicago: University of Chicago.

Denicolo, V. (1999). Pollution-reducing innovations under taxes or permits. *Oxford Economic Papers, 51*(1), 184–199.

Dernis, H., Guellec, D., & Van Pottelsberghe, B. (2001). Using Patent Counts for Cross-Country Comparisons of Technology Output. *STI Review, 27*, 128–146.

Directive 2009/29/EC of the European Parliament and of the Council of 23 April 2009, European Parliament; European Council 2009.

Dufour, C., Lanoie, P., & Patry, M. (1998). Regulation and Productivity. *Journal of Productivity Analysis, 9*, 233–247.

ECB. (2015). *Euro area 1999 - 2015.* October 3, 2015. Retrieved from https://www.ecb.europa.eu/euro/intro/html/map.en.html

Egger, P., & Pfaffermayr, M. (2003). The proper panel econometric specification of the gravity equation: A three-way model with bilateral interaction effects. *Empirical Economics, 28*, 571–580.

EIA. (2015). *International Energy Statistics.* April 7, 2015. Retrieved from http://www.eia.gov/cfapps/ipdbproject/iedindex3.cfm?tid=5&pid=53&aid=1

EPIA. (2009). *Global Market Outlook for Photovoltaics until 2013.* Brussels.

EPIA. (2001). *Global Market Outlook for Photovoltaics until 2015.* Brussels.

EPIA. (2012). *Global Market Outlook for Photovoltaics until 2016.* Brussels.

EPIA. (2014). *Global Market Outlook for Photovoltaics 2014 - 2018.* Brussels.

EPO. (2013). *Finding sustainable technologies in patents.* July 21, 2015. Retrieved from http://documents.epo.org/projects/babylon/eponet.nsf/0/6e41c0df0d85c0acc125773b005144de/$FILE/sustainable_technologies_brochure_en.pdf

EPO. (2015). *Patent statistics: 2015 Spring.* August 5, 2015. Retrieved from https://data.epo.org/expert-services/start.html

European Commission. (2015). *Europa: How the EU works.* Countries. August 28, 2015. Retrieved from http://europa.eu/about-eu/countries/index_de.htm

Evenett, S. J., & Keller, W. (2002). On Theories Explaining the Success of the Gravity Equation. *Journal of Political Economy, 110*(2), 281–316.

Fally, T. (2015). *Structural Gravity and Fixed Effects* (NBER Working Paper Series No. 21212). Cambridge, MA.

Feenstra, R. C. (2002). Border Effects and the Gravity Equation: Consistent Methods for Estimation. *Scottish Journal of Political Economy, 49*(5), 491–506.

Gray, W. B. (1997). *Manufacturing Plant Location: Does State Pollution Regulation Matter?* (NBER Working Paper Series No. 5880). Cambridge, MA.

Gray, W. B., & Shadbegian, R. J. (2003). Plant vintage, technology, and environmental regulation. *Journal of Environmental Economics and Management, 46*(3), 384–402.

Greenstone, M., List, J. A., & Syverson, C. (2012). *The effects of environmental regulation on the competitiveness of US manufacturing* (NBER Working Paper Series No. 18392). Cambridge, MA.

Griliches, Z. (1990). Patent statistics as economic indicators: A survey. *Journal of Economic Literature, 28*, 1661–1707.

Groba, F. (2013). *Renewable Energies Dissemination and International Trade. An Empirical Assessment of Policy, Markets and Innovation* (Doctoral Thesis). Technische Universität Berlin, Berlin.

Groba, F. (2014). Determinants of trade with solar energy technology components: evidence on the Porter hypothesis? *Applied Economics, 46*(5), 503–526.

Groba, F., & Breitschopf, B. (2013). *Impact of Renewable Energy Policy and Use on Innovation: A Literature Review* (DIW Discussion Papers No. 1318). Berlin.

Groba, F., & Kemfert, C. (2011). Erneuerbare Energien: Deutschland baut Technologie-Exporte aus. *DIW Wochenbericht, 78*(45), 23–29.

GWEC. (2006). *Global Wind Report 2006.* Brussels.

GWEC. (2008a). *Global Wind Report 2007, 2nd edition.* Brussels.

GWEC. (2008b). *Global Wind Report 2008.* Brussels.

GWEC. (2009). *Global Wind Report 2009.* Brussels.

GWEC. (2010). *Global Wind Report 2010: Annual Market Update.* Brussels.

GWEC. (2011). *Global Wind Report 2011: Annual Market Update.* Brussels.

GWEC. (2012). *Global Wind Report 2012: Annual Market Update.* Brussels.

GWEC. (2013). *Global Wind Report 2013: Annual Market Update.* Brussels.

Hamamoto, M. (2006). Environmental regulation and the productivity of Japanese manufacturing industries. *Resource and Energy Economics, 28*(4), 299–312.

Harhoff, D., Scherer, F. M., & Vopel, K. (2003). Citations, family size, opposition and the value of patent rights. *Research Policy, 32*(8), 1343–1363.

Harris, M. N., Kónya, L., & Mátyás, L. (2002). Modelling the Impact of Environmental Regulations on Bilateral Trade Flows: OECD, 1990-1996. *World Economy, 25*(3), 387–405.

Hart, S. L., & Ahuja, G. (1996). Does It Pay to Be Green? An Empirical Examination of the Relationship Between Emission Reduction and Firm Performance. *Business strategy and the Environment, 5*(1), 30–37.

Hausman, J. A., Hall, B., & Griliches, Z. (1984). Econometric Models for Count Data with an Application to the Patents-R&D Relationship. *Econometrica, 52*(4), 909–938.

Head, K., & Mayer, T. (2014). Gravity Equations: Workhorse, Toolkit, and Cookbook. In *Handbook of International Economics. Handbook of International Economics* (pp. 131–195). Elsevier.

Head, K., Mayer, T., & Ries, J. (2010). The erosion of colonial trade linkages after independence. *Journal of International Economics, 81*(1), 1–14.

Hicks, J. R. (1932). *The Theory of Wages.* London: Macmillan.

Hill, R. C., Griffiths, W. E., & Lim, G. C. (2012). *Principles of econometrics* (4th ed., international student version). Hoboken, N.J.: John Wiley & Sons.

Horbach, J. (2008). Determinants of environmental innovation—New evidence from German panel data sources. *Research Policy, 37*(1), 163–173.

IEA/IRENA. (2015). *Global Renewable Energy: Joint Policies and Measures database.* April 6, 2015. Retrieved from http://www.iea.org/policiesand measures/renewableenergy/

IRENA. (2012). *30 Years of Policies for Wind Energy: Lessons from 12 Markets.* Abu Dhabi.

IRENA. (2013a). *Renewable Power Generation Costs in 2012: An Overview.* Abu Dhabi.

IRENA. (2013b). *Intellectual Property Rights: The Role of Patents in Renewable Energy Technology Innovation* (Working Paper Series). Bonn.

Isaksson, L. H. (2005). Abatement costs in response to the Swedish charge on nitrogen oxide emissions. *Journal of Environmental Economics and Management, 50*(1), 102–120.

Jaffe, A. B., Newell, R. G., & Stavins, R. N. (2002). Environmental Policy and Technological Change. *Environmental and Resource Economics, 22*(1-2), 41–70.

Jaffe, A. B., Newell, R. G., & Stavins, R. N. (2003). Technological change and the Environment. In *Handbook of Environmental Economics. Environmental Degradation and Institutional Responses* (pp. 461–516). Elsevier.

Jaffe, A. B., Newell, R. G., & Stavins, R. N. (2005). A tale of two market failures: Technology and environmental policy. *Ecological Economics*, 54(2-3), 164–174.

Jaffe, A. B., & Palmer, K. (1997). Environmental Regulation and Innovation: A Panel Data Study. *Review of Economics and Statistics, 79*(4), 610–619.

Jaffe, A. B., Peterson, S. R., Portney, P. R., & Stavins, R. N. (1995). Environmental Regulation and the Competitiveness of U.S. Manufacturing: What Does the Evidence Tell Us? *Journal of Economic Literature, 33*(1), 132–163.

Jänicke, M., & Jacob, K. (2004). Lead Markets for Environmental Innovations: A New Role for the Nation State. *Global Environmental Politics, 4*(1), 29–46.

Jha, V. (2009). *Trade Flows, Barriers and Market Drivers in Renewable Energy Supply Goods: The Need to Level the Playing Field* (ICTSD Issue Paper No. 10). Geneva.

Johnstone, N., Haščič, I., Poirier, J., & Hemar, M. (2012). Environmental Policy Stringency and Technological Innovation: Evidence from Survey Data and Patent Counts. *Applied Economics, 44*(17), 2157–2170.

Johnstone, N., Haščič, I., & Popp, D. (2008). *Renewable Energy Policies and Technological Innovation: Evidence Based on Patent Counts* (NBER Working Paper Series No. 13760). Cambridge, MA. (published as: Johnstone, N., Haščič, I., & Popp, D. (2010). Renewable Energy Policies and Technological Innovation: Evidence Based on Patent Counts. *Environmental and Resource Economics, 45*(1), 133–155.).

Jug, J., & Mirza, D. (2005). Environmental Regulations in Gravity Equations: Evidence from Europe. *World Economy, 28*(11), 1591–1615.

Klinge Jacobsen, H. (1999). *Energy technology and foreign trade: The case of Denmark* (MPRA Paper No. 51796).

Kneller, R., & Manderson, E. (2012). Environmental regulations and innovation activity in UK manufacturing industries. *Resource and Energy Economics, 34*(2), 211–235.

Kyoto Protocol to the United Nations Framework Convention on Climate Change, United Nations 1998.

Lacerda, J. S., & van den Bergh, J. C. (2014). International Diffusion of Renewable *Energy Innovations. Energies, 7*(12), 8236–8263.

Lanjouw, J. O., & Mody, A. (1996). Innovation and the international diffusion of environmentally responsive technology. *Research Policy, 25*(4), 549–571.

Lanoie, P., Laurent-Lucchetti, J., Johnstone, N., & Ambec, S. (2011). Environmental Policy, Innovation and Performance: New Insights on the Porter Hypothesis. *Journal of Economics and Management Strategy, 20*, 803–841.

Lanoie, P., Patry, M., & Lajeunesse, R. (2008). Environmental regulation and productivity: testing the porter hypothesis. *Journal of Productivity Analysis, 30*(2), 121–128.

Levinson, A. (1996). Environmental regulations and manufacturers' location choices: Evidence from the Census of Manufactures. *Journal of Public Economics, 62*(1-2), 5–29.

Lewis, J. I. (2014). The Rise of Renewable Energy Protectionism: Emerging Trade Conflicts and Implications for Low Carbon Development. *Global Environmental Politics, 14*(4), 10–35.

Mäler, K.-G., & Vincent, J. R. (2005). Preface to the Handbook. In *Handbook of Environmental Economics. Economywide and International Environmental Issues, Volume 3* (pp. xiii–xviii). Elsevier.

Marklund, P.-O. (2003). *Environmental Regulation and Firm Efficiency: Studying the Porter Hypothesis using a Directional Output Distance Function* (Umeå Economic Studies No. 619). Umeå.

McCallum, J. (1995). National Border Matter: Canada US Regional Trade Patterns. *American Economic Review, 85*, 615–623.

McConnell, V. D., & Schwab, R. M. (1990). The Impact of Environmental Regulation on Industry Location Decisions: The Motor Vehicle Industry. *Land Economics, 66*(1), 67–81.

Millimet, D. L., & Roy, J. (2011). *Three New Empirical Tests of the Pollution Haven Hypothesis When Environmental Regulation is Endogenous* (IZA Discussion Paper Series No. 5911).

Murty, M. N., & Kumar, S. (2003). Win–win opportunities and environmental regulation: testing of porter hypothesis for Indian manufacturing industries. *Journal of Environmental Management, 67*(2), 139–144.

Nagaoka, S., Motohashi, K., & Goto, A. (2010). Patent Statistics as an Innovation Indicator. In *Handbook of the Economics of Innovation. Handbook of the Economics of Innovation, Volume 2* (pp. 1083–1127). Elsevier.

Nehrt, C. (1998). Maintainability of First Mover Advantages When Environmental Regulations Differ Between Countries. *Academy of Management Review, 23*(1), 77–97.

Nelson, R. A., Tietenberg, T., & Donihue, M. R. (1993). Differential Environmental Regulation: Effects on Electric Utility Capital Turnover and Emissions. *Review of Economics and Statistics, 75*(2), 368–373.

Nesta, L., Vona, F., & Nicolli, F. (2014). Environmental policies, competition and innovation in renewable energy. *Journal of Environmental Economics and Management, 67*(3), 396–411.

OECD. (2010). *Linkages between Environmental Policy and Competitiveness* (OECD Environmental Working Papers No. 13).

OECD. (2015). *IEA Energy Technology RD&D Statistics: RD&D Budget.* April 1, 2015. Retrieved from http://stats.oecd.org/BrandedView.aspx?oecd_bv_id =enetech-data-en&doi=data-00488-en

Palmer, K., Oates, W. E., & Portney, P. R. (1995). Tightening Environmental Standards: The Benefit-Cost or the No-Cost Paradigm? *Journal of Economic Perspectives, 9*(4), 119–132.

Pasurka, C. (2008). Perspectives on Pollution Abatement and Competitiveness: Theory, Data, and Analyses. *Review of Environmental Economics and Policy, 2*(2), 194–218.

Peters, M., Schneider, M., Griesshaber, T., & Hoffmann, V. H. (2012). The impact of technology-push and demand-pull policies on technical change – Does the locus of policies matter? *Research Policy, 41*(8), 1296–1308.

Popp, D. (2002). Induced Innovation and Energy Prices. *American Economic Review, 92(*1), 160–180.

Popp, D. (2003). Pollution Control Innovations and the Clean Air Act of 1990. Journal of Policy Analysis and Management, 22(4), 641–660.

Popp, D. (2005). Lessons from patents: Using patents to measure technological change in environmental models. *Ecological Economics, 54*(2-3), 209–226.

Popp, D. (2006). International innovation and diffusion of air pollution control technologies: the effects of NOX and SO2 regulation in the US, Japan, and Germany. *Journal of Environmental Economics and Management, 51*(1), 46–71.

Popp, D., Haščič, I., & Medhi, N. (2011). Technology and the diffusion of renewable energy. *Energy Economics, 33*(4), 648–662.

Popp, D., Newell, R. G., & Jaffe, A. B. (2010). Energy, the Environment, and Technological Change. In *Handbook of the Economics of Innovation. Handbook of the Economics of Innovation, Volume 2* (pp. 873–937). Elsevier.

Porter, M. E. (1990). *The Competitive Advantage of Nations.* New York: Free Press.

Porter, M. E. (1991). America's Green Strategy. *Scientific American, 264*, 168–171.

Porter, M. E., & van der Linde, C. (1995). Toward a New Conception of the Environment-Competitiveness Relationship. *Journal of Economic Perspectives, 9*(4), 97–118.

Pöyhönen, P. (1963). A Tentative Model for the Volume of Trade Between Countries. *Weltwirtschaftliches Archiv, 90,* 93–100.

Rassier, D. G., & Earnhart, D. (2010). The Effect of Clean Water Regulation on Profitability: Testing the Porter Hypothesis. *Land Economics, 86*(2), 329–344.

Rauscher, M. (2005). Chapter 27 International Trade, Foreign Investment, and the Environment. In *Handbook of Environmental Economics. Economywide and International Environmental Issues* (pp. 1403–1456). Elsevier.

REN21. (2005). *Renewables 2005 Global Status Report.* Paris: REN21 Secretariat.

REN21. (2006). *Renewables 2006 Global Status Report Update.* Paris: REN21 Secretariat.

REN21. (2007). *Renewables 2007 Global Status Report.* Paris: REN21 Secretariat.

REN21. (2009). *Renewables Global Status Report 2009 Update.* Paris: REN21 Secretariat.

REN21. (2010). *Renewables 2010 Global Status Report.* Paris: REN21 Secretariat.

REN21. (2011). *Renewables 2011 Global Status Report.* Paris: REN21 Secretariat.

REN21. (2012). *Renewables 2012 Global Status Report.* Paris: REN21 Secretariat.

REN21. (2013). *Renewables 2013 Global Status Report.* Paris: REN21 Secretariat.

REN21. (2014a). *The First Decade: 2004 - 2014: 10 Years of Renewable Energy Progress.* Paris: REN21 Secretariat.

REN21. (2014b). *Renewables 2014 Global Status Report.* Paris: REN21 Secretariat.

REN21. (2015). *Renewables Interactive Map.* March 10, 2015. Retrieved from http://map.ren21.net/

Rexhäuser, S., & Rammer, C. (2013). *Unmasking the Porter Hypothesis: Environmental Innovations and Firm-Profitability* (ZEW Discussion Papers No. 11-036).

Rubashkina, Y., Galeotti, M., & Verdolini, E. (2015). Environmental Regulation and Competitiveness: Empirical Evidence on the Porter Hypothesis from European Manufacturing Sectors. *Energy Policy, 83*, 288–300.

Santos-Silva, J. M., & Tenreyro, S. (2006). The log of Gravity. *Review of Economics and Statistics, 88*(4), 641–658.

Sauvage, J. (2014). *The Stringency of Environmental Regulations and Trade in Environmental Goods* (OECD Trade and Environment Working Papers No. 2014/03). OECD Publishing.

Scherer, F., & Harhoff, D. (2000). Technology policy for a world of skew-distributed outcomes. *Research Policy, 29*(4-5), 559–566.

Shrivastava, P. (1995). Environmental Technologies and Competitive Advantage. *Strategic Management Journal, 16*(S1), 183–200.

Simcoe, T. (2015). *Timothy Simcoe, Boston University Questrom School of Business: Data & Code.* September 28, 2015. Retrieved from http://people.bu.edu/tsimcoe/data.html

Stavins, R. N. (2003). Experience with Market-Based Environmental Policy Instruments. In *Handbook of Environmental Economics. Environmental Degradation and Institutional Responses, Volume 1* (pp. 355–435). Elsevier.

Sung, B., & Song, W.-Y. (2013). Causality between public policies and exports of renewable energy technologies. *Energy Policy, 55*, 95–104.

Sung, B., & Song, W.-Y. (2014). How government policies affect the export dynamics of renewable energy technologies: A subsectoral analysis. *Energy, 69*, 843–859.

Tenreyro, S. (2015). *The "Log of gravity" page*. September 29, 2015. Retrieved from http://personal.lse.ac.uk/tenreyro/LGW.html

Tinbergen, J. (1962). *Shaping the World Economy: Suggestions for an International Economic Policy.* New York: The Twentieth Century Fund. January 20, 2015. Retrieved from http://hdl.handle.net/1765/16826

United Nations Framework Convention on Climate Change, United Nations 1992.

UN. (2011). *Report of the Conference of the Parties on its sixteenth session, held in Cancun from 29 November to 10 December 2010.*

UN. (2015). *UN Comtrade Database.* February 25, 2015. Retrieved from http://comtrade.un.org/

Veefkind, V., Hurtado-Albir, J., Angelucci, S., Karachalios, K., & Thumm, N. (2012). A new EPO classification scheme for climate change mitigation technologies. *World Patent Information, 34*(2), 106–111.

Vlist, Arno J. van der, Withagen, C., & Folmer, H. (2007). Technical efficiency under alternative environmental regulatory regimes: The case of Dutch horticulture. *Ecological Economics, 63*(1), 165–173.

Vollebergh, H. R. (2007). *Differential Impact of Environmental Policy Instruments on Technological Change: A Review of the Empirical Literature* (Tinbergen Institute Discussion Paper No. TI 2007-042/3).

Vries, F. P. de, & Withagen, C. (2005). *Innovation and Environmental Stringency: The Case of Sulfur Dioxide Abatement* (CentER Discussion Paper Series No. 2005-18). Tilburg.

Walz, R., Schleich, J., & Ragwitz, M. (2011, April 6-8). *Regulation, Innovation and Wind Power Technologies – An empirical analysis for OECD countries*. Paper presented at the DIME Final Conference, Maastricht. July 14, 2015. Retrieved from http://final.dime-eu.org/files/Walz_C5.pdf

WIPO. (2015). *International Patent Classification (IPC) Official Publication: Version 2015.01*. July 24, 2015. Retrieved from http://web2.wipo.int/ipcpub/

Wooldridge, J. M. (2002). *Econometric Analysis of Cross Section and Panel Data*. Cambridge, MA: The MIT Press.

World Bank. (2015a). *World DataBank: World Development Indicators*. June 21, 2015. Retrieved from http://databank.worldbank.org/data//reports.aspx?source=2&country=&series=NY.GDP.MKTP.CD&period=

World Bank. (2015b). *World Integrated Trade Solutions: Tariff and Trade Analysis*. August 26, 2015. Retrieved from http://wits.worldbank.org/WITS/WITS/AdvanceQuery/TariffAndTradeAnalysis/AdvancedQueryDefinition.aspx?Page=TariffandTradeAnalysis

WTO, UNCTAD. (2012). *A practical guide to trade policy analysis*. New York, Geneva: United Nations Conference on Trade and Development; World Trade Organization.

Made in the USA
Monee, IL
13 September 2026

62973761R00164